GEOFFREY HARTMAN

CRITICS OF THE TWENTIETH CENTURY
General Editor: Christopher Norris
University of Wales

A. J. Greimas and the Nature of Meaning
Ronald Schleifer

Christopher Caudwell
Robert Sullivan

Figuring Lacan
Criticism and the Cultural Unconscious
Juliet Flower MacCannell

Harold Bloom
Towards Historical Rhetorics
Peter de Bolla

F. R. Leavis
Michael Bell

Postmodern Brecht
A Re-Presentation
Elizabeth Wright

Deleuze and Guattari
Ronald Bogue

The Ecstasies of Roland Barthes
Mary Bittner Wiseman

Julia Kristeva
John Lechte

Ezra Pound as Literary Critic
K. K. Ruthven

Introducing Lyotard
Bill Readings

GEOFFREY HARTMAN

Criticism as Answerable Style

G. Douglas Atkins

ROUTLEDGE
London and New York

First published 1990
by Routledge
11 New Fetter Lane, London EC4P 4EE

Simultaneously published in the USA and Canada
by Routledge
a division of Routledge, Chapman and Hall, Inc.
29 West 35th Street, New York, NY 10001

© 1990 G. Douglas Atkins

Typeset in 10/12pt Baskerville, Printed and Bound by
Redwood Press Limited, Melksham, Wiltshire

All rights reserved. No part of this book may be reprinted or
reproduced or utilized in any form or by any electronic,
mechanical, or other means, now known or hereafter invented,
including photocopying and recording, or in any information
storage or retrieval system, without permission in writing from
the publishers.

British Library Cataloguing in Publication Data
Atkins, G. Douglas (George Douglas)
Geoffrey Hartman: criticism as answerable style. –
(Critics of the twentieth century)
1. English literature. Criticism. Hartman, Geoffrey H. 1929–
I. Title   II. Series
820.9

ISBN 0–415–02094–8

Library of Congress Cataloging in Publication Data
Atkins, G. Douglas (George Douglas)
Geoffrey Hartman : criticism as answerable style / G. Douglas Atkins
p. cm. — (Critics of the twentieth century)
Includes bibliographical references.
ISBN 0–415–02094–8
1. Hartman, Geoffrey H.   2. Criticism—History—20th century.
3. Reader-response criticism.   I. Title.   II. Series: Critics of
the twentieth century (London, England)
PN75.H33A85   1990
820.9'145—dc20   90–8262

Lukács ... is as plastic as Kant or Schiller in his elaboration of distinctions, each of which is given its dignity. He is never trapped by categories.
Criticism in the Wilderness

[Wordsworth] wants his poetry to be like nature in function and effect. It should purge our imaginative belief in the necessity of apocalypse or violent renovation, and purge it gently.
Wordsworth's Poetry

[H]ere is a man whose mind moves as he writes, ... who thinks into the human heart ..., a poet, therefore, who confronts heuristically maze within maze.
Wordsworth's Poetry

The critic explicitly acknowledges his dependence on prior words that make his word a kind of answer. He calls to other texts "that they might answer him." His focus is on the activity of the receiver, on the possibility of drawing a timely response from "trembling ears."
Criticism in the Wilderness

[It] is not the individual poem that determines the meaning of indeterminate phrases but the poem as part of an intertextual corpus which the skilled interpreter supplies.... It is the reader who has to take responsibility.
The Unremarkable Wordsworth

The situation of the discourse we name *criticism* is ... no different from that of any other. If this recognition implies a reversal, then it is the master–servant relation between criticism and creation that is being overturned in favor of what Wordsworth, describing the interaction of nature and mind, called "mutual domination" or "interchangeable supremacy."
Criticism in the Wilderness

Contents

Editor's Foreword	ix
Preface	xiii
Acknowledgments	xv
Abbreviations of Hartman's texts	xvii
1 Reading Hartman	1
2 A matter of relation, a question of place: Hartman and contemporary criticism	13
3 The Wandering Jew: Hartman's relation to Judaism and Romanticism	31
4 Calling voices out of silence: criticism as echo-chamber	63
5 'Dying into the life of recollection': the burden of artistic vocation	82
6 Estranging the familiar: Hartman and the essay, or the cat Geoffrey at pranks	102
7 It's about time: negative hermeneutics and the fate of reading	127
Appendix I	148
Appendix II	151
Notes	156
Index	166

Editor's foreword

The twentieth century has produced a remarkable number of gifted and innovative literary critics. Indeed it could be argued that some of the finest literary minds of the age have turned to criticism as the medium best adapted to their complex and speculative range of interests. This has sometimes given rise to regret among those who insist on a clear demarcation between "creative" (primary) writing on the one hand and "critical" (secondary) texts on the other. Yet this distinction is far from self-evident. It is coming under strain at the moment as novelists and poets grow increasingly aware of the conventions that govern their writing and the challenge of consciously exploiting and subverting those conventions. And the critics for their part — some of them at least — are beginning to question their traditional role as humble servants of the literary text with no further claim upon the reader's interest or attention. Quite simply, there are texts of literary criticism and theory that for various reasons — stylistic complexity, historical influence, range of intellectual command — cannot be counted a mere appendage to those other "primary" texts.

Of course, there is a logical puzzle here, since (it will be argued) "literary criticism" would never have come into being, and could hardly exist as such, were it not for the body of creative writings that provide its *raison d'être*. But this is not quite the kind of knock-down argument that it might appear at first glance. For one thing, it conflates some very different orders of priority, assuming that literature always comes first (in the sense that Greek tragedy had to exist before Aristotle could formulate its rules), so that literary texts are for that very reason possessed of superior value. And this argument would seem to find commonsense support in the difficulty of thinking what "literary criticism" could *be* if it seriously renounced all sense of the distinction between literary and critical texts. Would it not then find itself in the unfortunate position of a discipline that had willed its own demise by declaring its subject non-existent?

But these objections would only hit their mark if there were indeed a special kind of writing called "literature" whose difference from other kinds of writing was enough to put criticism firmly in its place. Otherwise there is nothing in the least self-defeating or paradoxical about a discourse, nominally that of literary criticism, that accrues such interest on its own account as to force some fairly drastic rethinking of its proper powers and limits. The act of crossing over from commentary to literature – or of simply denying the difference between them – becomes quite explicit in the writing of a critic like Geoffrey Hartman. But the signs are already there in such classics as William Empson's *Seven Types of Ambiguity* (1928), a text whose transformative influence on our habits of reading must surely be ranked with the great creative moments of literary modernism. Only on the most dogmatic view of the difference between "literature" and "criticism" could a work like *Seven Types* be counted generically an inferior, sub-literary species of production. And the same can be said for many of the critics whose writings and influence this series sets out to explore.

Some, like Empson, are conspicuous individuals who belong to no particular school or larger movement. Others, like the Russian Formalists, were part of a communal enterprise and are therefore best understood as representative figures in a complex and evolving dialogue. Then again there are cases of collective identity (like the so-called "Yale deconstructors" where a mythical group image is invented for largely polemical purposes. (The volumes in this series on Hartman and Bloom should help to dispel the idea that "Yale deconstruction" is anything more than a handy device for collapsing differences and avoiding serious debate.) So there is no question of a series format or house-style that would seek to reduce these differences to a blandly homogeneous treatment. One consequence of recent critical theory is the realization that literary texts have no self-sufficient or autonomous meaning, no existence apart from their after-life of changing interpretations and values. And the same applies to those *critical* texts whose meaning and significance are subject to constant shifts and realignments of interest. This is not to say that trends in criticism are just a matter of intellectual fashion or the merry-go-round of rising and falling reputations. But it is important to grasp how complex are the forces – the conjunctions of historical and cultural motive – that affect the first reception and the subsequent fortunes of a critical text. This point has been raised into a systematic programme by critics like Hans-Robert Jauss, practitioners of so-called "reception theory" as a form of historical hermeneutics. The volumes in this series are therefore concerned not only to expound what is of lasting significance but also to set these critics in the context of present-day argument and debate. In some cases (as with Walter Benjamin) this debate takes the form of a struggle for interpretative power among disciplines with sharply opposed ideological view-points. Such controversies cannot simply be ignored in the interests of achieving a clear and balanced account. They point to unresolved tensions and problems which are there in the critic's work as well as in the rival appropriative readings. In the end there is no way of drawing a neat methodological line between "intrinsic" questions (what the critic really thought) and those other, supposedly "extrinsic" concerns that have to do with influence and reception history.

The volumes vary accordingly in their focus and range of coverage. They also reflect the ways in which a speculative approach to questions of literary theory has proved to have striking consequences for the human sciences at large. This breaking-down of disciplinary bounds is among the most significant developments in recent critical thinking. As philosophers and historians, among others, come to recognize the rhetorical complexity of the texts they deal with, so literary theory takes on a new dimension of interest and relevance. It is scarcely appropriate to think of a writer like Derrida as practising "literary criticism" in any conventional sense of the term. For one thing, he is as much concerned with "philosophical" as with "literary" texts, and has indeed actively sought to subvert (or deconstruct) such tidy distinctions. A principal object in planning this series was to take full stock of these shifts in the wider intellectual terrain (including the frequent boundary disputes) brought about by critical theory. And, of course, such changes are by no means confined to literary studies, philosophy, and the so-called "sciences of man". It is equally the case in (say) nuclear physics and molecular biology that advances in the one field have decisive implications for the other, so that specialized research often tends (paradoxically) to break down existing divisions of intellectual labour. Such work is typically many years ahead of the academic disciplines and teaching institutions that have obvious reasons of their own for adopting a business-as-usual attitude. One important aspect of modern critical theory is the

EDITOR'S FOREWORD

challenge it presents to these traditional ideas. And lest it be thought that this is merely a one-sided takeover bid by literary critics, the series includes a number of volumes by authors in those other disciplines, including, for instance, a study of Roland Barthes by an American analytical philosopher.

We shall not, however, cleave to theory as a matter of polemical or principled stance. The series extends to figures like F. R. Leavis, whose widespread influence went along with an express aversion to literary theory; scholars like Erich Auerbach in the mainstream European tradition; and others who resist assimilation to any clear-cut line of descent. There will also be authoritative volumes on critics such as Northrop Frye and Lionel Trilling, figures who, for various reasons, occupy an ambivalent or essentially contested place in modern critical tradition. Above all the series strives to resist that current polarization of attitudes that sees no common ground of interest between 'literary criticism' and 'critical theory'.

Christopher Norris

Preface

In this book I try to make clear the nature of the alternative Geoffrey Hartman offers contemporary criticism. It is, I think, a genuine alternative: not just another theory, method, or approach to the bewildering array of possibilities confronting late twentieth-century readers, nor, really, a way of reading but, rather, nothing less than the life of reading. Hartman witnesses to the power of art as he bodies forth a personal, unsystematic, but by no means impressionistic response to a wide range of texts – from Wordsworth to Heidegger and Lacan, Malraux to Alfred Hitchcock, Ross Macdonald to Derrida. Highly pressured, Hartman's readings, inextricable from a mind widely traveled and well stocked, are intertextual, unafraid to take risks, and productive of surprising, often stunning, insights. In other words, those of Susan A. Handelman, "reading Hartman, one does not feel as when reading Bloom, or de Man, or Derrida that texts are being processed through a pre-determined schema – and roughly forced to yield up their meanings." Instead, reading Hartman, we have an opportunity to observe – better: to participate in – what Paul H. Fry calls "the course of interpretive discovery. [Hartman's] criticism is the most *realistic* record we have of what literate reading is like." You can't imitate Hartman, and he doesn't want you to try; but you can admire, enjoy, and learn from him. One of his most important – and generous – lessons is to lead you somehow beyond him. Edward Said has recently put it this way, in "The Horizon of R. P. Blackmur": "rare are the critics for whom criticism is its own justification, and not an act for the gaining of adherents or for the persuasion of larger and larger audiences. Rarer still are critics whose work at its center cradles the paradox that whatever criticism urges or delivers must not, indeed cannot, be replicated, reproduced, re-used as a lesson learned and then applied." Such a critic is Geoffrey Hartman.

For reasons at least partially explained in the introductory chapter below, I offer these essays not so much as explication of Hartman's texts (which may be no more possible than desirable) as a response to them. Responding necessitates, among other things, close attention to what he has written, as well as recognition of what he is saying, and the form that response takes involves not so much straight, linear progression as a wandering (though not an aimlessness), a circling about that results in some repetition, certainly in not-infrequent returns to issues, concerns, and passages already remarked. In the quilt that this book is, I quote a lot from Hartman; that, I would claim, is both unavoidable and strategic: a tailor here, I piece together various patches, offering you something essayistic. Responding, moreover, I seek, neither to efface myself before Hartman's works, collapsing all difference, nor to distance myself from them, pretending to some specious objectivity and denying that I am writing *of* Hartman (as he does *of* Wordsworth). What I seek is relation rather than either identity or absolute difference.

For me, this book represents the second part of a tripartite effort that began with a book on and in deconstruction, in which I first wrote on (if not yet quite *of*) Hartman. The second part of this "trilogy" consists of three studies very different in appearance though related: my book on Alexander Pope, *Quests of Difference*, in which I acknowledged Hartman as the *genius loci*; a book on difference and relation as they bear on religion and pedagogy "in the wake of deconstruction"; and the volume you are reading. Since *Reading Deconstruction/Deconstructive Reading* I have been haunted by questions of difference and particularly by the relationality made possible by *différance*. In my estimation, Hartman's treatment of relation is the subtlest, most sophisticated, most satisfactory we have. His work, moreover, encourages me to begin the third and "final" part of the efforts I have mentioned: a collection of essays, critical and personal, in which I look towards a revitalized critical writing, at once theoretically informed and artful, one that seeks – such is its ambition – to overcome the ever-widening gap between the academic and the "general" reader, between – we might say – criticism and journalism. In that, I shall try to describe how theory, especially Hartman's work, has helped effect significant changes – and growth – in the person that I am: bringing theory to life.

Acknowledgments

I want, first and foremost, to express my appreciation – and debt – to the subject. This has been, I do not hesitate to say, a labor of love. Long before I began this study, Geoffrey Hartman was an inspiring teacher (at the School of Criticism and Theory, in 1978), a strong supporter, a good friend. That he suggested me to Chris Norris, editor of the series on twentieth-century critics, only increases my debt (without, however, obligating me). My second debt is to Chris Norris, who had faith in this project and who, likewise, supported me unstintingly. For institutional support, generous, timely, and gratefully received, I acknowledge the Hall Center for the Humanities, which provided a year-long fellowship as well as other assistance, and the General Research Fund at the University of Kansas, which gave me two summer grants. I also gratefully acknowledge, once again, my large debt to Beth Ridenour, who graciously and expertly processed the words, often barely legible, that I wrote, in longhand, in pencil, on yellow legal paper. I want, too, to acknowledge the continuing support of my department chair, Michael L. Johnson, friend and collaborator. I gratefully acknowledge as well the assistance, unstinting and gracious, of Lori Whitten, secretary-extraordinaire. Debts of various, often profound kinds are outstanding to other friends, former students, colleagues, and astute critics (of me), including Brenda Brueggemann, Patricia L. Douglass, Becky J. A. Eason, Randy Gordon, Jill Kruger-Robbins, Paul E. Northam, Brigitte Sandquist, and Cheryl B. Torshey. And once more I happily record my appreciation of and gratitude for Leslie and Christopher.

Abbreviations of Hartman's Texts

UnMV	The *Unmediated Vision: An Interpretation of Wordsworth, Hopkins, Rilke, and Valéry*, 1954, rpt New York: Harcourt, Brace and World, 1966.
M	*Malraux. Studies in Modern European Literature and Thought*, New York: Hillary House, 1960.
WP	*Wordsworth's Poetry 1787–1814*, 1964, rpt New Haven: Yale University Press, 1971.
BF	*Beyond Formalism: Literary Essays 1958–1970*, New Haven: Yale University Press, 1970.
FR	*The Fate of Reading and Other Essays*, Chicago: University of Chicago Press, 1975.
AC	*Akiba's Children*, Emory, VA: Iron Mountain Press, 1978.
PQT	*Psychoanalysis and the Question of the Text*, ed. Hartman. Selected Papers from the English Institute, 1976–77, Baltimore: Johns Hopkins University Press, 1978.
CW	*Criticism in the Wilderness: The Study of Literature Today*, New Haven: Yale University Press, 1980.
STT	*Saving the Text: Literature/Derrida/Philosophy*, Baltimore: Johns Hopkins University Press, 1981.
EP	*Easy Pieces*, New York: Columbia University Press, 1985.
"JI"	"On the Jewish Imagination," *Prooftexts* 5 (1985): 201–20.
"T and T"	"Tea and Totality: The Demand of Theory on Critical Style," in *After Strange Texts: The Role of Theory in the Study of Literature*, ed. Gregory S. Jay and David L. Miller, Tuscaloosa: University of Alabama Press, 1985.

ABBREVIATIONS OF HARTMAN'S TEXTS

B	*Bitburg in Moral and Political Perspective*, ed. Hartman, Bloomington: Indiana University Press, 1986.
UnRW	*The Unremarkable Wordsworth*. Theory and History of Literature 34. Foreword Donald G. Marshall, Minneapolis: University of Minnesota Press, 1987.
"BI"	"Blindness and Insight: Paul de Man, Fascism, and Deconstruction," *The New Republic*, 7 March 1988, 26–31.

1
Reading Hartman

[T]he so-called arbitrariness of the sign points once again to the free will of the users of language, placing the responsibility for the scrupulous reception and production of words on each person, whatever the odds.

Easy Pieces

A reader's responsibility is not easily defined. He must decide how much darkness is to be developed.... No one can remove the reader's responsibility entirely: in this, to each his own conscience.

The Unremarkable Wordsworth

Readers too have to recognize in themselves a will to power, or at least to knowledge, and must either achieve an empirical equilibrium or establish themselves on terra firma by means of theory. We are surprisingly close to an aristocratic type of reader-response (better: reader-responsibility) doctrine.... For each reader is an author in the sense of auctor, an augmenter who helps to "achieve" the work but who may also spoil or disestablish it. Reading... is "l'acte commun, l'opération commune du lisant et du lu"; it is "literally a cooperation, an intimate, inward collaboration... thus a disconcerting responsibility."

"The Culture of Criticism"

In *The Romance of Interpretation: Visionary Criticism from Pater to de Man*, Daniel T. O'Hara claims that Geoffrey Hartman "represents the future of the profession" of literary studies.[1] Though attractive and desirable, that prospect seems unlikely, given the responsibility

Hartman places on individual readers and critics and the severe demands he makes.

Reading Hartman, one encounters no such progressivistic expectation or hope. Certainly his own frequent asseverations against the usual or "plainstyle" critic point to the enormous difference between him and the vast majority of readers.[2] If Hartman is *sui generis* (having no characteristic "approach" or method, he has founded no school of criticism and is not likely to), "plainstyle" critics are legion. He has long argued that exegesis, which he regards as "puerile, or at most pedagogic" (BF 57), dominates critical activity: "The dominion of Exegesis is great," he declares in *Beyond Formalism*: "she is our whore of Babylon, sitting robed in Academic black on the great dragon of Criticism, and dispensing a repetitive and soporific balm from her pedantic cup" (56). In Hartman, practical criticism has grown up, but whether the profession is or ever will be able to follow him seems highly problematical.

What Hartman objects to – and usually his rhetoric is more controlled – is criticism's irresponsibility. That is, commentary so often fails to enact an "answerable style" or to meet the demands of responding to a text's call. Shifting the attention *of* critics *to* critics, he claims that they – we – are "scared to do anything except convert as quickly as possible the imaginative into a mode of the ordinary" (CW 27). Though aware that he "may be overstating the case," Hartman finds that "the spectacle of the polite critic dealing with an extravagant literature, trying so hard to come to terms with it in his own tempered language, verges on the ludicrous" (CW 155). To be answerable, according to Hartman, and responsible, criticism must be less timid, more assertive. It must "come out," appear as such: "the problem with criticism," he writes, "is . . . that it does not show enough of itself while claiming to show all" (CW 113). Not wanting to "come out," the interpreter may become "a pedagogue, or what Blake calls a 'horse of instruction'," but he or she may also become a critic "who judges only in order not to be judged." In the latter event, such a critic's "relation to art is like that of Man, in Blake, to the Divine Vision from which he has shrunk into his present, Rumpelstiltskin form. His professional demeanor," Hartman continues, "is the result of self-astonishment followed by self-retreat: he turns into a bundle of defensive reactions, into a scaly creature of the rock who conserves himself against the promptings of a diviner imagination" (FR 8–9).

The heavy rhetoric, which, as I have said, is uncharacteristic of

Hartman, reveals both an intensity of feeling and his critical difference: unlike the typical critic (at least as Hartman represents him or her), who successfully bypasses "the animal, infantile, or social basis of his needs" (CW 218), accepting "too readily his subordinate function," and so repressing "his own artistic impulses" (CW 216), Hartman cannot be cool and objective nor "methodically humble" (FR 9). But today's interpreter, Hartman wrote in 1975, generally

> subdues himself to commenting on work or writer, is effusive about the *integrity of the text*, and feels exalted by exhibiting art's controlled, fully organized energy of imagination. What passion yet what objectivity! What range yet what unity! What consistency of theme and style! His essays, called articles, merchandized in the depressed market place of academic periodicals, conform strictly to the cool element of scholarly prose. They are sober, literate, literal, pointed. Leave behind all fantasy, you who read these pages. (FR 9)

The essay from which I quote, "The Interpreter: A Self-Analysis," which opens *The Fate of Reading*, is anything but "sober, ... literal, pointed"; indeed, it is perhaps Hartman's most "fantastic" essay. It may also be dated, for in the years since 1975 critical style has changed somewhat, becoming more adventurous and risky. Still, plainstyle rules the critical waves.

Hartman's own way of writing, which, he grants, can be "difficult, or at least experimental" (EP ix), accounts for much of his difference, if not his importance. His style is, as he describes it, mixed and variable, consisting of different linguistic registers, multiform allusions and quotations, and often outrageous puns ("I must pun as I must sneeze," he declares at one point [STT 18]). Sometimes Hartman appears personal, conversational, and familiar, at other times oracular and prophetic. Such an uneasy mixture of "the conversational or 'friendship' style, and the oracular or priestly mode," he himself finds characteristic of modern writing (CW 136).

As difficult as we may find Hartman's mixed and impure style, so different from the plainstyle typical of academic criticism, both old-fashioned and poststructuralist, more unsettling is what might be called the paratactic quality of his writing. *That* he shares with such other writers in the European philosophical tradition as Theodor Adorno, whose style Martin Jay associates with a "refusal to subordinate arguments and observations in a hierarchically entailed manner," a refusal that "grew out of his unwillingness to privilege one element of the force-field or constellation over another."³ Somewhat similarly preferring alternatives to exclusions, Hartman engages in a way of thinking Wordsworthian in its adoption of reversal as "the very style of thought" (WP 273). Hartman may, in fact, wish his criticism to achieve what Wordsworth sought, who wanted "his poetry to be like nature in function and effect. It should purge our imaginative belief in the necessity of apocalypse or violent renovation, and purge it gently" (WP 252).

However that may be, Hartman's prose, like Wordsworth's poetry, normally reflects a gentleness deriving from avoidance of *point*. "Point" is a technical term denoting "concentrated reality or concentrated verbal meaning" (FR 229). Hartman describes the pointed style, at least as it developed in seventeenth-century England, as at once sinewy and masculine and "witty and antithetical: everything in it is sharp, nervy, *à pic*, and overtly like a hedgehog" (BF 47, 45). If, in England, neoclassicism "pruned the hedgehog and smoothed the prosody," it was Wordsworth who worked "to free the lyric from the tyranny of point" (BF 45). In a style simple and gentle, Wordsworth wrote poems that often have no point. Much more is involved, of course, than a question of style. What, Hartman wants to know, "is achieved by Wordsworth's creation of so pointless, so apparently simple a style?" (BF 49).

Hartman answers the question in a way that offers insight into his own writing. Noting the reduction entailed by pointing, "as if truth were here or there, as if life could be localized, as if revelation were a property," Hartman cites Wordsworth's question in *The Prelude*: who knows, he asks,

> the individual hour in which
> His habits were first sown, even as a seed?
> Who that shall point as with a wand and say
> "This portion of the river of my mind
> Came from yon fountain?"

"The error in such pointing," Hartman maintains, even if it "cannot be avoided," "is not only intellectual, due to that 'false secondary power . . . by which we multiply distinctions,' but it is also spiritual." For to point "is to encapsulate something: strength, mind, life. It is to overobjectify, to overformalize. It implies," writes Hartman, "that there is a fixed locus of revelation or a reified idolatrous content" (BF 50). We are, however, "greedy for the spoils of pointing," specifically the fixity and identity that it promises (UnRW 196). It is precisely here, in such monumentalizing, in which "the spirit continually comes to rest, or arrests itself, in an object," that we discern an important pattern, if not the core, in Hartman's thinking (STT 84). Belief in "a fixed locus of revelation or reified idolatrous content" is, of course, anathema to Hebraism, and Hartman's resistance to and repudiation of such idolatry reflects at once his Jewishness, his affinity with Romanticism (especially Wordsworth), and his commitment to a particular style with all that entails.

Though often witty and even epigrammatic, Hartman's style is hardly pointed, and that causes difficulty for readers accustomed to critical and scholarly writing that carefully marshals evidence to prove a definite thesis or point – accustomed to the article, in other words, rather than the essay. Reading Hartman is often frustrating and unsettling. Even the essays collected in *Easy Pieces*, and described as "journalistic," are, many of them, by no means easy (ix). Typically, Hartman broods intently on texts, often shuttling back and forth between exemplary texts and an idea in critical theory or literary history, *looking through* texts towards an illumination of some compelling idea. As we read him, or, perhaps better, journey with him in "the adventures of his soul among masterpieces," we feel in the presence of a mind thinking as it writes, rather than recording carefully prepared arguments or a prepackaged content. (Hartman *is* an essayist, his writing-thinking in this way recalling Montaigne.[4]) The journey itself bears significance: "thinking," Hartman contends, is "peripatetic" (STT 64), and "it is the *commentary process* that matters," the *work* of reading (CW 270). Intensely Hebraic, Hartman's spirit does not come to rest, or arrest itself, in an object. On the contrary, it wanders (and wonders), free. And as it does so, we wonder about his *point*: will he ever come to one, reach a destination, declare himself unequivocally, take a definite stand? Frustrated, we may conclude that he is a modern-day Hamlet sicklied o'er with the pale cast of thought. If that is our conclusion, more's the pity.

Resisting point results in both a slowing down of our reading and a "tender" or "affectionate" (STT 155) theorizing that, if gymnastic, produces minimal sting and reveals little if any arrogance of thought. In this, too, Hartman resembles Wordsworth, whom Keats branded as an example of the "egotistical sublime." For Hartman as for Wordsworth, *surmise* is crucial, and what Hartman writes of that poet applies to himself: "Wordsworth, under the impress of a powerful feeling, turns round both it and its apparent cause, respecting both and never reducing the one to the other." Surmise, moreover, "is fluid in nature; it likes 'whether ... or' formulations, alternatives rather than exclusions, echoing conjecture ... rather than blunt determinateness" (WP 8–9).

Hartman thus not only avoids assertion ('the aggressive summing up of a person or truth in words"), which is obviously a close kin of point, but he also offers writing permeated by "an atmosphere of thoughtfulness that rejects absolute positions" (EP 99, 134). Suspecting all one-way streets, he is wary of single solutions, stabilizing perspectives, and easy answers (UnRW 153). Typically, Hartman explores problems rather than provides answers; in fact, he *multiplies* questions and increases rather than resolves a mystery, able to live with "the malaise of never achieving a definitive or more than questioning way of stating things" (EP 218). His apparently offhand and plaintive remark in *Criticism in the Wilderness* reveals much: "I am not good at concluding" (131).

Continually "emphasiz[ing] the problem rather than pretend[ing] to solve it" (CW 211), Hartman reveals both an intellectual modesty – despite his enormous learning – and a remarkable capacity for remaining "in the wilderness," which he believes "is all we have," in fact (CW 15). Exhibiting the patience he urges on readers, Hartman manages, like Maurice Blanchot, whom he greatly admires, "to linger in uncertainty, to stay in the equivocal space of an embraced indeterminacy," and even to maintain himself "in the negative despite the strongest contrary pressure" (BF 106, 107). To questions hermeneutic, cultural, and political, Hartman's response is "deliberately hesitant": "To abide or not abide one's time, that is the question" (CW 32, 28). He suggests, in fact, that just as the humanities in general are characterized by their provision of "delay time" (EP 178 ff.) so hesitation "is almost the formal principle of literature itself" (STT 79). Thinking of art, Hartman says it is "no wonder some are scared witless by a mode of thinking that seems to offer no decidability, no resolution" (CW 283). Hartman is, fundamentally, essayistic.

It is, then, in and through such differences in style and thought that Hartman appears, "comes out." Rather than subordinate his commentary to the text being commented on, the critic should understand his or her work as a part of literature: criticism exists "within literature, not outside of it looking in" (CW 1). It in fact drives, Hartman believes, towards just such a recognition scene, implying a reversal whereby "the master–servant relation between criticism and creation" is "overturned in favor of what Wordsworth, describing the interaction of nature and mind, called 'mutual domination' or 'interchangeable supremacy'" (CW 259).

The individual interpreter thus bears considerable responsibility, and responsibility centrally if not primarily involves responsiveness to undeniable burdens and demands. As Hartman puts it, discussing the "echo structure" of Wordsworth's poetry, the reader

> must echo in himself a verse which he can only develop by the recognition that *de te fabula narratur*. The verse adjures him; demands grace of him; and no poet who reads so easily at first puts as resolute and lasting a demand on the reader. We are asked to read in ourselves. Thus Wordsworth's echo structure extends itself until we feel a relation between the poet looking "mutely" at the Boy of Winander's grave and the Stranger or Traveller – that is, Reader – on the horizon who will ponder this verse, the poet's inscription. Time stretches through this reader into a potentially infinite series of echoes. It is the reader who makes this verse responsive, however inward or buried its sounds: he also calls a voice out of silence. Alone, or as part of a family which includes Dorothy and Coleridge, he redeems the poet's voice from solitariness. In the ultimate pastoral, voice remains ghostly until it makes even the mute rock respond. "All things shall speak of Man." (FR 291)

Hartman understands understanding as involving a complex process that includes recognition, reception, and responsiveness to texts. A relationship exists that can only be described as one of "mutual domination" and "interchangeable supremacy," for the strength of books "is measured by our response, or not at all," and so "if certain works have become authoritative, it is because they at once sustain, and are sustained by, the readers they find" (CW 177, 170). In Virginia Woolf's words, "books continue each other, in spite of our habit of judging them separately."[5] The fate of books lies with us, who keep the dead alive, preserving them by elaboration as we accept our obligation to the concert of voices before, around, and presumably after us. "How much responsibility is on the respondent, on the interpreter" (STT 134), we exclaim with Hartman.

That is a burden difficult to bear. In a highly technological age, which prizes speed and efficiency (in *A Philosophy of Composition* E. D. Hirsch erects "relative readability" as the criterion for evaluating writing), the news Hartman brings, stressing the *work* of reading and the *labor* of the negative, as well as patience, is not good. Transmitted by this Bad News Angel is "the superficiality of all progressive schemes that cover up the old order, that try to lay it to rest" (CW 81). The "hermeneutic reflection" in which Hartman engages disables "the one-dimensional, progressive claims of conqueror or would-be conqueror" (CW 75). What remains, is precisely the issue, and Hartman is a profoundly *conservative* thinker, accepting the responsibilities of "the inspiring teacher in the humanities," represented at the close of *Criticism in the Wilderness*, who

> will always be pointing to something neglected by the dominant point of view, or something blunted by familiarity, or despised by fashion and social pressure. He is incurably a redeemer – not in the highflying sense but in the spirit-embedding sense. His active life is spent in uncovering and preserving traces of the contemplative life – those symbols and inscriptions buried in layers of change. Like Wordsworth's poet, the humanist recalls forgotten voices, arguments, artifacts, "things silently gone out of mind and things violently destroyed." (CW 300)

For Hartman, the Wandering Jew, there is no rest, only more travel, more travail, more work (of reading and writing) to be done.

Whether or not he "represents the future of the profession," the difference that Hartman's work of reading makes stems from the fact that he is not merely a critic, at least not as we are accustomed to regard critics. His concern does not come to rest in books, crucial though they be. What he is about was well described long ago by Georg Lukács in his well-known "On the Nature and Form of the Essay," to which Hartman has admitted being "drawn strongly" (CW 195): the true critic, writes Lukács, is "always speaking about the ultimate problems of life, but in a tone which implies that he is only discussing pictures and books, only the inessential and pretty ornaments of real life – and even then not their innermost substance but only their beautiful and useless surface."[6] Always concerned with "consciousness of consciousness," Hartman, however, never plays around the surface of texts. Reading him, on Wordsworth, say, we feel, in his scrupulous attention to the words within words, which he sounds out, that we are in the presence of a remarkably agile mind struggling also with emotions and human-heartedness. "In criticism," he writes, "we deal not with language as such, nor with the philosophy of language, but with how books or habits of reading *penetrate* our lives" (CW 202–3). The adventures we follow of Hartman's soul among masterpieces keep him in touch with human hopes and fears, possibilities and limits. And so when, for example, he writes, in *Beyond Formalism* about Andrew Marvell's "The Garden," its representation of false bodies of hope, and the interpreter's recognition of the necessity to chasten hope, which is hard to separate from haste and so can easily become apocalyptic, we soon realize that we are listening to something vital to the way we lead our lives (151–72).

In a review of *Criticism in the Wilderness*, originally published in *The New Yorker*, Helen Vendler sensitively reads Hartman's work as a (foreigner's) critique of American culture. She begins her review, in fact, as follows:

> We like to feel, in America, that we have lost that insularity which used to be a subject equally of jokes and of laments. With the world's books in our libraries, the world's art in our museums, the world's music in our concert halls, and, supremely, with so much twentieth-century art and literature our native product, we tend to think that the day when we had to be apologetic about our culture was over and gone. It comes, consequently, as something of a shock to have our insularity sharply, if suavely, taken to task by Geoffrey Hartman.[7]

Criticism in the Wilderness is the most pointed example of Hartman's critique, his most extended foray into cultural criticism. Vendler's achievement consists in showing that "Hartman's argument, though conducted on a literary-critical base, is really an argument against American taste in culture and American educational practice."[8] As Vendler acknowledges, "America is a child of England, in its thinking and its education in the humanities"; as a result, admits Vendler, generously, America is

> markedly impoverished in its capacity for thinking religiously, philosophically, or critically; the empiricism and positivism of the English philosophical tradition have governed our American intellectual procedures and styles, and divorced our critical thought from living connection with the largest questions of metaphysics, private ethics, and social responsibility.[9]

In *Criticism in the Wilderness*, Hartman brings to bear on Anglo-American empiricism, pragmatism, and formalism European philosophical thought, and the entire tradition of hermeneutics (including Rabbinical), confronting Matthew Arnold, T. S. Eliot, and Northrop Frye with Hegel, the Frankfurt School, and Walter Benjamin, as well as England's own maverick, Thomas Carlyle; *Sartor Resartus* he describes as "a nauseous cure or asafetida for British empiricism," its "remarkable," "crazy, mockingbird style" being an important part of Carlyle's "covert transfusion of Northern religious enthusiasm ... into German nature-enthusiasm and its transcendental symbolics" (CW 47, 48). "New Critical Reduction," hard on the heels of the "Arnoldian Concordat," reduced criticism to a secondary and service function, the critic to a mere pedagogue (as H. L. Mencken lamented). Against the "sublimated chatter" of the English tradition in criticism (CW 199), "a donnish discourse of civilized conversation, a restricted or accommodated style fearful of the more speculative extravagances of the mind, and a 'pastoral' model of criticism, which is based on the needs of the immature flock of students rather than on the 'theological' demands of sophisticated interpretation," Hartman places those engaged in the current "Revisionist Reversal." They refuse to accept the limitations imposed on them by the reigning conception of the critic's role and responsibilities. This is an expanded role for criticism, an understanding of critics as "being widely informed and broadly read, speaking in the public forum on matters of general concern and bringing the ethical and aesthetic perceptions gained from their reading into social discourse."[10] The desired model is European: in Europe, as Vendler puts it,

> Critic and artist were in the past more likely to be one and the same person; vernacular literature was not until rather recently a university subject, and the person writing an essay on a piece of art was likely himself to be what Eliot called "a practitioner" of that art – a poet or a novelist, or even a painter or a musician. An essay was simply one manifestation of the self as creator, and creative work another. The man of letters (to confine the case to literature) wrote in many different forms – some speculative, some critical, some creative; some public, some intimate; some formal, some informal. The man of letters felt able to write about issues other than literary ones; he read as naturally in historical or philosophical or legal or religious texts as he did in epic or pastoral. Milton is one of Hartman's examples of this ample reach; Pound appears as a writer who had the right notion of scope but went "bad in a good cause" – that of relating the realm of art to politics.[11]

But – and this is something Vendler fails to note – there is Jerusalem as well as Frankfurt and Paris. Hartman's thought owes as much to the Rabbis and midrash, to the peculiarly Jewish imagination, as it does to European (secular) philosophy.

In order to specify Hartman's place within such cultural criticism as Vendler discusses, we might consider the example of George Steiner. Cosmopolitan and well versed in philosophy European as well as Anglo-American, Steiner writes in a style obviously different from that of Hartman: if not exactly "teatotalling," that style is composed, urbane, dignified, rather than mixed and playful; it is therefore more accessible. Steiner's stylistic urbanity matches his arguments. Consider, in this regard, the essay "The Archives of Eden," in which Steiner essentially repudiates American claims for significant cultural achievement or originality. In literature, as in painting, music, and philosophy, claims Steiner, American efforts have been parasitical and at best second-rate, and the reason for that failure lies in democracy itself, the lack of an "elite model" to nurture genius. Now, no matter how simplistic my summary has made Steiner's position sound, it is by no means totalitarian ("The flowering of the humanities is not worth the circumstance of the inhuman. No play by Racine is worth a Bastille, no Mandelstam poem an hour of Stalinism"). At times, moreover, Steiner's language and ideas recall Hartman's: an "authentic culture ... makes 'response' 'responsibility,' it makes echo 'answerable to' the high occasions of the mind." Still, for all his elasticity, Steiner is not only less democratic than Hartman but also more negative.[12] If Hartman criticizes America, and he does, more implicitly than explicitly, it is not to put America down, but on the contrary to point in untried but potentially productive ways towards traditions we need to know better. Neither dismissive nor nostalgic, his aim is at once critical, recuperative, and generative.[13] A product of history and of the unique history that is Jewish, and (so) wary of apocalyptic dreams, Hartman is not much taken with "elite models" or, even if it be attractive, the notion of "authentic culture" (Steiner's terms). And that prospect, fueled by the promise of a style erudite and classical, is attractive. Hartman's efforts and effects are different: he unsettles, makes uncomfortable, leaves us with more questions than proposed solutions, more questions, in fact, than when we turned to him. It remains a question, therefore, whether such a strategy will prove productive.

Ambitious, yet not apocalyptic, his hopes tempered and seasoned, Hartman seeks a critical essay at once responsive and responsible, artful and culturally involved. What he seeks in bringing the European philosophical tradition and its union of hermeneutics and speculation to bear on our "cultural nakedness"[14] is not an overthrow of Anglo-Americanism by the Germans and the French but something very different, something that does not yet exist: "an independent American perspective" (CW 10). The pages that follow attempt to describe Hartman's own perspective and procedures and so the possibilities he holds out for a revitalized, responsible *criticism*.

2

A matter of relation, a question of place: Hartman and contemporary criticism

Psychoanalysis may seem ... a *Pardes*.... If we must enter it, let us not do it like most psychoanalysts. Instead of pretending to save literature for psychoanalysis, and showing a Pygmalion condescension toward all those beautiful works of art, let us rather claim to save psychoanalysis for literary studies.... I comment on the dangerous liaison between literary studies and psychoanalysis.

Equally dangerous is the liaison between rhetorical studies and literature.

... Some will accuse me, no doubt, of deconstructing without a license.

The Fate of Reading

[T]his final chapter becomes, among other things, a counter-statement to Derrida. It is not a refutation but rather a different turn in how to state the matter. A restored theory of representation should acknowledge the deconstructionist challenge as necessary and timely, if somewhat self-involved – that is, only occasionally reflective of analogies to its own project in religious writing and especially in literary writing.

Saving the Text

[T]he Yale critics had their own practice with roots in the New Criticism.... Their tendency, fed by many sources including Freud, was not so much to radicalize ambiguity and to delay closing the interpretation as to see *through* literary form to the way language or symbolic process makes or breaks meaning.... but the main thrust of this American deconstruction that did not know its name was to create a more dialectical and open view of how literature worked.

... The *practice* of deconstruction was forged in America, even if the *theory* had to await Derrida.

Easy Pieces

Though highly individualistic, Hartman spins no theory or system out of his own imagination. Instead, he ranges widely over texts "primary" and "secondary," taking from various theoretical positions without being taken over by any of them. Describing Hartman this way may call to mind the familiar distinction between the spider and the bee central to the ages-old Ancients–Moderns controversy, in which he believes we continue to be embroiled (CW 239). Whereas the spider, or Modern, as Swift elaborated on the Aristotelian distinction in *The Battle of the Books*, is "a domestick animal furnished with a native stock within [him] self," the materials for whose "large castle" are thus "extracted altogether out of [his] own person," the bee, or Ancient, engages, as his opponent puts it, in "an universal plunder upon nature," "stealing" from "a nettle as readily as a violet." For the bee, classical no less in his determinacy than in his precision – he always reaches a point and thus stings –

> the question comes all to this – which is the nobler being of the two, that which by a lazy contemplation of four inches round, by an overweening pride, feeding and engendering on itself, turns all into excrement and venom, produces nothing at last, but flybane and a cobweb; or that which, by an universal range, with long search, much study, true judgment, and distinction of things, brings home honey and wax.[1]

That the difference Swift thus describes is both applicable to Hartman and impossible to draw absolutely or unproblematically is precisely the point – one, moreover, valuable for understanding what the latter is all about. Like the bee, Hartman not only ranges widely over texts and theories and broods long over them, but he is also committed to "much study, true judgment, and distinction of things." He does not, however, normally sting nor so much plunder other texts as engage in responsive dialogue with them, producing as a result a kind of criticism that becomes difficult to di*sting*uish from the text being responded to. Whether or not his production is sweetness and light, it is, quite unlike the spider's, food for thought with power to sustain. That Hartman's work thus exhibits aspects of both the Ancients and the Moderns exemplifies the nature of his hermeneutic, or both/and, reflection. There is nothing pure, or simple, or uncontaminated, about Hartman's critical endeavor, which everywhere calls into question, as a matter of fact, our "innate purity perplex" (CW 292).

A MATTER OF RELATION, A QUESTION OF PLACE

From the very beginning of his career, Hartman has practiced a sophisticated strategy of close reading and responding to texts that both borrows from and goes considerably beyond reigning critical procedures and orthodoxies, challenging them in fundamental ways to be more open, dialectical, responsive, and responsible. The particular nature of the alternative Hartman offers, I attempt to make clear in this book. I begin, in this chapter, with his response to – and place in – contemporary criticism.

As I have noted elsewhere, Hartman's critical efforts bear important analogies to several other major voices that can be heard throughout his writing.[2] These include Ernst Gombrich and his work on the psychology of perception and "the beholder's share"; Jean Starobinski's *Words upon Words*, which presents Saussure's almost mystical work on anagrams; Bakhtin and his revolutionary sense of the dialogical nature of language; the entire Germanic tradition of hermeneutics, from Dilthey to Bultmann, the "new hermeneutic" of Ebeling and Fuchs, and, of course, both Heidegger and Gadamer; the "intellectual poetry" of Walter Benjamin and the "critical theory" of Theodor Adorno; Martin Buber, whose *I and Thou* is a call to relation that greatly influenced Harold Bloom's first book and significantly parallels much in Hartman; Jacques Lacan, whose psychoanalytical theories Hartman thinks through in *Saving the Text*, as he does Benjamin's cultural ones in *Criticism in the Wilderness*; and not least, Kenneth Burke, whose resemblances often appear but never more clearly than in *Criticism in the Wilderness* (most notably pp. 86–114). As even the most cursory reading suggests, Hartman's work is thus related to the widespread interest in correcting the imbalance suffered at the hands of the New Critics and restoring the reader to a deserved place of importance in the determination and even the creation of textual meaning. Yet Hartman must be distinguished from such "reader-oriented" and receptionist critics as Stanley Fish, Norman Holland, David Bleich, Wolfgang Iser, and Hans-Robert Jauss. Rather than on the reader, the reading process, or response as those are (differently) defined by reader-response critics, Hartman stresses, and values, obligation. Instead, then, of response, understood as an emotional or intellectual effect aroused in the process of reading, he emphasizes the reader's engagement, personal involvement, witness, and accountability, the burden and "stress of vocation" associated with the *work* of reading.

The indebted, responsive, and characteristically impure, or both/and, nature of Hartman's hermeneutic reflection appears, with particular vividness, in his relation to phenomenology and the so-called criticism of consciousness it inspired in the efforts of "Geneva critics" like Georges Poulet, Gaston Bachelard, and the early J. Hillis Miller.[3] When Hartman began writing in the early 1950s (*The Unmediated Vision* is a revision of his Yale dissertation), "criticism of consciousness" was just about the only mode of Continental criticism having any effect at all on the Anglo-American critical scene, and even that impact was slight. The European tradition, philosophical, speculative, and brooding, certainly affected not only Hartman's first book but also his focus in his 1964 study of Wordsworth's "consciousness of consciousness" (if mine is "phenomenological procedure," he added, "So be it" ["Retrospect 1971," WP xii]) and in his later experiment in "phenomenological thematics" proclaimed in "Evening Star and Evening Land," which is included in *The Fate of Reading*. But a central concern of the essays in *Beyond Formalism* is the difficulty, if not the impossibility, of transcending the study of forms, so important to Anglo-American critics but virtually dissolved in the "criticism of consciousness." In his preface to the last-mentioned volume, Hartman marks the complications attendant on our felt need somehow to decide between the rival claims of consciousness and those of form. I quote from an important paragraph evincing his respect for both claims: "Despite an allegiance to the Continental style of criticism," he begins, "I feel strongly what James called 'the coercive charm of form.'" Though the attractiveness of form is considerably more than a matter of charm, Hartman is by no means stranded, unable to choose and impotent, between the competing claims and their respective charms; on the contrary, he finds a dialectic at work within them. In his following sentences he elaborates on the reasons for both his "allegiance" and his refusal to make that allegiance exclusive:

> Continental criticism can be a lesson in how to subvert the specificity of literature. In attacking "the naive, egotistical idea of the work's unity" (Gaston Bachelard), it often neglects literary form and dissolves art into a reflex of consciousness, technology, or social process. In Anglo-America, respect for literary form is a priori, but not necessarily deeper.

No matter the strength of his early background (he was born and reared in Frankfurt-am-Main), Hartman writes as an Anglo-

American (he received his undergraduate education at the City University of New York, his graduate training at Yale University): "A more radical difference" between the study of forms and that of unconsciousness, he continues,

> centers on the presumed objectivity of the work of art: for us the reader in his selfhood is the problem, and he needs historical, philological, or similar correctives...; but for the Continental critic it is the objective form of art which seems problematic, and he seeks to liberate it, to release a hidden or repressed content. Not our subjectivity is to be feared but our overreaction to it, those pseudo-objective criteria which imprison both the work and ourselves. (BF xi)

About hermeneutics, whose association with phenomenology is, of course, close, Hartman has long harbored reservations, even as he has continually engaged in forms of hermeneutic activity. In *Saving the Text* he reflects on the nature of interpretation as both intuitive and counterintuitive, both (if you will) Pauline and Nietzschean (138 ff.) He is wary, in fact, of the frequent link between hermeneutics and accommodation, whereby reader and text, present and past, the known and the unfamiliar come to occupy the *same* space, differences somehow having been dissolved. In *The Fate of Reading*, Hartman goes so far as to claim that "we must set interpretation *against* hermeneutics." He distances himself from the latter because it "seeks to reconstruct, or get back to, an origin in the form of sacred text, archetypal unity or authentic story." Hartman thus finally diverges from the hermeneutics of Hans-Georg Gadamer, which, in its faith in a fusion of horizons between text and reader, past and present, explication and application, connotes an undialectical indiscriminateness and totalizing unacceptable to Hartman. He also rejects the rigid "distinction between a primary source and secondary literature, or between 'great Original' and its imitations" that "is the space in which traditional hermeneutics works" (16). The alternative he endorses is a "negative hermeneutics," which may be said to link the intuitive and the counterintuitive: "On its older function of saving the text, of tying it once again to the life of the mind, is superimposed the new one of doubting, by a parodistic or playful movement, master theories that claim to have overcome the past, the dead, the false" (CW 239 – the idea may derive from Paul Ricoeur).

While phenomenology and hermeneutics have long been influential on Hartman, psychoanalysis has come more and more to play a major role in his thinking. In *The Fate of Reading* Hartman recognized that psychoanalysis "may seem to future critics a *Pardes*" ("the 'paradise' of Biblical exegesis"), and for that reason he issued a caveat while acknowledging the potential for a fruitful relation between literature and psychoanalysis. If we must enter the paradise towards which psychoanalysis beckons us, he wrote in 1975, then "let us not do it like most psychoanalysts. Instead of pretending to save literature for psychoanalysis, and showing a Pygmalion condescension toward all those dumb if beautiful works of art, let us rather claim to save psychoanalysis for literary studies" (ix). Rather than imperialistic bombast, Hartman's point actually reflects his wariness of all totalitarian schemes – as well as his unshakeable belief in the power and insight of art. Having asserted the primacy of literature, he adds that the essays collected in The *Fate of Reading* "seek to lay the ground for a field of inquiry that might be called psychoesthetics." In the very next breath, however, he offers, typically, a counterremark or at least an important qualification, noting that in some of the other essays in the volume he comments on "the dangerous liaison between literary studies and psychoanalysis" (ix). Here and elsewhere Hartman finds that danger and promise are inseparable, cross over into one another – it is just such a chiasmus that always already "subvert[s] the very idea of winning" (CW 75). As to the issue at hand, the best that can be hoped for, as Hartman expresses it in the Preface to *Psychoanalysis and the Question of the Text*, is a "fruitful complication of psychoanalytic studies as they accept their mutual rather than masterful relation to language and literature" (vii). Such complicating is everywhere apparent in Hartman, characterizing his thinking; as with Wordsworth, so with Hartman, mutuality rather than mastery "triumphs."

After commenting on "the dangerous liaison between literary studies and psychoanalysis," Hartman proceeds, in The *Fate of Reading*, to declare that "equally dangerous is the liaison between rhetorical studies and literature." By the former term he refers to what is "newly imported from France, via Lacan and Derrida, though the work of Kenneth Burke, as well as that of Empson, Richards, and Frye, and even the academic revival of rhetorical studies in the period between roughly 1930 and 1960 (Curtius, Wallerstein, Tuve, Ong) resembles it" (ix). There is little doubt that Hartman has reservations concerning deconstruction's particular appropriation of rhetoric, even in the work of his late colleague and friend Paul de Man, which he greatly admires. Admiration, of course, does not entail acceptance and need not forestall doubt and criticism. Thus, as he readily acknowledges the necessity of rhetorical readings as well as the fundamentally figurative nature of language, Hartman worries that de Man's "monistic" position (FR 311) becomes "too absolute" (CW 108).[4] Brooding over Yeats's "Leda and the Swan" in the context of the rhetorical question, Hartman offers a brief and largely undeveloped counterstatement to de Man's "Semiology and Rhetoric," a *locus classicus* of rhetorical (i.e. deconstructive) reading strategies. Having earlier written, *pace* de Man, that "power tends to be associated not with language but with 'spirit,'" Hartman now manifests the "hermeneutical perplexity" that he fears de Man's rhetorical machinery forecloses. The final question in Yeats's poem, he writes,

> has somewhat of a finer tone, for it obliges the reader to become active, even to risk something. The question now is like a balance-point, which one unbalances by taking it up. Though it remains "rhetorical" in form, a reader can, perhaps must, develop it. What was rhetorical is no longer clearly on the side of inevitable, predetermined meaning, understood only *nachträglich*, *ex eventu*: after an event that seems to be the ground for the question. For what was rhetorical has moved through itself to the side of a more general meditative stance. We can *stand*, as it were, in that question, we can take our time and think of the relation of the human mind to what overthrows it.

He proceeds to claim that an accompanying indeterminacy

> turns rhetoric from a coefficient of power, which makes us victims also when we think we participate, to an imaginative or hermeneutic instrument of the pressured, time-haunted mind. Genuine rhetorical questions are therefore antirhetorical. Their "open-endedness, a refusal to speak the unspeakable, solve the unsolvable, resolve the unresolvable," discloses a freedom of thought that was in doubt. (CW 272–3)[5]

The importance of that reservation marks Hart-*m*an's significant difference from de *M*an, whose deconstructive machinery, while perhaps not tyrannical and certainly not terroristic, seems relentless and not so supportive of either hermeneutic reflection or the *tender* regard for "freedom of thought" that Hartman prizes.

Towards the Derridean and more conceptual form of deconstruction, as towards the de Manian and rhetorical, Hartman expresses both admiration and wariness, exactly the kind of balanced response we have noted *vis-à-vis* other theoretical positions. Even though Hartman wrote an elaborate and "answerable" book on Derrida's *Glas* and contributed to the "manifesto" published as *Deconstruction and Criticism*, for which he did the Preface and a long essay on Wordsworth, he can by no means be identified with this *bête noire* of contemporary criticism. The aforementioned Preface makes clear his (and Bloom's) difference from the more "orthodox" deconstructionists in the "Yale School," de Man, Derrida, and Miller. Emphasizing their differences, Hartman ends by writing that these critics

> amicably if not quite convincingly held together by the covers of this book differ considerably in their approach to literature and literary theory. *Caveat lector*. Derrida, de Man, and Miller are certainly boa-deconstructors, merciless and consequent, though each enjoys his own style of disclosing again and again the "abysm" of words. But Bloom and Hartman are barely deconstructionists. They even write against it on occasion. Though they understand Nietzsche when he says "the deepest pathos is still aesthetic play," they have a stake in that pathos: its persistence, its psychological provenance. For them the ethos of literature is not dissociable from its pathos, whereas for deconstructionist criticism literature is precisely that use of language which can purge pathos, which can show that it too is figurative, ironic, or aesthetic.[6]

Despite the dustjacket's vaunted claim, Hartman believes that *Deconstruction and Criticism* is less a manifesto than a book of essays retaining "the style and character of each writer" and addressing "a shared set of problems."[7] His characteristic emphasis on the evocation of human emotion, here associated with pathos and described as implicating the critic in any text studied, marks a significant difference among the "Yale critics." Hartman's reflections, moreover, manifest his particular version of both/and thinking, even if the precarious balance he typically achieves seems momentarily threatened by the pointed depiction of de Man, Derrida, and Miller as "boa-deconstructors," who, "merciless and consequent," crush the life – or pathos – out of texts, an act they repeat "again and again."

Hartman's family quarrel with deconstruction leads to a most important point. He implies it in *Deconstruction and Criticism* when he writes that, though it represents "more of a relentless focus on certain questions, and a new rigor when it comes to the discipline of close reading," deconstructive criticism "does not present itself as a novel enterprise" at all.[8] That deconstruction is neither new nor unprecedented Hartman has long recognized and argued. In 1975, as he wrote (again typically) "against" it while admitting to "deconstructing without a license," he reflected on "the historicity of even the most purified kinds of thinking. Hence my periodization of Derrida's philosophical antimasque," he adds, placing the "father" of deconstruction within *literary* tradition as an analogue of Mallarmé and a "cousin" of Borges (FR x) The analogy between deconstructive criticism, no matter how novel it seems, and other forms of writing is precisely the issue. It becomes the basis of Hartman's "counterstatement to Derrida" in the last chapter of *Saving the Text*. The "restored theory of representation" for which he strives "should acknowledge," writes Hartman, "the deconstructionist challenge as necessary and timely, if somewhat self-involved – that is, only occasionally reflective of analogies to its own project in religious writing and especially in literary writing" (121).

For Hartman, always insistent on extensive knowledge of history, it is not simply that the poets, and perhaps the Rabbis and patristic exegetes as well, were there before the theorists but also that at least some of the latter, who are above all *writers*, were there before Derrida. This point he drives home in an essay-review entitled "Wild, Fierce Yale," which uses Christopher Norris's book on deconstruction as the occasion for some unusually straightforward comments on the "Yale critics." Hartman is particularly interested in, and amenable to, Norris's way of "defining the intellectual milieu" of what Hartman describes as "a controversial array of writers active in America since about 1955, though not achieving full notoriety till the advent of Derrida and his invasion of American academic criticism in the 1970s" (EP 189). Acknowledging indebtedness while claiming some originality, Hartman asserts that "the Yale critics had their own practice with roots in the New Criticism, a movement they questioned long before Derrida arrived on the scene." Rejecting Frank Lentricchia's description of the "Yale critics" as merely "camp followers of changing philosophical fashions," Hartman maintains that their practice constituted an "earlier phase" of deconstruction. Even "if the *theory* had to await Derrida," "the *practice* of deconstruction was forged in America" as early as the mid-1950s (190).

What that practice was, at least as Hartman engaged in it, I want now to consider. In arguing that Hartman's earliest work, *The Unmediated Vision*, is proto-deconstructive in aim and strategies, I am interested not merely in that fact but in what that says about both Hartman and deconstruction. In other words, deconstruction is not a "novel enterprise" at all but instead a range of attitudes and recognitions with diverse and often surprising analogues. That Hartman's work, from the beginning, shares many of those attitudes and exhibits some of those recognitions, makes all the clearer his importance – not because he was doing deconstruction but because he was practicing a sophisticated, wary, open, and dialectical criticism that has some claim to originality. Of course, any originality is inseparable from the parallels and analogues with other writers, past, present, and future. The criticism Hartman has always done reflects the kinds of thinking I have been tracing throughout this chapter.

Though I focus in the remainder of this chapter on *The Unmediated Vision*, I shall look briefly at Hartman's contribution to the deconstructive "manifesto," "Words, Wish, Worth: Wordsworth," because the juxtaposition of these texts, written twenty-five years apart, will help us better to grasp the nature of Hartman's critical and often deconstructive efforts. Now, in suggesting that Hartman's earliest and his very recent work constitutes a continuum, I do not deny, nor do I mean to minimize, differences that certainly exist. There is no way, nor any need to try, to collapse his various texts into one.[9] Though the Introduction to *The Unmediated Vision* sounds themes developed later (e.g., "I am still not certain of my theme.... These essays leave certain things *in potentia*; and I hope this will not make for too much obscurity" [xi]), and though he already opposes easy accommodation of ideas (e.g., in the 1966 Prefatory Note to the Harbinger Edition reprint, he writes of his "hope that what follows is dry enough to prevent interpretation from being consolation, or merely that" [v]), Hartman is, at this early stage of his career, less variable stylistically than he became later, more straightforward and conventionally scholarly, but though not yet playful, certainly not dull or stuffy. "Words, Wish, Worth: Wordsworth," on the other hand, is brooding and speculative, less restrained, its movement reflective of "the course of interpretive discovery," rather than argumentative or ratiocinative.[10] It is, however, less pyrotechnical in its effects than the essays in *Saving the Text*, where Hartman adopts a style "answerable" to Derrida's *Glas*, the "subject" of his study.[11]

What is most clearly and specifically deconstructive in the 1979 essay has to do with the reversal and, indeed, oscillation of mastery that marks Wordsworth's familiar struggles with the rival claims of mind (or imagination) and nature. According to Hartman, recalling Wordsworth's epiphanic experience on Mount Snowdon (recorded in the fourteenth book of *The Prelude*), "the power in sound and the power in light, or ear and eye, or nature and mind, are asymmetrical elements that struggle toward ... 'interchangeable supremacy,' 'mutual domination.' There is no single locus of majesty or mastery...."[12] Here appears the close analogy between Wordsworth's insight and the now-familiar formulations that Derrida has labeled deconstruction.

That Hartman writes from *within* deconstruction though without being *of* it becomes all the more explicit when he describes in "Wild, Fierce Yale" the other "Yale critics'" relation to New Criticism, so I'll turn to that before resuming consideration of *The Unmediated Vision*. As he claims that the "Yale critics" were practicing a "deconstruction that did not know its name," Hartman proceeds to explain the symbiosis that exists between deconstruction and New Criticism, frequently figured as inveterate enemies. Having been taught by the poets, Hartman maintains that a "controversial array of writers active in America since about 1955" wrote both within and against New Criticism. This they did

> by a more rigorous application of its own emphasis on the text rather than on the text's historical frame. But even the text as its own frame is questioned by this group, which did not privilege unity by vesting it in the "achieved" or "coherent" form of a literary work. Their tendency, fed by many sources including Freud, was not so much to radicalize ambiguity and to delay closing the interpretation as to see *through* literary form to the way language or symbolic process makes or breaks meaning. To hold that making and breaking together risked, sometimes, giving the impression of enchanting disenchantment.

Continuing, Hartman offers a crucial distinction, which focuses on the openness and freedom he himself prizes and exhibits:

> the main thrust of this American deconstruction that did not know its name was to create a more dialectical and open view of how literature worked. The rhetoric of "tension," refined by the New Critics as irony, paradox, and controlled ambiguity, seemed too self-enclosing a version of literariness. It was felt that the New Critics promulgated under aesthetic cover a language ontology that made poetic and religious claims converge. (EP 190)

Seeing "through literary form to the way language or symbolic process makes or breaks meaning" and struggling "to break with incarnationist and imagistic theories" so as to "create a more dialectical and open view of how literature work[s]" – these figure among the important aims of *The Unmediated Vision*. Not only do the essays in that book, if more or less conventional in style and form – they are, in fact, articles rather than essays – , "leave certain things *in potentia*," but Hartman also advances the argument that literature, which he describes as "a distinctive mode of knowledge," enlists "in the service of no one, not even of truth" (xi). The openness this suggests, and with it an implied difference from New Criticism, appears clearly in the Introduction. The goal of *The Unmediated Vision*, Hartman writes, is nothing less than "complete interpretation" or a "criticism without approach," which "would respect both the persistent ideal unity of the work of art and the total human situation from which it springs" (x). Hartman looks, in fact, towards "a unified multiple interpretation of poetry," believing that "since the poem brings the complete man into activity, its symbols are open to various explanations equally valid as long as the unity or identity to which all tend is found" (xi–xii). Though traces of Coleridgean and New Critical "organic unity" surface in such remarks, Hartman goes considerably beyond the reigning orthodoxy of the 1950s, for the unity he seeks is much more encompassing than that envisioned by Brooks, Wimsatt, and company. The effect of his grounding in Continental modes of thought, particularly phenomenology and the "criticism of consciousness" it inspired, surfaces when, for example, he writes that since "there is no order of discrete things ... the poem should be taken as a whole, and the poet's work as a whole, or not at all" (xii).

Hartman proceeds to detail how Wordsworth, Hopkins, Rilke, and Valéry, in their individual quests for an "unmediated vision," "break with incarnationist or imagistic theories" of expression. Despite their differences, and the varying degrees of success they achieve, these poets "are at one in their quest for a pure representation. But as *modern* poets they are related by their effort to gain pure representation through the direct sensuous intuition of reality" (156). As moderns, in fact, according to Hartman, they have "suffered a distinct loss in the power to represent the world as a created thing" (157); there followed, in addition, an accompanying loss of belief in man as the apex of creation. A view of creation "as immanent and continual" replaces the biblical account, and consequent upon the irretrievable loss of the latter is "the modern poet's concern with the *inherent* arbitrariness of symbols" (158, 160–1). In the biblical and logocentric understanding (the Derridean term is exact here), Hartman notes,

> though words have a merely arbitrary or conventional relation to their referents, they are assured of a sacred origin. As words they are arbitrary, but as symbols divine; and the same holds for any other system of reference including that of the orders of creation, inasmuch as marked by the mark of God. (161)

Important among the consequences Hartman notes of Romantic developments is "the leveling of symbols or the fusion of *genres*," which accompanies the recognition of "the essential indifference of subject matter," a point that bears directly on his own later argument concerning the symbiotic rather than hierarchical relation between "literature" and commentary, "primary" texts and "secondary" (161, 162). This leveling means that

> nothing now declares God of itself, but all is the work of man, including the testaments; and all is profane as it is sacred, and cannot be more than his conceptions which remain conceptions. Symbols are only such by pretense, and the entirety of life is caught up in this pretense. Everything is *in potentia* equally sign and equally symbol. (161)

Entailed, in other words, is an immanentism, which J. Hillis Miller later explored in *The Disappearance of God* (1963) and *Poets of Reality* (1965), as well as an unavoidable acceptance of "the *inherent* arbitrariness of symbols," a condition that Saussure exploited and that became virtually foundational for deconstruction. With this discovered arbitrariness, "the bread and wine on the tongue is, like the word, only bread and wine, and yet, as Claudel says, 'Chair de Dieu sur ma langue, consacre mon coeur et mon principe'" (161). The paths thus open to modern poets, according to Hartman, were two: they could accept the arbitrariness of language and "make it both specific and total as in music," or else "effects which, though not as yet totally known, [might] be related to the imminent ... formations of consciousness." But this, Hartman adds, reflecting on the break with "imagistic" theories, bears on another way to overcome arbitrariness, and that involves "an exploration of the inner motion and incipient meanings of human speech as such: the discovery of the *voice* of the spoken word" (136). Voice – not *image* of voice but the spoken word's voice – continues to represent an effective alternative for

Hartman and is, in fact, a central concern of *Saving the Text* and of his recent essays on Wordsworth.

Considering more specifically now the proto-deconstructionism of *The Unmediated Vision*, I want to look at the reading strategies Hartman employs as well as at some of the local arguments. I turn first to his reading of an important passage in the fourth book of *The Excursion* (lines 1207-24). To begin with, Hartman notes Wordsworth's advocacy of "an ethic based on the 'constraint of love': *one cannot choose but love*, and seek the world in love, if one has communed with Nature." But this by no means tells the whole story, for in Hartman's words "the language does not entirely lend itself to the argument" (37). Those words sound familiar; they are the terms of deconstruction: though Hartman obviously did not set out to do deconstructive work, he has, in effect, discovered an *aporia*, the text's "navel," the point where the tapestry begins to unravel, Wordsworth's poem differing from "itself." Explaining how the text thus deconstructs, Hartman writes:

> It is said that a communion with Nature will gradually bring about a compulsive love. Yet the very word "communes" in the second line indicates a spirit of action already present which need only be set in motion; the phrase "with understanding heart" likewise. We thought at first that Nature would effect the change by her own agency, force the hard heart to love and spread love; we now perceive that the heart must already be understanding before love can come to it. At one point, the poet represents man as passive, "he by degrees perceives/ His feelings of aversion softened down;" at another point as active, already possessing what he is to possess, "who with understanding heart/ Both knows and loves." The very end is the only successful part. It betrays the real argument, which is that man acts, looks round, seeks, finds, not simply through the exercise of his will, but through a transcendent, pure principle of love that makes his heart understand before it has tried to understand. (37-8)

To apply Paul de Man's distinction, Hartman engages here not in paraphrase but in "genuinely analytical reading," which exposes how – in his own terms – *The Excursion* "betrays" its "real argument."[13] But unlike de Man's, despite the similarity in strategy, Hartman's reading is neither relentless nor merciless. The tender concern that surfaces for Wordsworth's own responsive *heart* marks

Hartman's ability to take from deconstruction, as from New Criticism and psychoanalysis, without being taken over by it.

Hartman's later points concerning relational knowledge require extended consideration, for they bear importantly on the analogies between Hartman's earliest thinking and deconstruction:

> Wordsworth's "understanding heart" forestalls and invalidates the entire logical sequence. "Understanding" is used in an absolute sense. We do not wish to ask what the heart understands, or how, etc. In one word, we would forgo relational knowledge. But the poet has put it into an argumentative context, so that we are forced to ask questions about "relatives," the what, how, and where, and so, finally, to disparage. Successful metaphysical statement, if it is to occur, must occur without prompting the mind to seek knowledge of relations. (UnMV 38)

Like Wordsworth, Hartman endorses an immediate, perhaps intuitive awareness of relatedness that is able to forgo *questions* of relation. The poet, he claims,

> feels himself, and is able to express himself, as fundamentally in relation, not with any particular, in any particular way, for any particular reason (though with some thing, in some way, for some reason), but *in relation*; so that poetry is more immediate, that is, less dependent on a relational use of symbols, than ordinary discourse. (39)

And the reason the poet can forgo relational thinking is simple: "he knows certainly that there is relation" (40).

This matter of relatedness, which Hartman identifies with poetic thinking, is central to if not characteristic of both structuralism and poststructuralism; it also cuts to the quick of Hartman's particular and highly individual – i.e., Romantic – thinking. I am not, however, concerned with thinking that is relational in the way Hartman privileges. My interest lies, instead, in the prior issue of relation itself, no matter how that came about, whether immediately and perhaps intuitively, or as a result of a series of probing questions. It is, of course, relation that I have been discussing throughout this chapter. Hartman's position *vis-à-vis* the various theories discussed, like his way of negotiating the rival claims of form and consciousness, exemplifies the very relationality he takes from Wordsworth, itself an analogue of deconstructive understanding.

In *The Unmediated Vision* the issue of relation emerges with striking clarity as Hartman discusses the fundamental Wordsworthian dilemma, figured as a wrenching struggle between the powers of nature and those of mind or imagination. Though it took years of anguished brooding to gain the wisdom, Wordsworth ultimately arrived at a "profound respect for both partners of the act of understanding," both mind and object (5). To sustain that respect proves extremely difficult, the temptation always being great to privilege one partner in the act of understanding rather than to stand in the precarious but essential play between them. Indeed, Hartman thought in 1954, it may be impossible to do so: the imagination, he writes, "cannot be true either to itself or to Nature, unless usurped by a third power ... at the moment when the creative will is at rest" (13). That third power, which Hartman defines variously as "a principle of generosity" (14) and "the dialectic of love" between man and nature (20), but which could be named *other-wise*, is "found now in Nature, now in man, [but] belongs ultimately neither to Nature as external nature nor to man" (15). However it is defined, the sustaining power ebbs and flows, oscillating between man and nature, creating a relation of reciprocity.

Such reciprocity is possible, it seems, only because of what the mind and its object share: that "an identical power sustains knower and known appears to be a necessary component of any true act of knowledge" (150), writes Hartman. Though he does not, of course, employ Derrida's notion of the "trace," his explanation certainly anticipates the idea, developed in *Of Grammatology*, that "without a retention in the minimal unit of temporal experience, without a trace retaining the other as other in the same, no difference would do its work and no meaning would appear."[14] Concerned with Wordsworth's answer to the question "what makes the act of knowledge possible," Hartman writes:

> There must be something which sustains thought, and something which sustains the object to thought. The existence of this something would not in itself explain knowledge unless that which sustains in the object to thought is identical to that which sustains thought itself. Only in the light of such a hypothesis can we understand all those dicta that relate to the possibility of intention, for example Aristotle's statement in the *Metaphysics*: "Actual knowledge is always at one with its object." This being true, we would find in every recorded experience of perfect knowledge a question implicit on the identity of knower with known and on the subject of this identity. (148–9)

The name of the reciprocal relation that Hartman discerns in *The Unmediated Vision* is what, along with "mutual domination," Wordsworth calls "interchangeable supremacy." Hardly any other idea can claim as much prominence in Hartman's thinking. Like Wordsworth's, Hartman's work typically takes as one of its major tasks the representation of "the mobile, responsive, reciprocal factor" in relationships conventionally figured as oppositions.[15] In its respect for the Other, Hartman's thinking may also be seen as richly and deeply Hebraic – the Jewish "heritage of a common historical experience," in short, their memory, produced an "imagination of reciprocity," an unHellenic ability "to imagine what it was to be the Other."[16] The notion of reciprocal mastery becomes, in any case, the basis of some of Hartman's most important contributions to literary criticism. Using the Wordsworthian terms in redefining the relationship of literature and commentary, he argues that since "the situation of the discourse we name *criticism* is . . . no different from that of any other . . . it is the master–servant relation between criticism and creation that is being overturned in favor of . . . 'mutual domination' or 'interchangeable supremacy' " (CW 259). Elsewhere Hartman elaborates on the tendency of writer and reader to "mutual domination," figuring it in the Wordsworthian terms crucial to both of them. Evoking the figure of chiasmus, Hartman contends that "criticism as commentary *de linea* always crosses the line and changes to one *trans lineam*." He then reflects on the relationship between the commentator's discourse and that of "source" text, which, he maintains, "cannot be neatly or methodically separated . . . the relation is contaminating and chiastic; source text and secondary text, though separable, enter into a mutually supportive, mutually dominating relation" (CW 206).

And so Hartman's place in the hotly contested field of contemporary criticism and theory? Even if he is not lionized like some more systematic theorists, around whom movements and even "schools" have sprung up, Hartman exercises tremendous influence as a critic of criticism and a writer of originality and power. But in quite another sense, Hartman's *place* is not secure at all; that is, he *occupies no place*. To be sure, place plays a prominent role in his thinking – he often talks about it in writing of Wordsworth and other poets – but its importance is as a site of demand or perhaps a recognition scene rather than as a locus of rest. Traveling among possibilities, considering alternatives, questioning all absolutes, Hartman – *bee*-like – alights only temporarily. The Wandering Jew, he chooses to be on the move, for he understands that the spirit must not, if indeed it can, come to rest in an object, system, or place.

The question of *place* obviously relates to *point* (and the sting it produces), which I discussed earlier: will Hartman ever come to a point, take a stand, occupy one place long enough for us unsettled readers to get a handle on him? (The rush of metaphors shifts attention momentarily to me and perhaps the relation between my desire to be a responsive interpreter and my drive towards a point.) Don't we expect from major critics something more than a ceaseless journeying among possibilities? In this chapter, I have indicated Hartman's ambivalent and balanced *relation* to such major theoretical stances as New Criticism, reader-response, hermeneutics, and psychoanalysis. That relation in its very negativity (better: "negative capability") constitutes, in fact, an alternative in contemporary criticism, one that Hartman has been offering since 1954, when he began to practice a deconstruction that would not know its name for another twelve years or so. Yet his relation to deconstruction *as a critical system*, no less than to other positions, has always been problematical.[17] At least in its American form, deconstruction may be "necessary for the survival of literary studies," Hartman believes, because it "refuses to shut literature in on itself or to abandon it for an ideological, text-transcendent position." He adds: "It is, I hope, this recuperative and truly conservative strength of deconstruction that appeals to the younger generation, rather than its esoteric and sophisticated mechanics" (EP 193).

From Hartman's "hermeneutic reflection" on – and relation to – contemporary criticism I move on to a fuller description of the alternative he offers. To understand that alternative better, we must consider at some length his way of responding to texts, as he calls voices out of silence; the burden of vocation he takes up, relating to the tradition he inherits and must sustain; the form a style answerable to those voices, that tradition, must assume as it estranges the familiar, and so the entire project of a "negative hermeneutics." First, though, we must consider Hartman's relation to both Hebraism and Romanticism, major examples of the analogues to deconstruction that he mentions in *Saving the Text*: "in religious writing, and especially in literary writing," appears what makes deconstruction not "a novel enterprise" at all. Whether or not for deconstruction, certainly for Hartman, Judaism and Romanticism are crucial contexts, analogues, and influences.

3

The Wandering Jew: Hartman's relation to Judaism and Romanticism

> [I]nterpretation, when problematic rather than doctrinaire, is always involved in ... "error."
> *"Meaning, Error, Text"*

> Unforeseen historical events and their interpretation keep meaning nomadic.
> *"Meaning, Error, Text"*

One of the themes which best expresses th[e] perilous nature of consciousness and which has haunted literature since the Romantic period is that of the Solitary, or Wandering Jew. He may appear as Cain, Ahasuerus, Ancient Mariner, and even Faust. He also resembles the later (and more static) figures of Tithonus, Gerontion, and *poète maudit*. These solitaries are separated from life in the midst of life, yet cannot die. They are doomed to live a middle or purgatorial existence which is neither life nor death, and as their knowledge increases so does their solitude. It is, ultimately, consciousness that alienates them from life and imposes the burden of a self which religion or death or a return to the state of nature might dissolve. Yet their heroism, or else their doom, is not to obtain this release. Rebels against God, like Cain, and men of God, like Vigny's Moses, are equally denied "le sommeil de la terre" and are shown to suffer the same despair, namely, "the self ... whose worm dieth not, and whose fire is not quenched" (Kierkegaard). And in Coleridge's Mariner, as in Conrad's Marlow, the figure of the wanderer approaches that of the poet. Both are storytellers who resubmit themselves to temporality and are compelled to repeat their experiences in the purgatorial form of words. Yeats, deeply affected by the theme of the Wandering Jew, records a marvelous comment of Mme. Blavatsky's: "I write, write, write, as the Wandering Jew walks, walks, walks."
> *Beyond Formalism*

Thinking is peripatetic, writes Hartman, who also believes that thinking occurs most productively in and as writing. If, as he also suggests, meaning is nomadic, and interpretation always implicated in and inseparable from error, thinking (or wondering), which for Hartman is thoroughly textual and material, involves erring because wandering. If thinking, like writing, did not err, it would amount to no more than the simple locating of identities and the drawing of absolute differences. Thinking, though, moves about, is, in fact, always *on the move*, never coming to rest or finding a place to settle down. Thinking explores – and thus is work for the essay, which is peripatetic.

An Ancient, Hartman travels among texts, theories, and positions, exploring them, and, bee-like, returns again and again to one of his principal feeding-sources – which he also helps sustain – the Romantic poets, especially Wordsworth ("I have never been able to get away from Wordsworth for any length of time," he has recently written [UnRW xxv]). A Modern given over to temporality and compelled to repeat his "experiences in the purgatorial form of words" (BF 304), he feels intensely the burden of consciousness as he relates the adventures of his soul among masterpieces. He writes, writes, writes, responding to the demands of consciousness in its encounters with the demands of texts, this Wandering Jew.

Having explored Hartman's "place" in contemporary criticism and theory, I turn now to his relation to both Judaism and Romanticism. I hope to show that many of Hartman's most important (and advanced) ideas, "poststructuralist" and often deconstructive in appearance, have parallels in, if they do not derive from, Judaism and Romanticism. I equivocate here, not sure whether to speak of analogues or influences. In a sense, of course, Judaism and Romanticism constitute both analogues of Hartman's thinking and definite influences on it. But, despite his strong commitment to Hebraism, like his returns to Romanticism, Hartman manages most often to avoid party spirit or partisan fashion. The thoughtfulness that marks his relation to hermeneutics, deconstruction, and psychoanalysis appears as well in his relation to Romanticism and Judaism.

I begin with Hartman's recent essay "On the Jewish Imagination," which allows us to glimpse what he finds noteworthy and perhaps distinctive about that way of being, that understanding, and which also provides us with a sharper sense of what Hartman is all about, itself inseparable from his Hebraism. That he focuses on *imagination* carries a certain significance: it is, of course, a prime concern of the Romantic poets, and Hartman has explored more carefully than anyone else its meaning in Wordsworth especially. So close is Hartman's own writing, in fact, to what he finds in "the Jewish imagination" generally that his essay may be considered a latent reflection on his own work. Doubtful that he can "insist that there is a single unified type of imagination that could be identified as Jewish," and wary of "essentialist perspectives that propose a uniquely Jewish or Hebraic factor," Hartman offers "a number of heuristic theses" (207, 208).

The first of these concerns the way "the Jewish imagination has been dominated by a turn to the written, and has developed within the orbit of the Hebrew Bible" (208). Echoing points made by writers like Emmanuel Levinas and Edmond Jabès and recent critics such as Susan A. Handelman, Herbert N. Schneidau, and José Faur, Hartman writes, "The Jews are a People of the Book, and their mind is text-dependent, even when it rebels against the text. They keep the word, not only the faith" (208).[1] The resonances of this description with Hartman's own writing are important. No less so is his later point that "Jewish writing is *liberated* by the broad encyclopedic form of biblical literature and a commentary process that circumvents such categorical distinctions as 'scholarly' and 'creative'; yet it is also *hemmed in* by an exemplary tradition which attributes everything to a divine source – refers it back to the Bible or to the chain of authority" (209). Notable here are a complexity and a problematic that reject any simple choice and manage instead to hold together apparent opposites (Jewish writing is both and at once "liberated" and "hemmed in"). Important too, of course, is the Hebraic circumvention of "categorical distinctions" such as "primary text" and "secondary" in favor of the symbiosis that Hartman himself both preaches and practices.

Writing raises other questions of relation. Though Christianity "attempted to set the 'spirit' against the 'letter' by treating the Bible as a transcended Book of Laws, or stories blind to what they prophesied," Judaism did not allow the split to occur, or else Jews repaired it "by inventive exegetical methods which kept the law-portion and the story-portion as a single, inalienable donation" (211). In Judaism, moreover, writing *remains*: it is material and "is lived through –

worked through – as writing, and does not cancel itself by a mythic or messianic sort of incarnation." Indeed, writing is "anti-incarnationist or counter-typological," characterized by a certain negativity rather than proffering fullness of presence (212). A "reserve" thus exists in Judaism, which further distinguishes it from Christianity and the typology that became its most effective interpretive strategy; the latter, Hartman claims, has always been intent on "expunging the reserve of Hebrew Scripture as if it were blindness rather than insight" ("M,E,T" 149). That assumption of progress, of insight displacing error once and for all, represents at once an arrogance and a sense of mastery (Hartman uses neither term) that he manages to avoid in his temperate revisionism.

Moreover, in his dependence upon, response to, and use of prior texts – in short, his intertextuality – Hartman participates in what he calls the "pseudoepigraphic impulse," characteristic of the Jewish imagination. What he means by this term is that in Jewish writing often "we do not find free-standing works of art but the retold tale, the recycled motif, a sense of time that plays with the illusion of time, and a style composed both of explicit and inner quotations" (210). Hartman shares other characteristics of Jewish writing as he describes it, including its penchant for humor and a paratactic rather than hypotactic structure. There is "an associative way of going from topic to topic," a procedure that links up with at least some aspects of Romanticism and that in the sacred text "mixes law and lore and produces astounding feats of memorization" (209). That particular mixing recalls Hartman's own shuttling between theory and specific texts, allowing "a formal idea within critical theory to elicit the analysis of a poem, and vice-versa" (CW 5).

Among the most important of the "heuristic theses" Hartman presents is that concerning a Jewish "reticence within its ascendental or messianic fervor," a "holding back" that may function as "a justifiable wariness of false promises or prophets, or more profoundly a knowledge that God is not above 'testing' his servants." That quality of reticence, about which he has some reservations, connects with the "reserve" I noted earlier, and it "contrasts vividly," Hartman writes, "with the relation between Word and Promise, or Scripture and Fulfillment, in Christianity." This restraint means "there is no doctrine that fixes itself in detailed pictures of heaven or hell, or other-worldly time" (214). Alongside this anti-iconic stance is an anti-apocalyptic tendency that accepts the necessity of waiting, even if in tempered and chastened hope (this is a wariness shared by

Wordsworth and Hartman). Yet as important as this reticence is, Hartman grants that "there is something incongruous in ascribing reticence to the Jewish imagination," which, as noted, is not lacking in messianic fervor. In this impasse, Hartman surmises that the "communicative bond," by means of which "the Jewish imagination gave us the God of the Bible as the Bible of God," "may be the determining feature, rather than a mysterious 'reticence'" (215). The focus in Judaism is squarely "on God, on what He will do, and what the community covenanted to Him must do – not on a redeemer figure," for "the imaginative center in Judaism is not the Person." There simply is "no other hand like that which brought the Jews out of bondage, and wrote what it wrought. Story and testimony prevail" (216).

At any rate, with extended reference to Franz Rosenzweig's *Star of Redemption*,[2] Hartman elaborates on this major characteristic of the Jewish imagination, this "reticence" or wariness. Rosenzweig, he writes, tries "to free religious thought from 'the tic of a timeless coming-to-knowledge' which has influenced both philosophy and theology – always resolved, always progressive – of the German idealist tradition by proposing a type of discourse he names *Sprechdenken* (speech-thought)" (216). Not unlike Hartman, elaborating in *Saving the Text* on Derrida's deconstruction of our quest of absolute knowledge (the *Sa* heard in Hegel, for example), nor unlike deconstruction as Hartman describes its opposition to German idealism (see below), Rosenzweig praises *Sprechdenken*: "that it is time-haunted, that it does not know in advance what will appear, that its key-words are given it by others (audience, dialogue partners, tradition), that it is, in sum, tempered rather than totalizing." Accordingly, Rosenzweig rebukes modern philosophy, criticizing it on two specific counts: in Hartman's words,

> as a science of history it presumes it can find out exactly what happened, and so entertains the thought that objective knowledge may help to make the past forgettably past; and as a philosophy of (replacing) religion it seeks despite itself a uniquely fulfilling moment in and beyond time.

Hartman too, everywhere, in various ways, opposes forms of mastery and totalitarian schemes and desires, as well as ventures seeking to transcend time, language, and history. According to Hartman, in fact, Rosenzweig substitutes the inconspicuous but significant term "and" for modern philosophy's "pet-term *eigentlich* (verily, really, authentically)" (216). He then explores some of the implications of Rosenzweig's substitution, and sets off more resonances with his own central (and often Wordsworthian) concerns. This "and," he quotes Rosenzweig as saying,

> "was the first deriving from experience; so it must return among the last of truth." The "and" signifies relation and drives us back from thought to experience: "God and world and man." Yet this "and," like the Hebrew "ve," is a connective that links episodes paratactically rather than hypotactically, and subverts any last word. Not "end" but "and." Rosenzweig posits, moreover, an "and" that allows a passing over of the book into what he punningly defines as dailiness and total day (*All-tag*). A redemptive rather than apocalyptic appropriation of time is evoked, a "door" leading out of books into a *Nichtmehrbuch* (No-longer-book), or the direct seeing of "the likeness of the world in God's face." (216–17)

That Hartman's own imagination would be richly Jewish is perhaps to be expected. He fled his native Germany in 1939 to avoid Hitler's persecution of the Jews. As has been noted, "the impact of European fascism and anti-Semitism" on his life was considerable, affecting him in subtle and long-term ways. *The Unmediated Vision* reflects, it has been argued by the same writer, Hartman's "implicit awareness of the way in which an *unqualified* romanticism, when the imagination has become a total circumference and a vehicle for final truths, can drift towards the intellectual habits of fascism."[3] Certainly the following sentences from the Introduction Hartman wrote to his first book offer a counterstatement to the totalitarianism from which he fled and about which he has continued to warn, no matter what its guise or form:

> Art... has this advantage over the other modes of knowledge: it, alone, is in the service of no one, not even of truth. For truth, even when sought for its own sake, will surely destroy in the searcher his consciousness of human responsibilities. Abstraction is never less than total. Great poetry, however, is written by men who have chosen to stay bound by experience, who would not – or could not – free themselves by an act of knowledge from the immediacy of good and evil. (xi)

No doubt also stemming from his own first-hand experience of anti-Semitism is Hartman's repudiation of all kinds of purity: he laments our "innate purity perplex" and claims, against Derrida, a Sephardic Jew born in north Africa, that purity "may be a more basic category than presence" (CW 292, 147).

Other characteristic Hartmanian themes and perspectives are at least related to, if they do not derive from, his Hebraism, including his esteem of the negative, his privileging of voice, and his emphasis on remembrance. Moreover, since he began writing in the mid-1950s, Hartman has played a pivotal role in the effort to dehellenize literary criticism. Paralleling the important theological effort at that time under way to liberate religion from Greek metaphysics, *The Unmediated Vision* represents Romantic and modern poets' immersion in experience itself at the expense of a putative transcendent vision. As the poets had embraced a "scattered" and immanent God – as we saw in the last chapter – and some critics an open and anti-incarnationist mode of reading texts, so theologians, Protestant and Catholic alike, came to reject the idea of order deriving from the sovereign Greek *logos*, that is, "the classical vision of a fixed center out there somewhere."[4]

In recent years, Hartman seems increasingly to have "come out" as a Jew. In 1978 appeared his collection of poems entitled *Akiba's Children* (Akiba was the first-century rabbi influential on interpretation theory), which contains a number of lyrics that treat specifically Jewish figures and themes, including "Abraham," "Ahasuerus," and "In Honor of the Master of the Good Name" (see Appendix I). More recently, Hartman was actively involved in the establishment of Judaic studies at Yale University and played a major role in founding and developing its Video Archive for Holocaust Testimonies. He has also published addresses, translations (e.g., of Martin Buber's poems), and reviews on Jewish and Hebraic issues;[5] has co-edited, with Sanford Budick, a collection of essays entitled *Midrash and Literature*; edited a volume on *Bitburg in Moral and Political Perspective*, which makes available documents and analyses related to President Reagan's 1985 visit to the cemetery of SS soldiers; and responded, poignantly, to the controversy surrounding his late friend Paul de Man, whose early collaborationist and occasionally anti-Semitic writings have recently come to light.

As early as 1969, however, when "Adam on the Grass with Balsamum" was first published (in *ELH*; it was later included in *Beyond Formalism*), Hartman was attempting a style and a structure that is basically that of a sacred hermeneutics. That is, even though Hartman increasingly seems drawn to midrash, his efforts to reinvigorate some of the virtues of the older hermeneutic mode, neglected and indeed displaced during the past 250 years, are by no means of recent vintage but instead point to a continuity in his thinking.[6] He says it himself near the beginning of "Adam on the Grass with Balsamum": his purpose, he writes, "is to imitate a more adventurous hermeneutic tradition, even at the risk of deepening, provisionally, the difference between criticism and interpretation" (BF 125). Hartman thus takes off from a brief passage in *Paradise Lost* (8. 253–6), broods on that, gives rein to his knowledge, imagination, and interpretive skills, then returns to the original lines and especially the image of "balmy sweat." By the time he ends ("finishes" is hardly the word), Hartman has unpacked and "heard" so much that he finds it necessary to issue a "disclaimer": "To see so much meaning in the text is not to overcharge it, because such meaning remains virtual and because we are dealing not with an extraordinary stylistic phenomenon but with ordinary, if poetical, modes of implication" (147) – a quite remarkable reading of an unremarkable passage, in other words. In Hartman's words: "Narrative conduct, in Milton, is subordinated to hermeneutic structure: inner light, the divining rod of the interpreter sounds scripture out" (150). *That* is precisely what Hartman has done in this essay and, in fact, often does: "Milton's poem makes us more into interpreters than readers" (150).

As Hartman puts it in a recent essay "Criticism and Restitution," published in *Tikkun* (vol. 4, no. 1), midrash "has always been exemplary for me. I am intrigued by its liberty and autonomy as well as by its strict adherence to prooftexts" (30). As indicated by the publication of the co-edited *Midrash and Literature*, midrash has become more and more important for Hartman. In the above-mentioned essay, he argues the importance of midrash for an enriched and reconstituted criticism. It is important for several reasons: "as a cultural achievement, as a work of the social imagination, and as a distinctive mode of reading" (31).

"By including midrash," Hartman argues, "criticism would exercise its power to revalue an alienated practice, and it would enlarge itself at the same time." There is much to learn, he insists, "from a religious culture in which the creative energies went almost totally into commentary and the same basic method of reading was used for law (halakha) and lore (haggada)" (31). Particularly striking, given Hartman's commitment, is the tone and balance he manages in his treatment of Jewish issues. Take his introduction to *Bitburg in Moral and Political Perspective*, a collection of essays and articles that both resist "simplifying the historical record" and "fanning resentment or settling a score" (7). President Reagan's decision to visit the SS cemetery, after turning down a visit to Dachau, was hailed by his supporters as a gesture of reconciliation, even of forgiveness, but for others it raised disturbing questions. Hartman asks, "What does 'forgiveness' or 'reconciliation' mean? Especially in circumstances where the offense may not be forgotten?" His reply, in terms both judicious and genuinely questioning, follows:

> This issue of *response* cannot be separated ... from that of *responsibility*. How do we handle the imputation of collective guilt? Can the offended and injured evolve a statute of limitations, not of course toward individual criminals but toward the perpetrator nation, or bystanders (the church and others, not just the average German) who did so little to help? We surely cannot invoke a collective guilt of the kind that bloodied the record of history long before the Nazis translated it into their atrocious practices against the Jews. (4)

Hartman decries the loss of memory, of the *felt* experience of that atrocity, maintaining that "the worst attitude we could take is to persuade ourselves that it might not happen again *or* that it is something that happened before – that the Holocaust was one catastrophe among others." In the face of the Presidential "blunder" (if that is not too mild an assessment), Hartman writes, "It needs a particular courage not to overcome the past but to live with it still."[7] What he asks for, though it may seem little, is actually much.

In the remaining pages of this section, I want to look closely at two other recent essays that bear on Jewish concerns, both thoughtful rather than polemical responses to highly pressured demands. The first is a brief essay, "Meaning, Error, Text," in the special edition of *Yale French Studies* entitled *The Lesson of Paul de Man*, which was both a *festschrift* and a series of memorial tributes. Hartman opens "Meaning, Error, Text" with the pronouncement that "meaning, despite the efforts of *maîtres-penseurs*, does not remain stable" (143). That ideas of mastery concern him almost as much as the obviously related matter of meaning's instability becomes immediately clear: "The meaning, for example, of this French phrase is shifted when Foucault applies it, ironically, to German thinkers like Hegel and Nietzsche, who reappear in Nazi doctrines about the *master* race. Unforeseen historical events and their interpretation keep meaning nomadic" (145). They prevent totalization and so keep meaning temporal. Hartman's own discussion now appears ironic, for "unforeseen historical events" have intervened since its publication in the 1985 tribute to de Man to imbue *it* with new meaning.

In "Meaning, Error, Text," Hartman provides two examples of the instability of meaning, two instances of "the impossibility of making truth and text coincide" (146). The first concerns the trial of Hitler, Ludendorff, and their associates in March 1924, which a Boston newspaper interpreted as a farce deserving "international volleys of laughter" (quoted 145). The second example is "the Christian era, which has its first trial transcripts in the Gospels" (146), and particularly the relation of the New Testament to the Old. The issue here is, in part, blindness and insight, the possibility of progress, and especially the relation of a supposedly enlightened present to a benighted past. About the New Testament Hartman writes with characteristic balance, refusing to adopt a simple either/or stance: "we can admire it," he writes, "for struggling with the incumbency of what it calls 'old'; we can also blame it for trying to liquidate a precursor text by degrading it as the shadowy prefiguration of its own truth" (146).

Hartman's two examples raise the question of error. "Can we talk of meaning and error together," he asks, "as if error were part of the structure of meaning? Why is it so difficult for truth and text to coincide? Or, what is equally surprising, why should anyone think they could come together?" (146). One reason, of course, why text and truth do not coincide is the fact of readers, what Hartman here calls the "precarious and spiritually burdened view of the relation between letter (text) and reader." At least in sacred matters, "the truth of the text is the text, but only as it inspires" a "transactive relation" between text and readers. The very fact (and "scandal") of error provided the opportunity to fashion "a triumphant mode of interpretation, masterful toward the Hebrew text and consoling toward historical time." That interpretive strategy is figural typology, which differs radically from the Rabbinic, whose relation to "the Messianic event as a fulfillment of time and of the Word" is "negative" (147). Indeed, typology identifies error with unfulfillment, rather than as a necessary structural component of meaning. Speaking the "truth" once and for all, typology stabilizes meaning. Rabbinical exegesis, however, like deconstructive literary criticism, takes "a more temporal or temporizing view" (149).

The then-unforeseen relevance of "Meaning, Error, Text" to the very person in whose memory and honor it was published emerges in

"Blindness and Insight." Hartman published the latter in *The New Republic* a few months after the story broke of de Man's collaborationist writings (including some anti-Semitic work) in the early 1940s, when he was twenty-one or so. The title given to the essay carries considerable irony, since it is also the title of de Man's first book, which established him as a major critic and a rigorous deconstructive thinker. Hartman thus signals that he will apply de Man to the situation surrounding de Man – and we should apply, I am suggesting, "Meaning, Error, Text" to Hartman's response to the de Man "scandal."

The news of de Man's complicity was startling to Hartman and painful, particularly in view of their long-term friendship and Hartman's intense involvement with the Holocaust. In the tribute he delivered at the memorial service at Yale, he talked about how close they had been, and described his friend as "the most gracious of persons, never dismissive, even if he knew 'de Trut,' the most considerate and engaged teacher, the most agreeable conversationalist."[8] In "Blindness and Insight," following a brief consideration of de Man's collaborationist writings, he declares, "There was no trace of anti-Semitism in the de Man I knew" (29). But, he adds, "I cannot ignore these expressions of anti-Jewish sentiment, even if they remained polite, even if they were limited to suave cultural essays and never spilled over into exhortatory rhetoric or demagoguery" (29). The restraint and balance Hartman shows does not let de Man off the hook, though the criticism is tempered, the commentary tender. De Man's failure to "mention the Nazi years" Hartman labels "an evasion" (31), but some of his arguments smack of special pleading (e.g., that de Man was doing, and writing, what other intellectuals were doing, and writing). And Hartman fails to pick up on his friend's claim to know "'de Trut,'" itself perhaps related to the "monism" (FR 311) and a tendency to become "too absolute" (CW 108) that he himself has noted in de Man's writing. In any case, Hartman implies that de Manian deconstruction is not without some responsibility, since in his rigorously deconstructive essays de Man never placed himself "in historical context, and he should have done so" (30).

That failure represents what Hartman calls a "purity" (obviously a loaded term), and his critique leads to a more general consideration of deconstruction, whose power and influence may be undermined by the discoveries of de Man's early writings. At least the sensationalized accounts of those discoveries in the popular media, which have always represented deconstruction as nihilistic, claim to have heard its death-rattle. Hartman's criticism of deconstruction is different. Deconstructive reasoning, he acknowledges, elaborating on his earlier point, "does not reveal, not in de Man at least, its situatedness, its personal or ideological context. The method acts as if it had no relatives" (30). Hartman echoes here the point made in *Saving the Text*, which I quoted earlier, concerning deconstruction's self-involvement. It is, he continues in "Blindness and Insight," "this *purity* of deconstructive thought, not its power, that can now be questioned" (30; italics added). That power Hartman traces to deconstruction's "significant critique of German idealism ('identity philosophy'), insofar as the latter resulted in various kinds of organicism, including fascism" (29). So despite the charges widely bruited about, deconstruction has much to tell us, Hartman suggests, about attempts at mastery and totalization, perhaps indeed about totalitarianism in all its forms. In Hartman's account, rather than somehow aiding and abetting fascism, deconstruction confronts and effectively undercuts it.

Deconstruction also has something to tell us about error, progress, and the relation of early (or "original") and later writing, including de Man's own. Though de Man's "method insists on excluding the biographical ('extralinguistic') reference" (30), Hartman suggested in the Yale memorial service that his friend's writings "have more of personal stamp than we may presently see."[9] In "Blindness and Insight" he makes a similar point. He believes that "one crucial and hurtful problem is that de Man did not address his past. We do not have his thoughts" (29). Hartman proceeds to wonder, however: "Did he avoid confession (he was without a religious bone in his body, except for the subdued religious feelings that were still perceptible in his early enthusiastic emphasis on the *âme particulière* of nationalities), and instead work out his totalitarian temptation in a purely intellectual and impersonal manner?" (29). The "postwar writing may constitute an avowal of error, a kind of repudiation in its very methodology of a philosophy of reading" (30). At any rate, the remainder of Hartman's essay may be seen as, in part, a deconstruction of the *purity* of de Man's deconstructive reasoning.

Hartman begins with de Man's controversial statement that "what stands under indictment is language itself and not somebody's philosophical error," which has always been controversial and which now sounds rationalizing and self-serving. Reading de Man with the help of de Man, but at the same time sympathetically, Hartman maintains that that statement

all of a sudden becomes a reflection by de Man on de Man. The
earlier self is not off the hook, but the emphasis shifts to the way
language operates. The later self acknowledges an error, yet it
does not attribute it to an earlier self, to a self involved in ideas
and responsible for the error, because that would perpetuate its
blindness to the linguistic nature of the predicament. (30)

Hartman grants the convenience of such a view, but he stays with de
Man, continuing his analysis, which closely parallels that in "Meaning, Error, Text." According to de Man's understanding, he writes,

> enlightenment as such cannot resolve error, and even repeats it,
> if one is deluded into thinking that the new position stands in a
> progressive and sounder relation to language, that it has corrected a historical mistake once and for all. Even to say, quite
> simply, "I was young, I made a mistake, I've changed by mind"
> remains blind if it overlooks the narrative shape of this or any
> confession. (30)

Hartman thus shifts attention from the past to the present and the
blindness that characterizes it in its claim of progress or enlightenment (recall his account of Christian "progress" over Jewish "darkness," in "Meaning, Error, Text"). In his study of self-analysis,
Hartman continues, de Man rejected the "'pathos of history,'" including personal history, and insisted on a suffering 'specifically
linguistic.'" That linguistic pathos, Hartman quotes de Man as
saying, "must not be confused with an 'elegiac gesture, by which one
looks back on the past as a period that is lost, which then gives you the
hope of another future that might occur'" (30). Recall here Hartman's distinction between Bloom and himself, on the one hand, and
the other "Yale critics": whereas such "boa-deconstructors" as de
Man believe that literature is "precisely that use of language which
purges pathos," Hartman and Bloom, differently, hold that "the
ethos of literature is not dissociable from its pathos."[10]

What about de Man's own past, which was hidden to us but now
stands revealed in its error? The moral force of Hartman's analysis
lies in his refusal to condemn *or* to exonerate, *and* in his caution to us
who come later. Referring again to the statement I quoted concerning
language and personal error, Hartman writes:

> The personal history behind this passage was hidden to us, but
> now we can see more clearly de Man's attitude toward his past.

> He places himself beyond nostalgia, yet he does not say that the past can be overcome. Germans still talk of the Nazi era as a "past that will not pass away," that resists being worked through. De Man does not mention the exceptional Nazi years, and that is an evasion; but he makes a general statement that to mourn the past as lost in order to guarantee ourselves an unencumbered future will not succeed. There cannot be, he suggests, a future that will not prove to have been a past like that. His essay on Benjamin envisages a temporal repetition that subverts the hope in new beginnings, in a New Era: it subverts a hope, ultimately messianic, that always revives. (The political culture he championed in the *Le Soir* articles, a culture that claimed to be modern and revolutionary, was based on such a hope.) (31)

Thus, Hartman surmises, in subverting hope in a New Era, in the possibility of some ultimate truth or absolute progress, de Man was at once commenting on his own past and effectively criticizing the hope that figured prominently in that past and that fanned the fires of such "progressive" schemes as Nazism.

However we respond to Hartman's words, we must remember, among other things, that he was addressing a highly charged situation where de Man stood condemned. Hartman insists that we latecomers bear considerable responsibility too.

> We can accuse de Man of lacking foresight or civil courage, or of underestimating the ruthlessness of the Nazi regime. And we abhor the anti-Semitism, and any collaboration that occurred. Once again we feel betrayed by the intellectuals. The accusations we bring, however, are a warning to ourselves. They do not justify complacency or easy judgments about the relation of political ideas to moral conduct. Many on the left also welcomed what Kenneth Burke called "sinister unifying," and succumbed to xenophobic and anti-Jewish sentiment. De Man's "dirty secret" was the dirty secret of a good part of civilized Europe. In the light of what we now know, however, his work appears more and more as a deepening reflection on the rhetoric of totalitarianism. His turn from the politics of culture to the language of art was not an escape into, but an escape out of, aestheticism: a disenchantment with that fatal aestheticizing of politics, blatant in his own early articles, that gave fascism its false brilliance. De Man's critique of every

tendency to totalize literature or language, to see unity where there is no unity, looks like a belated, but still powerful, act of conscience. (31)

In spite, then, of the early collaborationist writings, the later de Man was, in Hartman's reading, a man of conscience. This is a strong and controversial position, in which a past sin no more negates a distinguished future than an enlightened present guarantees progress, and in which Hartman's power as interpreter is strongly felt. Is it *his reading*, in fact, indebted though it be to de Man's own theory, that exculpates his friend?

Given what Hartman has written about Bitburg and the desire on the part of some to have us forgive and forget, any effort to minimize collaborationist activities would be not only a change of heart too massive to be believed but also a violation of conscience. I at least am left with but two conclusions. Hartman seeks to focus attention, not on the sensationalized aspects of the "case," but on deeper, more difficult, and perhaps more important issues. Moreover, though I may at points quarrel with Hartman's reading of de Man's early writings, and even believe him on the whole too easy on his friend, I find his assessment sincere: he sees that those writings are puerile, sadly deluded, and offensive but mild in comparison with what else was then being written. They are not forgivable, but they may be understandable. For *Hartman* to imply as much, in his typically indirect and unpointed way, is to say a great deal.

One other point emerges clearly and powerfully when "Blindness and Insight" is read in the context of Hartman's Judaism and his efforts on its behalf. As a Jew, he everywhere confronts and combats tendencies and desires that are at bottom absolute, unifying, and totalizing, messianic and apocalyptic, and he claims that de Man, as a deconstructionist, led an analogous effort, engaging in an ideological critique, in fact, of former beliefs and allegiances. Even if tempted by messianic impulses and (occasional) opportunities, Judaism, not unlike deconstruction, maintains a reserve and a reticence – as does Hartman and as does Romanticism, as a matter of fact, especially in a poet like Wordsworth. Like the Romantic poets, indeed, Hartman resists the siren song of abstract, disembodied thought.[11]

Sometimes, with the pressures of contemporary life what they are, Wordsworth's poetry may seem too reflective or low-powered. Yet we rarely cease to feel the agony or urgency from which it sprang. It mediates between the modern world and a desperate imagination, one that sees itself deprived of genuine relations with that world. The tempo of industrialization seemed to Wordsworth to encourage a rootless and abstract kind of existence, a man-made nature alienating us from Nature. Love, or the sympathetic imagination, could not flourish long in that artificial environment: imagination, indeed, could not even grow to become love in that soil. It needed a slower birth and a more generous nurture, for the imaginative spirit in us is wild, and only gradually humanized. Wordsworth's sense of apocalypse is simply his pre-vision of the failure of that process of humanization. The modern imagination, stronger than ever, but also more homeless than ever, falls back into itself, or endlessly outward. It becomes solipsistic or seeming-mad. We understand Wordsworth best when we are too near ourselves, too naked in our self-consciousness. Then his poetry, its strange spiritual calculus, its balancing of imaginative failure with elemental gratitudes, can still infuse a modest and rocky strength: "O joy! That in our embers/ Is something that doth live" (*Intimations Ode*).

The Unremarkable Wordsworth

Some of what may seem most Jewish about Hartman's writing is also Romantic (as well as often deconstructive). I have already suggested some of the connections between Romanticism and Judaism. Hartman himself makes the point in writing, for example, that Wordsworth's "'spots of time'" erupt from their hiding-places like the Hebraic God" (FR 144) and, more importantly, in averring that Wordsworth "relived on the very ground of his senses the religious struggle between Hellenic (fixed and definite) and Hebraic (indefinite, anti-anthropomorphic) representations of the divine" (WP xii). It is Hartman's treatment of and relation to Romanticism, and especially Wordsworth, that I want to explore in the remainder of this chapter. The Wandering Jew is a Romantic figure.

Though Hartman has never been a narrow practical critic, even *The Unmediated Vision* evincing considerable breadth and impressive theoretical sophistication, his reputation was made as a scholar of Romanticism. *Wordsworth's Poetry 1787–1814* established Hartman as probably the preeminent Wordsworthian, and subsequent essays on a variety of topics crucial to Romanticism and published in *Beyond Formalism* and *The Fate of Reading*, as well as elsewhere, enhanced his reputation and extended his influence. The essays in the 1970 collection perform the valuable, indeed essential, function of contextualizing Romanticism, reading Romantic poetry within literary history, recovering traditions and conventions that the great Romantics confronted and addressed, and taking them seriously as thinkers as well as visionaries. The later collection often returns, bee-like, to Romanticism, abetted by certain theoretical texts, notably those of psychoanalysis, and reflects deeply and richly on major Romantic poems and concerns. When, in subsequent work, especially *Criticism in the Wilderness* and *Saving the Text*, Hartman focuses more directly on theoretical issues, he never leaves Romanticism far behind or strays far from Wordsworth, to whom he returns yet again in his most recent book. As a matter of fact, Hartman points to the important relation of contemporary theory to Romanticism, despite some theorists' vociferous rejection of the latter. A revaluation of Romanticism, he contends, "is a special feature of post-New Critical or revisionist criticism in America":

> The term *revisionist* . . . is perhaps most appropriately applied to the rethinking of literary history now going on, which questions a periodization that has given "modernity" a polemical and prestigious life separated from Romantic origins. But the revision that is occurring is not a matter of redressing the balance, or adjusting claims, or seeing continuities rather than discontinuities: it thrusts us back into an awareness of the problematic persistence of enthusiastic, poetic, and even archaic forms in contemporary life. (CW 44–5)

As a result, Hartman believes, "If there is one criterion that distinguishes the present movement in criticism from that prevailing, more or less since Eliot, it is a better understanding and higher evaluation of the Romantic and nineteenth-century writers" (CW 46). This important revisionist effort appears vividly in *Deconstruction and Criticism*, the so-called manifesto of the "Yale School." In the Preface, in fact, Hartman points to "the important place taken in the essays by Romantic poetry," particularly that of Shelley. He surmises that we may "have begun to understand what kind of thinking poetry is, especially Romantic poetry that was often held to be intellectually confused or idle."[12]

Hartman has lent a major voice to this revisionist effort, showing, as has Harold Bloom, the pressing claims Romanticism has on our attention. At the center of Hartman's effort, of course, has always been Wordsworth, just as Blake has been crucial for Bloom. In the

Introduction to *The Unremarkable Wordsworth*, Hartman explains what initially attracted him to "the giant Wordsworth," who, he says elsewhere, "preempts them all" (FR 168):

> The moment I was obliged to read him during high school in England, he reflected back my own sense of nature: rural nature, but more generally a world that felt as ancient and immemorial as "rocks, and stones, and trees," that encompassed, inanimate yet animating, the mind in its earth-walks. But the discovery prompting me to write about him was that he could brood about himself in a way that nurtured rather than violated a "culture of feeling." No one before him had so naturally brought perception and consciousness together, had charted the growth of the mind without over-objectifying it; and so not only anticipated developmental psychology but made us inherit unforgettably, after the Enlightenment, and in the dawn of the Industrial Revolution, a sense of "unknown modes of being." (xxv)

All of these points, and others, are important: a shared sense of nature; a brooding self-consciousness that also looks outward, strengthening human-heartedness and nurturing a "culture of feeling"; an achieved crossing or interchange of perception and consciousness; a focus, in the face of enlightened and technological pressures, on the mysterious, on "unknown modes of being."

The problems Wordsworth confronted and the responses he made deserve our attention, in part, because, according to Hartman, our era is the same as his. For Wordsworth the problems confronting the modern world stem from "a convergence of factors: urbanization, a 'degrading' thirst for news incited by the Napoleonic Wars, and the heady hopes of ideologists of the French Revolution, who parted the new order from the old 'as by a gulph' " (UnRW xxvi). Also contributing to the crisis, if less dramatically, was the Enlightenment, which was crucial to the revolution in France and menacing to the future of imagination and poetry. Though Hartman regards Romanticism as "a viable *poetic* form of enlightenment (or poet-enlightenment) thought" (FR 277), he believes that the Romantics criticized even as they fulfilled the Enlightenment (BF 311). For the Enlightenment was (en)lightening: "it eased certain burdens weighing on the human spirit, and especially the 'burden of the mystery'" (FR 118).

In part, the question that Hartman calls to our attention concerns the fate of the poetical character in an Age of Reason. Since "the growth of reason and the decline of imagination are linked" (BF 197), does enlightenment doom the poetical genius? Could poetry, in other words, "outlive the Enlightenment, when it was perfectly clear that the great works of the past had been based on 'Superstition'?" (BF 319). Threatened, therefore, was the very idea of fiction, as well as vision, prophecy, and myth, all of which appeared to the enlightened mind as resembling superstition. Well aware that "it does not prove easy to give up the sophisticated superstitions by which literature had always amused, shocked, or instructed," Hartman shows how writers became "intensely conscious of the primitive nature of these beliefs but also ingenious in accommodating them to rationality" (BF 283). What had to be overcome, if the wish was to be realized for fiction and reason to kiss, was the created "dichotomy of 'gentle mind' and 'false themes' " (BF 284), the latter referring to the materials of romance. Romance figures centrally in "pre-Romantic" and Romantic struggles with Enlightenment, and Hartman's contribution revolves around his demonstration that "Romanticism is genuinely a rebirth of Romance," revealing "the depth of the enchantments in which we live" (BF 307). The Romantics' attempt to deal with romance in an enlightened age

> is a moving, intense, and endless one. They knew that light must be fought with light and that the great intellectual movement which preceded them, and in which they continued to participate, could not be reversed.... [T]he fate of poetry seemed to depend on poetry's revaluation of its founding superstitions. (BF 311)

Evincing the range of his knowledge and critical abilities and exemplifying the way he grounds Romanticism in literary history, Hartman opens his story of this revaluation with Milton. The "romantic struggle with Romance," Hartman argues, starts with Milton, who, in fact, "marks the beginning of modern Romanticism" (BF 285). With Milton, claims Hartman, "the spirit of Romance begins to simplify itself. It becomes the creative spirit and frees itself from the great mass of medieval and post-medieval romances in the same way as the Spirit of Protestantism frees itself from the formalism of temples" (FR 288). Milton's achievement includes a "new and sweeter style," constituting "a gentler fiction," which offers a "romantic machinery ... grounded in the reasonableness of a specific national temperament" (BF 287). This new machinery is translated into the idea of the *genius loci* and so the kind of fiction likely to survive in an enlightened *British* climate. Though both enlightened and accommodated, that machinery retains its basis in the demonic, however transformed were Milton's allegoric persons into "pleasures of the imagination." Even if the "gentle mind" thinks itself free of demons, enlightened and liberated, they sit "far within/ And in their own dimensions like themselves" (*Paradise Lost* 1.792–3). What Milton begins is a "romantic purification of Romance," and that, Hartman claims, is "the true and unceasing spiritual combat" (BF 289).

Of course, Hartman is by no means alone in telling the story of romance's importance – nor of Milton's importance for Romanticism. A student of Blake, as Hartman is of Wordsworth, Northrop Frye has developed, in the *Anatomy of Criticism*, *The Secular Scripture*, and elsewhere a general theory of literature owing much to romance modes and the possibility of their survival. As Hartman writes in "Ghostlier Demarcations: The Sweet Science of Northrop Frye" (the telling allusion is to Blake's notion that "the dark Religions are departed and sweet Science reigns"), "The more we read in him the more we understand how essential the romance tradition is, both in itself and in its modern afterlife" (BF 39). To consider briefly Hartman's interpretation of Frye will enable us to specify Hartman's positions as well as better to understand him as both a student of Romanticism and a latter-day Romantic.

In the above-mentioned essay, first published in 1966, Hartman writes that Frye has emerged as the "most ambitious exponent of a systematic criticism," one that offers "a new vantage point with its promise of mastery and also its enormously expanded burden of sight." From Hartman's perspective, we now know, these are not purely honorific terms, the idea of mastery and the systematic lying close to the heart of what he most fears and everywhere confronts. In fact, he calls Frye "an overreacher, a man with hubris," even if it be "a methodical hubris, a heuristic and applied attitude" (BF 24). As he recovers romance, Frye, unlike Hartman, advances the work of the Enlightenment, not that of Romanticism, whose relation to the Enlightenment is certainly problematic. What Frye wants, Hartman believes, is "to democratize criticism and demystify the muse." Hartman describes Frye as "our most radical demystifier of criticism, even though his great accomplishment is the recovery of the demon or of the intrinsic role of romance in the human imagination." If Frye's "importance to literary history proper is as a topographer of the romance imagination in its direct and displaced forms," his larger social contribution is "to the ongoing need to have greater numbers of persons participate in the imaginative life, to open the covenant of education...." In Frye, argues Hartman, demystification derives from the embraced idea of system, and "to systematize criticism is to universalize it, to put its intellectual or spiritual techniques into the hands of every intelligent person, even every child" (BF 25). Hartman believes that Frye's "critical system moves in the same direction as the history of art it seeks to liberate – away from the closed culture, the closed society, the priest-interpreter, the critic's critic." Properly understood, then, Frye appears as "a knight in a continuing quest: that of removing the dragon from the hoard, or mystery from the communion" (BF 28).[13] Frye's difference from Hartman is palpable.

The demystifying that Hartman questions, is, of course, traceable to more than Frye's systematizing, as important as that is. Frye's central sense of archetypes is similarly unmysterious. "There is no mystery about archetype," Hartman writes; "the archetype is simply the typical at the highest power of literary generalization" (BF 29). The flattening-out of mythic substance that archetypes achieve, is, according to Hartman, "like transforming a landscape into a map, but also like opening a closed book" (BF 30). As Hartman's figures indicate, Frye's "system" is "consciously spatial" and thus insensitive to temporality and therefore unhistorical (BF 33, 38). Frye gives us a mapped landscape, Hartman charts a wilderness.

In Hartman's judgment, other problems exist, including the "superductive" nature of Frye's work, whereby "the aura of the individual work" is sacrificed to the system that incorporates it (BF 31). Hartman also faults Frye because he does not "make us feel the problematic situation of either writer or critic, or any sign of that divided consciousness which the mythical method affirms by remaining an artifice in Yeats and Joyce" (BF 32). Unlike Frye, Hartman everywhere problematizes, complicates, and even estranges texts as he relates them to both himself and history; indeed, he witnesses to textual calls, taking texts seriously in their particularity, preserving their individual *aura*, and relating their art to society as a whole. In *Criticism in the Wilderness*, moreover, Hartman claims that Frye "lightens [the] burden – specifically, the yoke of the imagination, creative energy as it bears down on the wary critic and teacher in the minute particulars of great writing"; Frye's "problem (ours too)," Hartman continues, "is that major art in its very negativity or terrifying respect for exact witness cannot be co-opted. There is no accommodating it," despite Frye's impressive effort to rescue "criticism as accommodation" (BF 182–3). In what may stand as a conclusion to our brief consideration of Frye, Hartman declares that "the great work of fiction (or criticism)" – his placement of criticism alongside fiction is important –

> recalls the origin of civilization in dialogic acts of naming, cursing, blessing, consoling, laughing, lamenting, and beseeching. These speak to us more openly than myth or archetype because they are the firstborn children of the human voice. Myth and metaphor are endued with the acts, the gesta, of speech; and if there is a mediator for our experience of literature, it is something as simply with us as the human body, namely the human voice. It is here that one possibility of progress lies: in honoring the problematic relation of words to a reality they mediate rather than imitate. To envision "ghostlier demarcations," a poet must utter keener sounds. (BF 39)

Hartman's difference from Frye appears dramatically in these remarks: rather than a totalized system, he offers personal, highly individualistic, responses to basic human needs and desires that materialize rather than spiritualize.

Hartman's sensitivity to individual – and problematic – poetic response is mirrored in other aspects of his treatment of the Enlightenment and its aftermath. Following Wordsworth, he shifts attention from old-style Romance and mythic machinery to the travails of consciousness. The "romantic purification of Romance," we might say, climaxes in "Wordsworth's animism, his consciousness of a consciousness in nature, [which] is the last noble superstition of a demythologized mind. All nature-spirits are dissolved by him," Hartman notes, "except the spirit of Nature" (BF 296).

Interested, from his youth, in the way Wordsworth "charted the growth of the mind" and so "anticipated developmental psychology," Hartman explores, in *Wordsworth's Poetry* and elsewhere, the poet's process of maturation, leading from "love of nature" to "love of man"; "the drama of consciousness and maturation," he writes in the Preface to that book, "... is what I attempted to follow" (xxiii). The process is indeed dramatic and precarious, Wordsworth struggling with the angel of consciousness itself. As *The Prelude* makes clear, having lost the sustaining power of nature, Wordsworth "passed through a depression clearly linked to the ravage of self-consciousness and the 'strong disease' of self-analysis." For the Romantics in general, Hartman observes, "every increase in consciousness is accompanied by an increase in self-consciousness," and "analysis," he adds, "can easily become a passion that 'murders to dissect'" (BF 298, 299). Analysis, and the reason that nourishes it, finally appeared as the problem, indeed as "a modern kind of fanaticism" (UnRW 6). Hope emerged as *reason*, which had questioned everything, began to question itself.

Certainly there could be no going back to a simple naïveté, though there might be the possibility of "a return, via knowledge, to naïveté – to a second naïveté" (BF 300). The antidote to self-consciousness, the Romantics discovered, lies within consciousness itself, "the strait through which everything must pass" (BF 303). The Romantic discovery is complicated and important, not least because it carries religious implications, indeed a transvaluation of crucial religious ideas. Suggesting what is at stake, Hartman writes that "the traditional scheme of Eden, Fall, and Redemption merges with the new triad of Nature, Self-Consciousness, and Imagination – the last term in both involving a kind of return to the first" (BF 307).

Those who, in Hartman's terms, "first explored the dangerous passageways of maturation" (BF 299), the Romantics *lived* the transition from consciousness to imagination. What imagination is, is difficult to say, with any exactness. Hartman describes it, in *Wordsworth's Poetry*, as "consciousness of the self at its highest pitch (or an immediate imaginal reaction to this)" (18); it may stand for the "sympathetic imagination." Elsewhere he notes that Wordsworth "cites with approval Charles Lamb's definition of imagination as that power which 'draws all things to one; which makes things animate or inanimate, beings with their attributes, subjects with their accessories, take one colour and serve to one effect'" (UnRW 143). Related to this definition is Hartman's brief account of the *Ancient Mariner*, in "Romanticism and Anti-Self-Consciousness," as "a poem that depicts the soul after its birth to the sense of separate (and segregated) being." In this poem, which "generically converts self-consciousness into imagination, Coleridge describes the travail of a soul passing from self-consciousness to imagination." To explore that "transition from self-consciousness to imagination and to achieve that transition while exploring it (and so to prove it still possible) is," writes Hartman, "the Romantic purpose I find most crucial" (BF 307). His account of the *Ancient Mariner* then proceeds as follows:

> The slaying of an innocent creature, the horror of stasis, the weight of conscience or of the vertical eye (the sun), the appearance of the theme of deathlessness, and the terrible repetitive process of penitence whereby the wanderer becomes aware through the spirits above and the creatures below of his focal solitude between both – these point with archetypal force to the burden of selfhood, the straits of solitude, and the compensating plenary imagination that grows inwardly. The poem opens by evoking that *rite de passage* we call a wedding and which leads to full human communion, but the Mariner's story interposes itself as a reminder of human separateness and of the intellectual love (in Spinoza's sense) made possible by it. (306–7)

As adumbrated in Coleridge's poem, the transition from self-consciousness to imagination, in its precariousness, "naturally evokes the idea of a journey," but one that "does not lead to what is generally called a truth: some final station for the mind. It remains as problematic a crossing as that from death to second life or from exile to redemption." These religious ideas remind us yet again that "Romantic art has a function analogous to that of religion" (307).

Only part of the process of self-development, the necessary transition from consciousness to imagination must proceed and effect a return to nature – that hoped-for "second naïveté." For Wordsworth, the dream of nature does not, as in Keats, lead to formal Romance but "is an early, developmental step in converting the solipsistic into the sympathetic imagination. It entices the brooding soul out of itself, toward nature first, then toward humanity" (BF 308). What heals the wound consciousness inflicts upon the self is "unconscious intercourse" with a nature "old as creation." Wordsworth thus "evokes a type of consciousness more integrated than ordinary consciousness, though deeply dependent on its early – and continuing – life in rural surroundings" (BF 309).

In returning to Wordsworth in his most recent book, Hartman succinctly describes the way the poet himself "returned consciously and devotedly to Nature – to rediscovering his roots," finding "inner continuities," including the integral and sustaining role played by the past in the "stream of life" (UnRW 6). Through a painful process, Wordsworth discovers "the idea which dominates his poetry," that of nature as "the nurse, / The guide, the guardian of my heart, and soul/ Of all my moral being" (*Tintern Abbey*)(UnRW 8). For Wordsworth, nature means, according to Hartman, "chiefly rural nature, the abiding presences of mountain, lake, and field under the influence of the changing seasons," and "sensuous contact" with nature is essential if the self is to come through the painful travails of self-consciousness and its often terrible wounding (UnRW 3).

Wordsworth understood, with remarkable literalness, Hartman believes, "the concept of *culture* as *cultivation*." He thus returned "to the idea of a ground out of which things grew slowly, precariously; where accident was important, some grew and some didn't, but where there were, for humanity generically considered, infinite chances of birth and rebirth. The literalism of 'Fair seed-time had my soul' (*Prelude* I. 301)," writes Hartman, "shocks us into a view of culture as nature" (FR 292) – it may also remind us of "eine gewichtige Pranke" that suddenly, enigmatically rises up to impede progress and doom intention (CW 80–1). In describing this relation to nature, Hartman uses the Hebraic term *akedah* (literally, "binding"), which he contrasts with the (Christian) term "apocalypse" (WP 225 ff.) – here Judaism and Romanticism appear clearly linked in Hartman's thinking. The term "apocalypse" denotes the impatience and haste, as well as the craving for "gross and outrageous stimulation," apparent in the *uncultivated* mind or imagination.

Wordsworth's enduring trust in nature, Hartman contends, remains, despite insidious temptations, "a trust in the human mind, which finds inexhaustible rewards in the world, and is renewed by natural rather than supernatural means. His poetry substitutes, therefore, the 'produce of the common day' for sensationalism and supernaturalism..." (WP 259). Poetic attention shifts, accordingly, from the extraordinary or mythic, populated perhaps by romance figures of exceptional quality, to the simply human, ordinary, and quotidian. Wordsworth's greatness, in fact, may consist in his recovery of "elemental situations" (BF 224). The extraordinary, or mysterious, is not, however, branded as merely superstitious and dismissed, as was the tendency in the wake of the Enlightenment. As Wordsworth "considers man in his own and in his ordinary life" – to quote his own words in the Preface to the *Lyrical Ballads* – he respects not only ordinary experience but also its "extraordinary potential" (UnRW 11). Uninterested in "the supernatural as such," the poet, or at least the Wordsworthian, "deals with a contagion of the mind by human materials that exert a supernatural effect" (FR 188).

All of this is obviously related to the religious and the possibility of its survival in the wake of Enlightenment. The Romantic period, according to Hartman, constitutes the time when "art frees itself from its subordination to religion or religiously inspired myth and continues or even replaces them." As Hartman puts it, "if Romantic poetry appears to the orthodox as misplaced religious feeling ('spilt religion'), to the Romantics themselves it redeems religion" (BF 305). How it does so is, obviously, the question. Accepting completely "the spirit of Enlightenment critique of all organized religion," Wordsworth lives through "that experience of the sacred which can only be laid bare and made available after not just sects, but virtually everything that goes under the name 'religion,' has been stripped away."[14] Rejecting, like the Jews, "any continuity between human and divine assured by intermediaries or intermediate forms" (WP 192), as well as any "personal intermediary" (WP 289), Wordsworth "converts nature into a paraclete, *the* paraclete" (WP 50). He also, notes Hartman, opens religion once more "to all, as in the primitive Christianity of St. Paul. Wordsworth extends Romans 1:19 to its limit and supports the simplest affirmation of the New Testament, that immortal life is in every man's reach" (WP 153).

The basic question is, how is human being renewed? In his 1964 book, Hartman explains Wordsworth's answer, contextualizing and distinguishing it from Blake's. Involving the concept of nature, it

> modifies the personalistic and apocalyptic views of divine agency, but without approving the deistic God ... against whom Blake prophesies. Blake, of course, remains an uncompromising personalist, who would have denied that Wordsworth was capable of sowing regeneration, since the more than human is the more-human, and a nature which is not humanized ... is but the "deistic abstract void." Wordsworth's view is closer to Goethe's. Man can never know, says Goethe, how anthropomorphic he is; and anthropomorphism is a prison-house. Influenced by Spinoza, Goethe wished to reconcile a divinely impersonal Nature with a personal Mediation. (290)

Similar to the Hebraic rejection of a "personal intermediary," Wordsworth's position reflects a characteristic wariness of apocalyptic tendencies and temptations. According to Hartman, Wordsworth

> thinks of nature as chastening imagination, as purging it of a too personal "master folded in his fire." His attitude may be quite unknowingly a renascence of negative theology. To see only the human in nature (or, for that matter, in man) is like seeing only

the personal God: it must produce an apocalyptic self-consciousness, a too-human or superhuman image, and so fix the person to one self-image. (290)

What Wordsworth broke through to, and what Hartman's phenomenological perspective manages to lay bare, is "a mode of experience more deeply integral to human existence than either the conventionally 'sacred' or secular."[15] This point Hartman develops in "The Poetics of Prophecy," in which he uncovers the vital link between Wordsworth's "secular" yet prophetic writing and that of Hebraic figures like Jeremiah. On the level of interpretation, this "more deeply integral" experience is what Schleiermacher called *Verstehen*, "on the basis of which a hermeneutic is projected that seeks to transcend the dichotomizing of religious and nonreligious modes of understanding and of earlier (prophetic) and later (poetic-visionary) texts" (UnRW 178). The interpreter thus repeats the poet's struggle to overcome the "obsession with analysis" that "murders to dissect."

At any rate, a confluence of effects emerges, and they point to a new understanding of religion. Supported by the shift away from mythic machinery and the supernatural and towards the human and ordinary, the new triad of Nature, Self-Consciousness, and Imagination, which merged with "the traditional scheme of Eden, Fall, and Redemption," puts "religion in a new dress, the dress of feeling" (WP 153). According to Hartman, Wordsworth's "call to save nature ... expresses not only a residual agrarian sensibility but a response to apocalyptic stirrings which institutionalized religions cannot always bind or subdue. He knew that religion, like poetry itself, arises from imaginative sensations that might be channeled into human-heartedness" (UnRW xxvii). Human-heartedness is the lesson Nature teaches, the object of her ministrations. Expanding the heart and so enhancing relation, "love of nature" leads to "love of man." Enlightened critique of systems, sects, and institutions joins with religious feelings in this humanization – a *humanizing* of the heart – that does not end in glorification or apotheosis of the human but rather directs attention to the heart as the locus of significance. Reinterpreting both the source and the end of religious feelings, Wordsworth, who Keats said thought deeply into the human heart (Hartman calls him "a poet of the human heart" [WP 74]), offers a vision at once fundamental and revolutionary, though revolutionary in the slow and gentle way that nature teaches.

The object of Wordsworth's efforts was, then, to channel "imaginative sensations" into the human-heartedness dependent on the ministrations of nature in danger of being neglected by, if even available to, modern men and women. "Without a filial relation to Nature," Hartman writes, "to that animate earth and heaven which plays so crucial a role in ancient myth," we become

> unimaginative or require increasingly personal and violent stimuli.... The result is that revolutionary or self-alienating, rather than creative, personality in which Wordsworth saw the great temptation of his epoch, and to which he almost succumbed. His poetry, with its emphasis on "the infinite variety of natural appearances" and on the way the simplest event can enrich mind, sets itself against "gross and violent stimulants" in the realm of the senses or of public action. (UnRW 3–4)

It remains the case, whether or not we are ready to receive him, that Wordsworth *"considers man in his own nature and in his ordinary life"* (UnRW 13). The lesson Wordsworth teaches is one that Hartman now teaches himself.

Though the foregoing suggests that Hartman learned much from the Romantics, especially Wordsworth, whose work he not only elaborates but also extends, I want, in closing, to redirect attention to some major points. Actually, I remain unsure how much Hartman *learned* from the poets he admires: as suggested by the passage I quoted earlier concerning his initial attraction to Wordsworth, the possibility is good that reading the Romantics, particularly Wordsworth, merely confirmed – and nurtured – feelings, perspectives, and concerns he had in common with them. This question leads us back to Wordsworth, via Hartman: who knows, the poet asks in *The Prelude*,

> the individual hour in which
> His habits were first sown, even as a seed?
> Who that shall point as with a wand and say
> "This portion of the river of my mind
> Came from yon fountain?"

Thus the error lies in pointing, which is "to encapsulate something... to overobjectify, to overformulize. It implies that there is a fixed locus of revelation or a reified idolatrous content" (BF 50).

It may be that something more is involved in Hartman's initial – and continuing, indeed inescapable or binding – attraction to Wordsworth than those reasons he lists in the Preface to *The Unremarkable Wordsworth*, as important as they unquestionably are. Imre

Salusinszky, for one, thinks so. Introducing a recent interview, Salusinszky writes that

> By the time he arrived in the United States in 1946, Hartman had probably seen too much of apocalyptic yearnings and unconstrained idealisms to be much attracted by Blake. Instead, he turned to a poet in whom an apocalyptic idealism is being continually qualified by a recognition of those things – nature, other people, experience – which are always outside the imagination, and will not be controlled by it.[16]

Whether or not as a major reason for Hartman's initial attraction to Wordsworth, wariness of the apocalyptic in all its forms is certainly fundamental to Hartman's thinking. In *Wordsworth's Poetry*, with reference to the Book of Revelation, Hartman defines the apocalyptic as "the kind of imagination that is concerned with the supernatural and essentially the Last Things," as "a mind which actively desires the inauguration of a totally new epoch," and as "any strong desire to cast out nature and to achieve an unmediated contact with the principle of things" (xxvii). Elsewhere, Hartman avers that the apocalyptic, manifested as excessive hope, represents a turning against time as well as against nature (UnRW 167). For both Wordsworth and his critic, however, "there is no apocalyptic or revolutionary change, just due process of time and nature" (BF 296). With Benjamin, Hartman looks towards a new understanding of history, one that robs hope of the apocalyptic. It is at once revolutionary and critical, because it looks not towards the future but towards the past. Hartman makes the point most clearly in the recent essay "Religious Literacy":

> "Hope in the past" means refusing to associate hope exclusively with the future, as if the past were inert and unredeemable, nothing but bare, ruined choirs. In the eyes of hope (a more revolutionary virtue than faith) there are alternative, even plural, versions of the past in the past, archaic or repressed currents retrieved by the revolutionary thinker.[17]

Hartman's opposition to "apocalyptic stirrings" takes several forms, including his critique of the often-thoughtless haste implicit in hope, expressed in such essays as "Marvell, St. Paul, and the Body of Hope" and in his discussion of the chiasmus of hope and catastrophe in *Criticism in the Wilderness*. Hartman's account of the humanities, especially in several essays collected in *Easy Pieces*, as a valorization of and provision for "delay time" stands as an implicit critique of those pressured activities that fuel apocalyptic dreams and desires. His description of "the inspiring teacher in the humanities," which closes *Criticism in the Wilderness*, represents the thoughtfulness and patience that the apocalyptic imagination cannot abide. Indeed, Hartman's advocacy of "hermeneutic reflection," which, he says, "disables the one-dimensional, progressive claims of conqueror or would-be conqueror," manifests his pervasive wariness of the apocalyptic (CW 75). That wariness appears as well in Hartman's important, if somewhat surprising, recent account of the "aesthetic" as "a structure of postponement" and "the doubting or delaying of closure, the insistence on remainders or of a return to the past"; the "aesthetic" Hartman juxtaposes with action, which he claims, "idealizes interpretation and keeps moving relentlessly toward an all-consuming point which is the new regime, the new order" (UnRW 186). Since "there is always a remainder that cannot be purged, whatever violence of intellect we apply" (UnRW 192), purity, which may be one aim of the apocalyptic, is rendered impossible. Hartman's (Jewish) reticence or reserve, like Wordsworth's concerning the pointed style, appears an analogue of his wariness of apocalyptic drives.

Just as patience and thoughtfulness represent the opposite of apocalyptic hope and haste, so *akedah* represents opposition to apocalyptic violence against nature. The tie that binds poetry to nature is, however, no more confining than the analogous one that binds interpreter to text. In both cases, nothing replaces responsibility, for like the poet before nature, the interpreter, who must respond to the always-prior call of texts, enjoys real freedom.

That the interpreter/text relation corresponds to that of poet/nature and, properly understood, displays the same patience and care appears clearly in "The Use and Abuse of Structural Analysis," reprinted in *The Unremarkable Wordsworth*. In this essay, Hartman considers Wordsworth's "Yew-Trees" in relation to the structuralist reading of the poem offered by Michael Riffaterre. Though he calls Riffaterre's "the best commentary on that poem yet written," one that "ranks with the best commentaries on any Wordsworth poem" (130), he implies there is something almost apocalyptic about it: "The progression of Wordsworth's poem (noted by Riffaterre) toward a final perspective that alleviates the burden of the mystery is, it seems to me, a halting one, and as precarious as that final perspective itself" (137). After noting, against Riffaterre, the several "impediments to easy progression" that the poem presents, Hartman himself halts on the word "united," "the most intriguing case" (138); he is, like Wordsworth, "the halted traveler." Hartman's "more intuitive" (131) and "personal" (135) reading specifically links texts and nature as well as reader and poet and makes clear the analogous effort in which the latter engage. Brooding over the word "united," like the Rabbis practicing midrash, Hartman begins by observing an equivocation in sound: "The *un* sequence may lead to a momentary and illusory reading of it as *un-ited*." Though the reader "resolves the riddle word *un-ited* by the proper, forward movement," "once the word has been slowed or foregrounded in this way, a new, less commonsensical deciphering may suggest itself. It again brings the poem to a halt or condenses it as one riddling phrase. *United* could be read *U*nited, that is, *Yew*nited (Yewnighted)" (138–9). Hartman thus enacts a strategy or procedure, better, a brooding, that slows down reading and *binds* the reader *to* the poem rather than moves quickly to supposed meanings. Moreover, referring to the analogies between nature and language, Hartman explains that

> slowing the reader makes him aware that the forms of language, like those of nature, "have a passion in themselves." ... The slowing of reading also makes him aware of time. Like language, time is more than a medium. There seems to be no way to force its growth or to subdue it to the predictable. Time has the erratic motion of a snake coiled up. There is something treacherous in the flow of time or of words which makes Wordsworth exceedingly cautious. (139)

Hartman proceeds to other important points. Invoking Wordsworth's idea that the mind participates *with* nature, perception and creation being interimplicated, Hartman clearly indicates how the interpretive situation mirrors that of mind confronting nature. He also suggests that a responsible way of reading parallels nature's own processes.

> Wordsworth's "yewnity," a dream word disturbing further the not undisturbed realism of the poem, has the dark appeal of its double or compound character. Half-perceived, half-created by the reader, it is a centaur shape guiding him to a new understanding of how words and things, signifier and signified, connect. It suggests the possibility of a strangely mimetic or organic literary form, of a language of nature: here is a kernel, out of which, however unconsciously – by vegetable genius – the poem

grows. "Yewnity" suggests a model for analysis imitating the branchings of tree or flower from a deeply nurtured, perhaps covert, point. (139)

Not unlike the way in which Wordsworth, in the face of increasing pressures to avoid or void her, tries to preserve nature as nurse, guide, guardian, and indeed anchor of our moral being, Hartman works to save texts by thoughtfully elaborating on them, cooperating with them, and preserving them in our memory. The relationship of reader to text exactly parallels that of (the poet's) mind to nature, as Wordsworth comes to understand it in the climactic experience on Mount Snowdon, represented in the last book of *The Prelude*. That experience constitutes the focus of my next chapter.

Whether Hartman's work may be considered the literature of "imaginative reason" that both the Romantics and Matthew Arnold, somewhat differently, hoped for, it certainly recognizes and takes into account the post-Enlightenment importance of analysis, irony, and prose (BF 310). The burden the Romantics shouldered was considerable, and it is a burden Hartman feels: the burden of responding to major demands; of being "on the spot"; of preserving not just individual texts but also an entire tradition, perhaps of criticism itself if not also of poetry; of being able to abide time; perhaps above all else, of bearing what Wordsworth in *Tintern Abbey* calls "the burthen of the mystery." If Wordsworth, as Keats believed, bore "'the burthen of the mystery' more intensely than previous poets" (UnRW 15), Hartman bears that burden more intensely than many other contemporary critics. Change the single word "verse" to "prose" in the following passage, and what Hartman writes of Wordsworth seems to apply to himself:

> here is a man whose mind moves as he writes, who thinks aloud in verse (as Matthew Arnold remarked disparagingly), or who thinks into the human heart (as Keats said approvingly), a poet, therefore, who confronts heuristically maze within maze. (WP 209)

4

Calling voices out of silence: criticism as echo-chamber

Whether or not there is a language of nature there is a language of the heart that goes out to nature.
The Unremarkable Wordsworth

Take away the play of allusion, the comforting ground of literary-historical texture, and you place the burden of responsiveness directly on the reader. He must echo in himself a verse which he can only develop by the recognition that *de te fabula narratur*. The verse adjures him; demands grace of him; and no poet who reads so easily at first [as Wordsworth does] puts as resolute and lasting a demand on the reader. We are asked to read in ourselves.... It is the reader who makes the verse responsive, however inward or buried its sounds: he also calls a voice out of silence.... he redeems the poet's voice from solitariness.
The Fate of Reading

The critic explicitly acknowledges his dependence on prior words that make his word a kind of answer. He calls to other texts "that they might answer him." His focus is on the activity of the receiver, on the possibility of drawing a timely response from "trembling ears."
Criticism in the Wilderness

[I]t is not the individual poem that determines the meaning of indeterminate phrases but the poem as part of an intertextual corpus which the skilled interpreter supplies.... It is the reader who has to take responsibility.
The Unremarkable Wordsworth

In the Foreword to *The Unremarkable Wordsworth*, Donald G. Marshall struggles to define Hartman's appeal as a critical reader. Not so different from my earlier description of Hartman's open and dialectical procedures that, I add, produce an "art of antitheses" resistant to "straight-line interpretations" (M 64, 62), that article emphasizes how Hartman raises "the voltage of reading by sustaining a polar tension" between encountered "alien modes of thought." Responsible for their (electric) power, Marshall correctly notes, is no "method" or particular "approach," the desirability of which Hartman questioned as early as *The Unmediated Vision*; "any separation of the critic from the poet being read," writes Marshall, "will interrupt and still the reverberations which animate the reading" (ix). Marshall claims, in fact, that in Hartman's hands the very idea of "critical method" is "strangely transmuted. It is not that Hartman measures theory by its usefulness for interpretation, nor even that he 'tests' it against poems. Rather, he opens an interchange between contemporary currents and Wordsworth which has the reciprocal and dialogical character of genuine thought" (viii). Having no "method," Hartman, according to Marshall, simply *thinks* with and about texts; as a result, reading and thinking appear "one and inseparable." Providing the ground that connects reading and thinking is, Marshall maintains, "Hartman's feeling for language" and especially his "uncanny ear for sounds." That ground "has a perplexingly shadowy materiality," due to "a strangely physical grasp of every utterance's openness to and resonance with other utterances, present and – above all – past." Marshall proceeds to define Hartman's gift as "the power to hear echoes and to write a criticism as echo-chamber." That is not, he rightly says, "quite what is called 'intertextuality,' for what is at stake is not the disseminated play of signifiers, but having 'ears to hear' (ix)." Those ears allow the skilled and knowledgeable interpreter to hear the "intertextual echoes" of words, which, Hartman claims, not only bring out their peculiar spirit but also, paradoxically, materialize them. By focusing on Hartman's contributions to a "criticism as echo-chamber," I want, in this chapter, both to elaborate on his analogues with Wordsworth and to explore the specific responsiveness – and responsibility – that characterize his "intertextual leaping."

Lacking a "method" or definable "approach," and neither wanting nor needing one, Hartman has described his way of reading as "intuitive" and "personal" (UnRW 131, 135). Just as news of the death of the author is premature (echoing, indeed quoting Milton, Hartman regards the great poem as the "life-blood of a master-spirit" [FR 255]), so is that concerning the *de rigueur* impersonalism of critical commentary. In Hartman's words, "methods are backed up by methodizers: there is a person in the machine" (UnRW 130); and with all his erudition, hermeneutical speculation, and highjinks, Hartman never loses sight, or lets his reader lose sight, of the person responding. Without embracing impressionism, despite his fondness for Anatole France's definition of the critic as one who "relates the adventures of his soul among masterpieces" (CW 11), Hartman thus maintains that understanding is more than "a matter of rules or techniques" (STT 137), which, in "modern 'rithmatics' – semiotics, linguistics, and technical structuralism," "convert all expression into generative codes needing operators rather than readers." With so much of culture in his head and heart, Hartman laments that "a sophisticated technique is accompanied too often by a barbarous or parochial narrowness of culture" (FR 272–3). Adapting Martin Buber, Hartman considers the text a Thou understood as "a relation and not an object," not a "naturalized and neutered 'It'" (CW 102). Indebted to phenomenology as well as to the entire hermeneutical tradition, Hartman directs attention to "the life-situation of the interpreter," which in his terms, has to do "with riddles as well as puzzles" (STT 137).

What is sought in "the language-exchange" that constitutes human communication, literary as well as ordinary, "is often," Hartman claims, "the readiness to take and give words in trust, rather than the answer to a problem." In fact, Hartman seeks "troth rather than truth: the ability to exchange thoughts in the form of words; to recognize words of the other; or to trust in the words to be exchanged." Pointing to the *communion* involved, Hartman avers that "one breaks words with the other as one breaks bread" (STT 139).[1] It comes as no surprise, then, that he believes that "no method can guarantee an interpretation" (UnRW 130).

Crucial to the notion of interpretation as troth or trust is, as Hartman indicates, the idea of *recognition*, which like Hartman's criticism, is intuitive rather than positivistic or methodological, and which sustains the language-exchange. Though he acknowledges them, Hartman's understanding differs somewhat from Gilles Deleuze's juxtaposition of recognition with encounter as well as from Heidegger's depiction of hermeneutics as *"re-cognitio, Wieder-erkennung,"* or "the working out, the unfolding of a preunderstanding, ...

the recovery of a prior understanding for which we have hitherto lacked the words."² For Hartman, moreover, whether the text be Wordsworth's or Derrida's, Christopher Smart's or Ross Macdonald's, a scene of recognition is always being played out. Marking that scene, and indeed serving as its apparent ground, is the *evocative* nature of language. In Jacques Lacan's formulation, "the Word always subjectively includes its own reply.... The function of language is not to inform but to evoke. What I seek in the Word is the response of the other."³ After quoting these remarks himself, Hartman proceeds to describe the literary text as "a gift for which the interpreter must find words, both to recognize the gift, and then to allow it to create a reciprocating dialogue, one that might overcome the embarrassment inspired by art's riddling strength" (STT 136). He contends, moreover, that "recognition must precede as well as follow cognition. To put the entire emphasis on the cognitive function (*connaissance*) will damage the recognitive function (*reconnaissance*) and the language exchange as a whole" (STT 137). The necessity of sustaining dialogue, or the language exchange, puts major "responsibility ... on the respondent" (STT 134).

Perhaps nowhere is Hartman's relationship to Lacan closer, his use of and debt to Lacan greater – though here, too, that use appears as digestion, elaboration, and even counterstatement. Still, it is important to recognize what Hartman is doing, how he does it, what texts lie behind and within his own reading and writing. In this case, it is, at least in part, Lacan's reading of Melanie Klein's account of "little Dick" and her use of Oedipus as therapeutic intervention in the child's inability to respond "normally." What Klein effects in Dick is verbalization, a relationship, his passage from the Imaginary to the Symbolic, this latter being

> the differential situating of the subject in a *third position*; it is at once the place *from which* a dual relation is apprehended, the place *through which* it is articulated, and that which makes the subject (as, precisely, this symbolic, third place) into a linguistic signifier in a system, which thereby permits him to relate symbolically to other signifiers, that is, at once to relate to other humans and to articulate his own desire, his own unconscious, unawares.[4]

In short, what happens is, in every sense, performative (instead of constative): the analyst engages in a speech act that produces in the child "the call that was lacking, the address that then becomes his motivation for the introjection of human discourse (language)."⁵ Let Lacan explain these loaded terms "call," "response," and so forth, words that carry religious weight though they derive for Lacan – and Hartman – from a situation that is secular and analytical:

> ... if I call the person to whom I am speaking by whatever name I choose to give him, I intimate to him the subjective function that he will take on in order to reply to me, even if it is to repudiate this function.
>
> What I seek in speech is the response – the reply – of the other. What constitutes me as subject is my question. In order to be recognized by the other, I utter what was only in function of what will be. In order to find him, I call him by a name that he must assume or refuse in order to reply to me.
>
> A reaction is not a reply.... There is no reply except for *my* desire.... There is no question except for my anticipation....
>
> Henceforth, the decisive function of my own reply [as analyst] appears, and this function is not, as has been said, simply to be received by the subject as acceptance or rejection of his discourse, but really to recognize him or to abolish him as subject. Such is the *responsibility* of the analyst, each time he intervenes by means of speech.⁶

The gift the analyst thus offers is a reply, not superior knowledge (he or she is only in the *position* of "the one who is supposed to know," put there by the analysand). Since "the reply addresses not so much what the patient says (or means), but his call," "the interpretive gift is not constative (cognitive) but performative: the gift is not so much a gift of truth, of understanding or of meaning: it is, essentially, a gift of language."⁷ Literary texts work in similar fashion, in Hartman's formulation, attempting to evoke a response to a call the interpreter apparently precipitates.

At least part of what reader-responsibility entails in Hartman's terms is sketched out in "Understanding Criticism," the first chapter of *Criticism in the Wilderness*. Exemplifying the way he constantly "shuttles" between theoretical issues and the reading of (or brooding upon) particular poems, Hartman constructs out of "Leda and the Swan," "I wandered lonely as a cloud," and "Resolution and Independence" "a fable for the hermeneutical situation" (5, 35). Represented in these poems is a reception of the strange and extraordinary, perhaps even of otherness: by Leda of the swan-god, by Wordsworth of "a crowd,/ A host, of golden daffodils" and of the mysterious, decrepit old leech-gatherer. In each poem, in fact, despite their differences "the situation is intrinsically a hermeneutic one" (30). That situation the interpreter repeats in responding to the extra-ordinary representation the poet has made of the extra-ordinary event encountered. The work of the interpreter thus involves *receiving* the extra-ordinary language-event that constitutes the poem, itself a representation of the poet's reception of an extra-ordinary event. Reception, as Hartman makes clear, need not entail acceptance: "To receive is not to accept; between these, as between active and passive, critical thinking takes place, makes its place. We cannot solve, a priori, the issue of strange or other; we can only deal with it, in the mode of 'resonance' that writing is" (27). Struggling with what is received – a text or texts, as well as "the burden of tradition" one inherits – is what criticism is about.

Such a poem as "Leda and the Swan," according to Hartman, exacts a price of its recipient, obliging the reader "to become active, even to risk something" (CW 272–3). The form of that activity, of course, is *response*, which the idea of reception implies as a correlate. The question of style enters as soon as the matter of response is broached, especially since, as Hartman believes, "the difference that reading makes is, most generally, writing" (CW 19): "How can the critic," he wonders, "respond to the extraordinary language-event and still maintain a prose of the center?" (CW 157). With response, in any case, the emphasis shifts, obviously, to the reader or receiver. In *Saving the Text*, Hartman goes so far as to claim that "critical reading is not only the reception (*Rezeption*) of a text, but also its conception (*Empfängnis*) through the ear" (STT 141–2).

Linked to responsibility, response is key to an appreciation of Hartman's way of reading. Here too his understanding parallels Wordsworth's, as well as Lacan's. Hartman repeats structurally in his response to Wordsworth the poet's response to nature. These echoing responses are rich and complex activities that deserve close attention. Apparent since *The Unmediated Vision*, Hartman's emphasis on the role of the ear and what is heard, which "counter-balances... the immediacy of the eye" and threatens its tyranny, represents another analogue with Hebraism (STT 142).

For Hartman, as for Wordsworth, "responsibility begins with the ability to respond" (FR 21). The "burden of responsiveness" is related to what Wordsworth in the Intimations Ode calls a "timely utterance." Whether or not poetry is that "timely utterance," which in that poem problematically brings to "a thought of grief" some "relief," what matters, according to Hartman, "is the sense of a *bond* between mind and nature, of a *responsiveness* that overcomes the difference of speech and muteness, or articulate and inarticulate utterance" (UnRW 156). Entailed, specifically, is a "reciprocal response," that is, "an inward and meeting echo" (UnRW 156). The poet must gain (or regain) the capacity to "answer or echo nature," just as the critic must answer or echo the text whose call he or she recognizes and receives. Wordsworth's version of "ecchoing song" is his antiphonal style (a poet's words "are always antiphonal to the phoné of a prior experience. Or, the prior experience is the phoné" [UnRW 101]). That alerts us to the way "poetry is echo humanized, a responsive movement" (UnRW 103).

The idea of *echoing response* is one that Hartman frequently treats. The *locus classicus* of that idea is probably the fragment concerning the Boy of Winander, included in *Lyrical Ballads*. The poem represents the poet gazing "mutely" upon the grave of the Boy, whose efforts to make nature "echo responsively" we might take, echoing Wordsworth's vision on Mount Snowdon, as "a grand emblem of responsive" criticism. Because of its importance, I quote the entire fragment:

> There was a Boy, ye knew him well, ye Cliffs
> And Islands of Winander! many a time,
> At evening, when the stars had just begun
> To move along the edges of the hills,
> Rising or setting, would he stand alone,
> Beneath the trees, or by the glimmering lake;
> And there, with fingers interwoven, both hands
> Pressed closely palm to palm and to his mouth
> Uplifted, he, as through an instrument,
> Blew mimic hootings to the silent owls
> That they might answer him. And they would shout
> Across the watery vale, and shout again
> Responsive to his call, with quivering peals,
> And long halloos, and screams, and echoes loud
> Redoubled and redoubled; concourse wild
> Of mirth and jocund din! And, when it chanced
> That pauses of deep silence, while he hung
> Listening, a gentle shock of mild surprise
> Has carried far into his heart the voice
> Of mountain torrents; or the visible scene
> Would enter unawares into his mind

> With all its solemn imagery, its rocks,
> Its woods, and that uncertain heaven, received
> Into the bosom of the steady lake.
>
> This Boy was taken from his Mates, and died
> In childhood, ere he was ten years old.
> Fair are the woods, and beauteous is the spot,
> The Vale where he was born: the Church-yard hangs
> Upon a slope above the Village School,
> And there, along that bank, when I have passed
> At evening, I believe, that oftentimes
> A full half-hour together I have stood
> Mute – looking at the grave in which he lies.
>
> (quoted in FR 293)

Wordsworth depicts the Boy of Winander as engaged in only one act: "he makes nature – its hidden life – echo responsively." In pointing out that "the reflective man standing over the boy's grave does a similar thing," Hartman establishes the analogy with the interpreter's situation, for he or she too makes texts – their "hidden life" – "echo responsively" (FR 289). Poet and reader alike are engaged in "calling a voice out of silence" (FR 289). Referring to the "Boy of Winander" fragment in particular, Hartman contends that the reader

> must echo in himself a verse which he can only develop by the recognition that *de te fabula narratur*. The verse adjures him; demands grace of him; and no poet who reads so easily at first [as Wordsworth does] puts as resolute and lasting a demand on the reader. We are asked to read in ourselves.

It is, in short, "the reader who makes the verse responsive, however inward or buried its sounds: he also calls a voice out of silence" and in so doing "redeems the poet's voice from solitariness" (FR 291).

However it may appear, it is "not mystical," Hartman insists, "to call poetic language the voices of silence" (BF 343). Rather than mystical, what Hartman means is more like "historical" and recalls Saussure's "scientific" research on anagrams that Jean Starobinski presents in *Words upon Words*. If, in fact, "reading a poem is like walking on silence," as Hartman believes, that is because in reading "we feel the historical ground; the buried life of words. Like fallen gods, like visions of the night, words are erectile" (BF 342–3). In any case, poetry makes "a curious alliance with critical reading, in order to reactivate the ear. Both are auscultations that have the capacity of putting us on the alert toward the silence in us: the wrongly silenced words as well as the noisy words that get in their way and prevent thoughtfulness. The words of a text, in their silence," Hartman continues, "are but divining rods to disclose other words, perhaps words of the other" (STT 142). Too often conceived of simply as "a scrutiny of content or form," reading, at least of the kind that Hartman both advocates and practices, discloses that "structure of *words within words*, a structure ... deeply mediated, ghostly, and echoic" (STT 129). Various hermeneutical modes thus come together, including psychoanalysis and midrash. In literature, Hartman agrees with Lacan, so much "depends on hearing what is said in what is being said," and reading is, or can (indeed, should) be "an active kind of hearing. We really do 'look with ears' when we read a book of some complexity." Thus "when literary critics remark of literature, 'There's magic in the web,' they characterize not only what distinguishes the literary from the merely verbal, but what distinguishes critical from passive kinds of reading" (STT 128).

The responsibility that devolves upon the reader able and willing to shoulder "the burden of responsiveness" necessitates an "intertextual awareness" (UnRW 160) that engages him or her in "an active kind of hearing." Though that awareness, Hartman insists, does not "divorce us from deeply beloved experience, or Wordsworth's 'the world, which is the world of all of us,'" it does produce what he acknowledges as his own "intertextual leaping" (UnRW 160, 162). That phrase occurs at the close of "'Timely Utterance' Once More," which offers a particularly clear window onto Hartman's way of reading, his own "echoing song," as well as allowing us better to estimate any reader's share in literary understanding.

Hartman's essay, included in *The Unremarkable Wordsworth*, proceeds from an opening citation of Lionel Trilling to a wide-ranging speculation on what "timely utterance" gave Wordsworth's "thought of grief" a welcome and hoped-for "relief," in the Intimations Ode. Hartman's *speculations*, or "hermeneutic reflections," lead to several other Wordsworth poems as well as to *The Aeneid*, Shelley's "Adonais," Spenser's *Shepheardes Calendar* and *Epithalamion*, the Book of Genesis, *Lycidas*, *The Rime of the Ancient Mariner*, and the work of Kenneth Burke and Jacques Lacan. Hartman's *focus* centers on the echo-structure the Ode reveals, as Wordsworth looks toward "an inward and meeting echo, a reciprocal response" to nature's ministering efforts (155). Hartman describes his reading of Wordsworth's poem as "mildly deconstructive," in that it "discloses in words 'a "spirit" peculiar to their nature as words' (Kenneth Burke). Such a reading refuses to substitute ideas for words" (159). Whether or not the "timely utterance" refers to God's first words in the Bible, the *fiat lux* of Genesis, as he suggests, Hartman moves nimbly and widely, providing a record of critical thinking and an engaging account of interpretive discovery. "I have taken one phrase as my starting point," he acknowledges, "and made many angels dance on it." But, he adds, "these revels would be in vain if Wordsworth's Ode were not involved in the question of ... what connection there might be between poetry and prophecy" (161). Hartman's essay thus has to do with the response that poetry represents, perhaps as a renewal of the covenant that *binds* mind or imagination and nature. In unpacking the meanings that surround the phrase "timely utterance," Hartman has "echoed responsively" Wordsworth's own responsiveness. The critic's "intertextual leaping" has indeed brought the Word (*davar*) out of silence.

In "'Timely Utterance' Once More," Hartman's uncanny ability to discern "intertextual echoes" in various texts leads to his own "timely" disclosures. In "The Use and Abuse of Structural Analysis," which I noted in the previous chapter, it is Hartman's ability, somewhat differently, to hear strange, even ghostly, reverberations in words taken alone that produces surprising insights. Recall the term "United" in "Yew-Trees," over which Hartman broods. Hartman hears in that word "*U*nited," "*Yew*nited," and "Yew*night*ed." A strange sort of "*yew*nity" thus emerges for the mind hooked on, and "drugged" by, words. The term "yewnity," in fact, Hartman writes, "dream word disturbing further the not undisturbed realism" of this particular poem, "has the dark appeal of its double or compound character" (139). Elaborating on that character, he outlines what appears to be a theory of reading, deriving, of course, from Wordsworth's poem, which he looks *through*: "Half-perceived, half-created by the reader, it is a centaur shape guiding him to a new understanding of how words and things, signifier and signified, connect." After then quoting from *Paradise Lost*, Hartman writes: "Paradigm Lost, something echoes in us" (139). Aware of the charges this (kind of) reading engenders, he asks why view Wordsworth's poem "through the focus of a quack linguistic compound 'yewnity'?" (140). His response addresses the issue of "responsibility" raised by such word-play and, in fact, sketches a general theory of the "reader's responsibility." That, he admits, is not easily defined. The reader must decide how much darkness is to be developed. It is always a matter of "yewnity" versus "unity," whoever wrote the poem. For a "yewnifying" critic darkness is of the essence: the persephonic food cannot be separated from the bright cereal. In some interpreters, of course, there are three parts of light to one of darkness, as in the Persephone myth itself. Only one season is given to Hades. Some interpreters are more evangelical still, and reduce the part of darkness to that which allows the light to shine or the grain to die in order to ripen. Others are more willing to be badnewsmen. No one can remove the reader's responsibility entirely. In this, to each his own conscience. But Wordsworth's poem taken as a model suggests that the relation between dark and light or heliotropic and melantropic readings, is only precariously "unificent." In fact, to deny imagination its darker food, to seek and make it a "Shape all light," is to wish imagination away. (140–1)

The responsibility to know how far to carry interpretive freedom rests with the individual reader, whose imagination Hartman honors. Reader-responsibility criticism looks not to the individual poem to determine the meaning of indeterminate phrases but rather to "the poem as part of an intertextual corpus which the skilled interpreter supplies" (UnRW 213). The skilled interpreter is like those Rabbis who engaged in "hermeneutical highjinks" while maintaining a scrupulousness regarding the text read.

How far Hartman himself will go is perhaps clearest in *Saving the Text*, which presents his most extended, and elaborate, account of *echo* and which becomes a "counterstatement" to Derrida. As he offers striking readings of *Glas*, particularly in the opening essays "Monsieur Texte" and "Epiphony in Echoland," Hartman acknowledges Derrida as "the most radical critic of naïve, phonocentric materialism; at the same time he claims that "nothing could be more mistaken than to think of Derrida as derogating what he calls the 'cas de la phonè.' The case of the *phonè* is never closed; its cadence cannot be encased in grammar or meaning. It falls through, into, both. Writing manifests it as ambiguity, irony, equivocation" (35, 14). Prizing, as he has throughout his career, "openness of thought and inquiry," Hartman believes that "the fullness of equivocation in literary structures should now be thought about to the point where Joyce's word-play seems normal and Empson's *Seven Types* archaic" (23). As he explores Derrida's word-play, in which he too engages, he takes on what he calls "the *task* of equivocation" that "the French critical tradition" has accepted but that "Anglo-American criticism still seeks to limit" (60).

Equivocation follows, of course, from *dissemination*, which, according to Hartman, "enters a new phase" with Derrida.

> It is now directed *analytically* – prosaically, if you wish – against the mimetic principle (the "collect" or "legein" of the logos) in major texts of the Western tradition. They are so separated from a direct logo-imitative intention by his deconstructive readings that they cannot be returned to their father: their author, or their author in heaven. Instead of converting the straying text to a central truth by a mode of interpretation similar to allegoresis or sacred parody, Derrida absolutizes the text's "error." (STT 51)

Thanks to *dissemination*, reading becomes "an *errance joyeuse*, rather than the capitalization of great books by interpretive safeguards" (STT 52). Difficult to formalize, and perhaps happily so, *dissemination*, according to Hartman, involves not interpretive licentiousness but rather "a *travail de textes*, their working-through, in which the texts themselves undergo a renewed birth-labor" (STT 52). Let there be no mistake, however: what Hartman, in *Saving the Text*, following Derrida, advocates – and practices – represents a radical departure from traditional New Critical or scholarly protocols of reading. It is not enough, he declares, to be attentive to "the multiplicity of themes or the polysemy of a work of art," though that "constitutes a progress over 'linear' exposition." Nothing less than "the horizon of criticism, which is the assumption of *uni'y* of meaning, has itself to be breached" (STT 52; my italics).

A mazy, joyous, and spermatic writing, equivocally dedicated to "the subject," *Saving the Text* makes no bow to "linear" exposition, which, in the case of *Glas*, hardly seems possible or desirable. Different from a narrow and impersonal structuralism or poststructuralism, it celebrates not only words but the (human) imagination that makes them play. Brooding over a limited number of (carefully selected) passages, and being attentive to words as words rather than jumping to meaning, Hartman suggests how "the horizon of criticism" might be breached (the central chapter is entitled "How to Reap a Page"). With his alert and "erectile" ear, Hartman hears in Derrida's words resonances that evoke a sense of the latter's entire project. He accomplishes more than that, however, for he discerns echoes that allow us not only to glimpse a sense of the (non)whole of *Glas* but also to catch at the significance of that text as at once commentary and art with the power to unsettle our understanding of writing – and so much more. As Hartman puts it, "only when writing discloses an echo rather than an image, so that the sounding word has reverberations that transcend the economy of clarity and form, do contradictions arise that shake the 'temples of wisdom and science'" (xxii).

To exemplify Hartman's "criticism as echo-chamber," consider an important, dense, and rich passage where it becomes impossible to separate Hartman from Derrida, commentator from text(s) commented on, echoed: STT 60–2, a section entitled "Derrida's Knot" in "Epiphony in Echoland." Who can point to a spot where Hartman's exposition of Derrida ends and his own contribution begins? Such merging of text and metatext as occurs here is difficult to achieve – and it represents difficulty for the perplexed reader unable to determine whose position is being described. Thus this passage illustrates both the positive achievements of "criticism as echo-chamber" and its problematics. About halfway through, after five paragraphs, the reader is not merely unsettled but perhaps wondering whether the critic has gone too far, his own text outstripping that commented on. Hartman suggests that problem himself, beginning the next paragraph, "Enough, you say." At issue is Derrida's acronym IC for the Immaculate Conception, on which Hartman has been brooding. I quote the remainder of this remarkable section:

> In his pamphlet on Adami, Derrida plays further on IC, which now reappears in the form of ICH ("I" or "Je"), the abbreviated ICH(TOS) symbol for Christ (see the fish of Adami's picture), and by chiastic reversal both the chiasmus itself (X) transliterated as CHI, and the querulous pronoun QUI. Free-play reaches here a methodical craziness that parallels Christopher Smart's. But taken altogether a series of slippery signifiers has now established itself on the basis of the problematics of the subject, its construction and subversion. Though this verbal gematria is no more, no less, persuasive than Lacan's diagrammatia, it has the same treacherously memorable effect, as if Lacan's imaginary and symbolic realms had finally come together in a sort of *specular script*.

Now it becomes clear that Hartman is *elaborating* on Derrida, taking his cue from *Glas*, looking through it, and seeing perhaps more than, perhaps seeing things differently from, Derrida, though we can wish that Hartman had made clear – such may be our commitment to pointing – where and how much is his, where and how much is Derrida's.

Let me try to formulate this basic mirror-writing as
IC(ICH/CHI)INRI

I have added the last term, the acronym of Christ on the Cross, to that crossing or chiasmic middle term, which stands for the problematics of subject or ego, and to the first term, which evokes, together with the initials of Christ and the first syllable of ICarus (as in "la voie/voix d'Icare"), the Immaculate Conception.

The three terms in series repeat a scene of nomination. It focuses on ICH, the narcissistic shifter, a mere text-figure when CHI. It focuses equally on the "Name of the Game," whether "Je," "Jeu," or "Je est un autre." But if to enter language is not the same as to enter the law, it is also not merely to learn the rules of a game. As in Kafka's parable, we remain "before" the law, a situation that keeps us "profane" yet engages us in a hermeneutics based on hope even when we resist that hope. It is, in short, the relation of language and law that is always being worked out in "symbolic" situations.

To enter language means to risk being named, or recognized by name, to struggle against false names or identities, to live in the knowledge that *reconnaissance* and *mépris(e)* are intertwined, and that self and other are terms that glide eccentrically about an always improper ("metaphoric") naming of things or persons. There is no ultimate recognition scene. *Glas* keeps us looking in a glass, darkly. It disenchants the hope it expresses by playing language against itself, by dividing, spacing, splitting, joycing, tachygraphing, equivocating, reversing its charged words. This then is Derrida's crucifixion of the Word, that is, cruci-fiction: his crosswordings rag the story of Christ, tear a seamless garment into semes. For many this will cheapen or overintellectualize a sacred text. Yet Derrida's negative labor can also be understood as an anamnesis of the journey of the self from IC to INRI, from a scene of ideal or spectral naming to the slander of identity. (60–2)

From "the equivocal, echo-nature of language" that Derrida exploits in *Glas*, Hartman derives what again approaches a theory. The focus is, as Hartman playfully notes, "sound reasoning," which does not so much as "dally ... with closure" (111). In *Glas*, in particular, as curious as *Finnegans Wake* or Smart's *Jubilate Agno*, which Hartman admiringly treated in *The Fate of Reading* as "responsive poetry" and as a "poetics of relation,"

> the rhyming properties of language, the sonic rings and resonances always potentially there, are like Poe's "Bells" (cited by Derrida) and their telltale symptoms of a vertiginous *glissement* of language toward an uncontrollable echoing: a mad round of verbal associations of signifier-signifying signifiers. The anxiety roused by language *as* language is that this echoing movement cannot be economized, that it is a fluid curse, a telling that is merely that of time, whose wasting becomes a tolling: *Glas*. (111)

The strange, estranging amalgam, or crazy-quilt, called *Glas* evokes a response that echoes: Hartman *recognizes* what Derrida is up to, *receives* that equivocating "message," and repeats it *productively*, in an "answerable style" that merges response and creation, text and metatext. To receive is, however, I repeat, not (necessarily) to accept, as Hartman says, and the last essay in *Saving the Text* becomes a declared "counterstatement" to Derrida.

From Derrida I return now to "the unremarkable Wordsworth" and the closing episode in *The Prelude*. Wordsworth's account of a magical and serendipitous experience on Mount Snowdon, given in Book Fourteen, is one to which Hartman (bee-like) returns time and again, though with a difference each time. There, writes Wordsworth, he "beheld the emblem of a mind/ That feeds upon infinity, that broods/ Over the dark abyss, intent to hear/ Its voices issuing to silent light/ In one continuous stream..." (70–4). As Hartman shows, the poet emerges from Snowdon with a renewed appreciation and richer understanding of the relation between creation and response. That insight follows from Wordsworth's recovery of the "fellowship of silent light/ With speaking darkness." As Hartman puts it, "the poet ascends the mountain and brings back the word." Sound, however, does not come first but only as "an antiphonal response from the abyss. What Wordsworth brings back, therefore, is actually a second that becomes a first: an antiphony that reverses the priority of 'silent light' and shows itself to be coeval, even ante-phonal." The poet thereby "brings the speaking darkness to light; he transforms the power in sound into enlightened sound" (103). There is, in other words, a "first" text to which Wordsworth's "stands as a 'second,' but this relation is reversible, and the late utterance achieves its own firstness." Wordsworth has thus raised "the antiphonal cues in his own precursor text(s) to a new, a 'second' power. He has created his own text by a verbal geometry that extends the lines of force in a prior scripture" (104) – not unlike Hartman on *Glas*. We might conclude, then, that Snowdon represents "a vision of mastery," though "a peculiar one." That peculiarity resides in the reversal of powers that Wordsworth depicts:

> The power in sound and the power in light, or ear and eye, or nature and mind, are asymmetrical elements that struggle toward ... "interchangeable supremacy," "mutual domination." There is no single locus of majesty or mastery: it is doubled and troubled by shifts in the poet's interpretation of what he experienced. (103)

Thus creation and response merge, and the spectacle on Snowdon appears as "a grand emblem of responsive verse," in which Wordsworth represents the mind, or imagination, in its reciprocal and reciprocating power (105).

For Hartman, echoing Wordsworth in "Tintern Abbey," the work of the interpreter matches that of mind relating to nature: Hartman too, that is, talks of what is "half-perceived, half-created" by the responding imagination. Active, rather than passive, the interpreter engages texts in such a way that response becomes creative, as Hartman's does in echoing Derrida in *Glas*. Appropriately enough, Hartman uses the key Wordsworthian notions from the Snowdon episode to describe the relation of commentary and text commented on: "The situation of the discourse we name *criticism* is," he writes in *Criticism in the Wilderness*, "no different from that of any other. If this recognition implies a reversal, then it is the master–servant relation between criticism and creation that is being overturned in favor of what Wordsworth, describing the interaction of nature and mind, called 'mutual domination' or 'interchangeable supremacy'" (259).

Elsewhere Hartman ponders the implications of this described chiastic situation. It may not be possible, he conjectures in *The Fate of Reading*, "to distinguish ... what is the reader's and what the author's share in 'producing' the complex understanding which surrounds a literary work" (vii). All we can be certain of, despite our mania for analysis and pointing, he believes, is that "literary understanding is bipartite, requiring both literary discourse (texts) and literary-critical discourse (commentary, or associated texts)" (FR 271). In *Criticism in the Wilderness*, Hartman borrows from Heidegger in elaborating on the irreducibly dialogical nature of literary understanding. "The circle of understanding," he writes, "encompasses both the interpreter and the given text; the text, in fact, is never something radically other except insofar as it is radically near. As the 'fore-structure' of the very act of reading," he adds, "it tends to coincide with the innermost thoughts of the reader. The question What is disclosed by reading? invokes therefore a double text that remains a hendiadys: the text referred to by the interpreter, and the text on the text created by the referring act of criticism" (167).

If these points now seem obvious and incontrovertible, they look in a radical direction, perhaps still difficult for the traditional Anglo-American critic to follow. For Hartman literally means what he says: "the commentator's discourse, that is, cannot be neatly or methodically separated from that of the author: the relation is contaminating and chiastic; source text and secondary text, though separable, enter into a mutually supportive, mutually dominating relation" (CW 206). The relation is so intimate, in fact, that Hartman even claims that the critic is "'of' the writer he is discussing, a creation 'of' the Book he is ... writing about" (CW 255). Hartman certainly seems to be "of" Wordsworth, and the passage I noted above in *Saving the Text* shows how his own discourse "cannot be neatly or methodically separated" from Derrida's. Like all other forms of good love, however, the revealed intimacy does not lead to subjugation, let alone to destruction of the self infused with or flooded by a great writer. Difference remains, as manifested, for example, in Hartman's venture of "a counterstatement to Derrida" in the last chapter of *Saving the Text*.

The symbiotic, rather than subordinate or parasitic, situation of criticism places severe demands on the respondent. The considerable responsibilities faced derive precisely from the mutuality, or responsive echoing, that characterizes the relationship Hartman describes as a hendiadys. If, as he puts it, "certain works have become authoritative, it is because they at once sustain, and are sustained by, the readers they find"; the strength of books, in other words, "is measured by our response, or not at all" (CW 170, 177). Poems, even great ones, must be redeemed by a "responsive interpreter." Moreover, though we are all, as human beings, "in a basically responsive situation" (FR 29), texts, including the "responsive voice" (UnRW 149) that is poetry, exact other demands. They "place" us. What this entails Hartman explains, with reference to Heidegger, whose understanding of *Erörterung* (another word for commentary, synonymous with *Erläuterung*), he writes,

> helps to formalize the work of reading. *Erörterung* has the same structure as Abraham's "Here I am" responding to God's call. ("And what am I, that I am here?" is Matthew Arnold's complex fusion, in "Stanzas from the Grande Chartreuse," of that response, and a covertly blasphemous "I am that I am.") The patriarch's answer is more than an immediate act of obeisance. It clarifies an existential situation: it places the respondent who accepts the "point" or "charge" (*Ort* in the archaic sense of a point of convergence, particularly spear-head or battle-wedge.) The answer is so forceful that each act signifies the other: *Agen-Word* becomes part of the Word. (CW 171)

Another way of describing the demand placed on the respondent is with the help of the psychoesthetics Hartman sketches in "I.A. Richards and the Dream of Communication," included in *The Fate of Reading*. He opposes to Richards's "idealized stimulus and response pattern" of communication one involving "an unbalanced 'excess' (of demand) and 'defect' of response" (37, 36). Though the ideal is, of course, "perfect reciprocity, ... giving and taking humanely balanced" (40), Hartman recognizes that "no complete harmony between demand and response is really possible" (38). In the interpretive situation, no such harmony is possible because, "though art can temper demand or strengthen the responsiveness of the (language) source, it must itself enter the cycle of demand and response; art, that is, "becomes a demand as well as responding to one" (38). *That* demand the reader must, somehow, respond to, in an "answerable style." Hearing the "call" of a text, and so placed "on the spot," the interpreter bears the burden of "echoing responsively."

Even if creation and response merge in a reciprocal, reciprocating act, there is always something prior. The poet's words remain "antiphonal to the phonè of a prior experience," nature being there to guide, educate, and nourish Wordsworth. Similarly, a text and the tradition surrounding it precede the interpreter. "*Someone was there before us*," Hartman agrees with Harold Bloom in his review of *The Anxiety of Influence* (FR 51). Because interpretation is anaclitic, "the art of leaning, of falling back, on something given" (FR 14), the critic "acknowledges his dependence on prior words that make his words a kind of answer. He calls to other texts," like the Boy of Winander blowing "mimic hootings to the silent owls/ That they might answer him" (CW 223). More is involved in this question of priority than chronology, however; it includes authority: "The presence of greatness is what matters, a beforeness which makes readers, like poets, see for a moment nothing but one master-spirit" (FR 51). Without that, "without a greatness prior to our own," Hartman continues, "there would be nothing to respond to and so no dialogue, let alone dialectic." In that case, "culture and tradition would be vain concepts. 'Das leblose Einsame' would remain, playing with skulls in the Golgotha of imagination" (FR 123). The very opposite of solipsistic, the responsible critic must be immersed in the tradition that represents "prior greatness"; he or she must be both skillful and learned enough to supply the "intertextual corpus" in which the individual poem acquires its meaning and without which it has or is precious little.

5

"Dying into the life of recollection": the burden of artistic vocation

[I]s it possible to esteem poems that do not feel liable – responsible to the great makers gone before?
Beyond Formalism

[E]very artist is like Hamlet. The artist must always find his own way to "appear": he has no ritual to guide him. The presumption of his act, the daring of his art, is all. The conventions at his disposal do not lessen the agony of self-election: if he admires the ancients, he trembles to rival them; if he does not admire, he trembles before a void he must fill. No wonder art continually questions the hopes for art.
Beyond Formalism

The fledgling god's dying into the life of recollection is ... comparable to Adam's falling into knowledge or the ambiguous career of the soul in Wordsworth's Intimations Ode, its humanizing passage from a birth which is "a sleep and a forgetting" to the compensating radiance of the philosophic mind.
Beyond Formalism

[T]he literary consciousness as such, the consciousness a poet has of his vocation, not the programmatic statements only, in letters and manifestoes, but principally the opus operatum, the poem as recapitulating a vision of literary destiny or constitutive of it.... [E]very great spirit is subject to that glorified bully, tradition.
The Fate of Reading

English, when it gets beyond spelling and grammar, is not a technique but a cultural acquisition of great complexity: a literature as well as a basic literacy.
Criticism in the Wilderness

"Without a greatness prior to our own," we have heard Hartman claim, "there may be nothing to respond to... no dialogue, let alone dialectic" (FR 123). And in a review of Harold Bloom's *The Anxiety of Influence*, sounding very much like his friend, he acknowledges that "if there were no precursor he would have to be invented. The imagination needs a blocking-agent to raise itself, or not to fall into solipsism. We become great, Kierkegaard said, in proportion to striven-with greatness." Greatness begins, in fact, "by choosing a worthy obstacle" (FR 49).

As much as he admires Bloom as a reader, one perhaps with enough strength to *save* poetry, Hartman is not totally convinced by the psychomachia his fellow "Yale critic" describes. In the review, entitled "War in Heaven," he expresses a number of reservations, but his strongest objection centers on the closed and totalizing nature of the system "the planet Bloom" erects. "There is something overcondensed" in Bloom's account, he writes, and indeed his theory, Hartman maintains, is vulnerable

> because *priority* (a concept from the natural order) and *authority* (from the spiritual order) are not clearly distinguished; in fact, they merge and become a single, overwhelming *proton pseudos*. By seeking to overcome priority, art fights nature on nature's own ground, and is bound to lose. Nothing *could* grow in the shadow of this first principle except by delusion or misrepresentation. The awareness of a prior greatness is unanswerably strong, and the argument that art – or its survival – is based on misprision looks suspiciously like one which holds that blasphemy is an acknowledgment of God. Disconnection proves to be impossible: each slap is an antithetical embrace. Where is the joyous franchise of art? Hermeneutic freedom becomes misinterpretation, the wit of poetry a compulsive "swerving" from identity, and family romance the nightmare of always walking into parents. (FR 49–50)

Concerned about the survival of art, valuable, in part, for its gift of "hermeneutic freedom," and seeking to save imagination, threatened, as Wordsworth knew, by nature, Hartman adds that "Bloom's overcondensing takes away the second chance: literary history is for him like human life, a polymorphous quest-romance collapsing always into one tragic recognition." Thus in Bloom's rigorous and relentless system, "flight from the precursor leads to him by fatal prolepsis, nature always defeats imagination, history is the repetition of 'one story and one story only'" (FR 50). A powerful indictment of what he has opposed since *The Unmediated Vision*, Hartman's critique of his friend, like that of another friend (Paul de Man), nevertheless lacks the pointedness and sting of his asseverations against Northrop Frye, to whom he returns again and again.

Another difference from Bloom requires mention. Whereas Bloom focuses on the ephebe's determining quest of (individual) greatness, Hartman is more interested in the greatness with which one must struggle. This is not to dismiss Bloom's strong theory nor to minimize Hartman's admiration of it but, rather, to understand what he means in claiming that without a "prior greatness" "culture and tradition could be vain concepts. 'Das leblose Einsame' would remain, playing with skulls in the Golgotha of imagination" (FR 123). That more is involved than the mere presence of otherness becomes all the clearer when Hartman writes, *pace* Bloom, that "the presence of greatness is what matters, a beforeness which makes readers, like poets, see for a moment nothing but one master-spirit" (FR 51). By this last term Hartman means, I take it, not a single artist or great precursor but *poetry*: the entire tradition, the various traditions, spanning the entirety of literary history. It is that sense of a "larger life" to which the individual artist must join his or hers. For young, aspiring artists, "prior greatness" "may be a burden or a bait: an angel they must wrestle, a double or secret sharer that haunts them" (EP 30). The struggle with tradition in which the artist engages is no less intense, demanding, and problematic than the wrestling with a single, great, and unacknowledged precursor that Bloom laboriously describes. Hartman's account of that struggle, focused in several texts as the burden of artistic vocation, is broader, more generous, and ultimately more responsible than Bloom's single-minded attention to the lonely artist caught in a psychomachia the result of which is always the same. When Hartman writes, a bit prankishly, that "every great spirit is subject to that glorified bully, tradition," he adds another dimension to the requirement to "echo responsively" a calling and demanding text. As he makes clear in discussing reasons for including theory in the canon and the curriculum, what matters is immersion in that "greater life" that constitutes tradition: "it is not a matter of 'knowing' Derrida or Heidegger but of reading and steeping oneself in a corpus of critical, philosophical, and literary texts that they incorporate and revise" (CW 255).

"Incorporate and revise" – those words reflect an understanding of the individual's relation to tradition or literary history similar to yet different from that expressed by T. S. Eliot in his almost-epochal essay "Tradition and the Individual Talent" (1919), later included in *The Sacred Wood*. A good deal of Hartman's work stands as a forceful counterstatement to Eliot's account. Opposing expressive, and particularly Romantic, theories of literature, Eliot finds genuine poetry to be "an escape from emotion" and lauds in the "mature" poet "a continual surrender of himself as he is at the moment to something which is more valuable. The progress of an artist," insists Eliot, rejecting Wordsworthian notions, "is a continual self-sacrifice, a continual extinction of personality." His personality thus reined in, the poet becomes a "finely perfected medium in which special, or very varied, feelings are at liberty to enter into new combinations."[1] Once this "medium" acquires a necessary "historical sense," moreover, he or she is compelled "to write not merely with his own generation in his bones, but with a feeling that the whole of the literature of Europe from Homer and within it the whole of the literature of his own country has a simultaneous existence and composes a simultaneous order."[2] Adding his own testimony modifies the pre-existing order or tradition, no matter how imposing and magnificent it may appear and no matter how small and weak by comparison the new work seems. As Eliot puts it, "What happens when a new work of art is created is something that happens simultaneously to all the works of art which preceded it. The existing monuments form an ideal order among themselves, which is modified by the introduction of the new (the really new) work of art among them." Though "the existing order is complete before the new work arrives," Eliot carefully if stiffly explains, "for order to persist after the supervention of novelty, the *whole* existing order must be, if ever so slightly, altered."[3]

Now, despite the insistence on a "historical sense," which Eliot maintains is essential, he himself flattens differences, sacrificing diachrony to synchrony and in effect collapsing history. His statement, for example, that "the whole of the literature of [one's] own country has a *simultaneous* existence and composes a *simultaneous* order" (italics added) reflects a totalizing prominent throughout "Tradition and the Individual Talent." Eliot is, moreover, obviously committed to the notion of civilization as order (Hartman, puckishly, relates ["Burkes"] order to ordure). No wonder that Eliot insists on subordinating the "personality" of the artist to the amorphousness and cleanliness of the whole, to "something which is more valuable" than the individual and his or her unruly emotions. No wonder, either, that Eliot offers a selective and narrow notion of tradition, to which the artist must continually sacrifice himself or herself, extinguishing the very individuality that we might think essential for the creation of the "really new" work of art.

Hartman's most extensive critique of Eliot's essay occurs in "The Sacred Jungle 1: Carlyle, Eliot, Bloom" in *Criticism in the Wilderness*. The title is, obviously, pointed – Eliot's "sacred wood" becomes here something altogether different: threatening and dangerous (rather than orderly and "civilized"), echoing with wild, disruptive voices, and including critics as well as poets. For an understanding of tradition, Hartman prefers Bloom, whose treatment of *kabbalah*, a Hebrew word for "tradition" (it means, literally, "reception"), does not "inhabit the same world of discourse as Eliot's," so different are "the language, the materials, the mode of self-presentation" (54). Hartman prefers Bloom's Hebraizing because "the model of reception he takes from the Kabbalists is at once more systematic (theological) than anything in Eliot, and more personal" (54–5).

Furthermore, Bloom possesses, in Hartman's estimation, a richer understanding of the importance – and inevitability – of trespass or profanation. With reference to one of Kafka's parables, Hartman illustrates how the (deeply Hebraic) profanation "is structured into the critical ritual, into the model as contemplated or applied": "'Leopards break into the temple and drink the sacrificial chalices dry; this occurs repeatedly, again and again: finally it can be reckoned on beforehand and becomes part of the ceremony.'" From this parable Hartman draws an important lesson for literary criticism: what it leads us to understand, he writes,

> when we consider a canon of secular authors rather than the Bible is that the "spiritual form" (Blake) of the dead writers returns upon the living, like those leopards. It has to be incorporated or appeased by tricks that resemble Freudian defense mechanisms. And in this there can be no progress, only repetition and elaboration – more ceremonies, sacrifices, lies, defenses. That we esteem these is the woe and wonder Bloom constantly commemorates. The literature of the past is an unquiet grave. (55)

Anglo-Catholic and Hellenic, Eliot trusts in the power of the original (unprofaned) ritual to *contain* such voices as rise from the sprouting corpses in *The Waste Land* but can only move "symphonically through a poem that acts as their requiem"; the erupting, disruptive voices "are kept within the locus of the poem, shut up there as in a daemonic wood. In their asylum is our peace" (55–6). Unlike Bloom, then, or Hartman, though the psychic problem of doing so "startles the economy of his prose" (CW 81), Eliot "buries the dead and orders all things well" (CW 55).

Acknowledging the "return of the dead" upon the living, and respecting the voices that break the silence and disturb our peace, Hartman differs radically from Eliot. Those voices break out of whatever wood we try to keep them in, unsettling us, not so unlike the Hebrew God, who shatters the monuments to our magnificence we busily erect all around us. But the question Eliot posed still haunts: what is the relation of the individual talent to tradition? Though Eliot grants that the "truly great" artist changes a pre-existent order, he does not acknowledge the precarious nature of absorption and sacrifice, a partially unassimilated "subjective state always on the point of vacillation or revolt" (CW 218), even the *possibility* of struggle and resistance. Differently from Eliot, Hartman argues that individual artists (I would say, critical as well as "creative") "incorporate and revise" a body of texts that constitute literary history; he recognizes, that is, the physical, material nature of artistic endeavor and is aware, too, that the individual writer not merely "alters" tradition but actually revises it as he/she incorporates it.

Consisting of acknowledged works of art – the "secular canon" – tradition Hartman describes as "something like a museum, something like a pantheon," that "gathers together those structured spiritual forces that have guided men in the past" and that hold out the promise of continuing to do so now and in the future (EP 30). Whereas, I would argue, Eliot depicts tradition as legislative and regulating, Hartman understands it as creative, liberating, and open, with the power, in fact, to sustain us (and not merely contain us). Thus, Hartman writes that "the burden of history is that we must make sense of our lives by assimilating them to a larger life" (FR xi). Immersing ourselves in tradition, or better, history, is, therefore, at once potentially redemptive and demanding, exacting a heavy price even as it holds out the possibility of rendering our hearts and minds more capacious. For all of us, the burden, of assimilation, is heavy, but we know, do we not, that there is no meaning apart from relation, perhaps no significance apart from "prior greatness." For the artist, however, the burden is especially acute; it involves what Walter

Jackson Bate calls, in a book published three years before *The Anxiety of Influence*, "the burden of the past": the artist, that is, has to bear "the 'giant forms' of tradition," "the mighty abstractions of a craft with thirty centuries behind it" (BF 270), in other words, nothing less than "poetry – poetry as it impinges on those who seek to continue it" (FR 166). Struggle is inevitable, but what is art, Hartman asks, but "a genuine mediation: a wrestling with, and separating of, the dead" (FR 112). Even if some of us be spared the intense struggle with "giant forms" that artists experience, there is a real "*burden* of knowledge" (CW 254) to be borne by everyone concerned with art and its survival, and Hartman calls attention to "the entailed responsibilities" on critic, poet, and "ordinary" reader alike, when he says that that burden "must be carried by someone" (CW 254).

In his various accounts of tradition or literary history, its burdens and our "entailed responsibilities," Hartman displays the "historical sense" Eliot preaches (but fails to practice). Richly integumented, Hartman's reflections focus on the poet's struggles with his or her vocation, its possibility, opportunities, and demands. As I observed earlier, this focus differs from Bloom's, who is not so much concerned with the *vocation* of art as with the individual artist's particular psychological and rhetorical strategies to defend against and overcome a powerful and influential precursor. Yet Hartman, like Bloom, Bate, and other recent scholars, traces the "origins" of the artist's struggle with the vocation of art and his or her anxiety concerning "the burden of the past" to the awesome strength of Milton, felt (whether or not fully acknowledged) by all succeeding poets. Himself influenced by Bloom, especially in *The Fate of Reading*, Hartman writes in "Evening Star and Evening Land": "The burden of creativity became both ineluctable and as heavy as the pack Christian wore. After Milton, poetry joins or even rivals divinity in pressing its claim on the artist." In this situation, religious notions are very much involved. "As soon as greatness is acknowledged," Hartman writes, "it raises the question of succession," and so

> a theological element enters; a reflection on who is – or could be – worthy to continue the line. In these circumstances literary criticism can take the form of a theologico-poetical examination of the pretender. Is he apostolic? The question need not be imposed from the outside: indeed, it generally comes from within the visionary poet, and leads to self-doubt as easily as to self-justification. (FR 167)

"DYING INTO THE LIFE OF RECOLLECTION"

In the history Hartman makes available, the Enlightenment was a watershed, precipitating a crisis that deeply affected poets both in England and on the Continent. The threat to poetry was palpable: could poetry "outlive the Enlightenment, when it was perfectly clear that the great works of the past had been based on 'Superstition'" (BF 319)? A "powerful combination of an intellectual and a religious movement," the Protestant Enlightenment, moreover, "incited a new and prophetic consciousness in the vocation it wished to demystify: the vocation of poetry" (BF 318). In England, Hartman observes, it was "only with Collins, Smart, and the great Romantics" that the poets' struggle with the artistic vocation became "religious in intensity and direct[ed] their voice. What is at stake" in these writers, Hartman claims, "is, in fact, the erection of voice. 'Would to God all the Lord's people were prophets'" (FR 167). In France, the situation was different. There "a *vocation* was not in sight; available was only the idea of a career," and as Hartman says, "a career is not – or no longer – a calling." An added burden thus fell on art: only it "could now renew the image of a vocation that was more than careerist, or of a heroism tied to inward or social reform rather than political ambition" (EP 30).

Various factors thus coalesced, in the wake of the Enlightenment, to insure the aggrandizement of art. Prominent among them was the transformation of political hopes following the collapse of the French Revolution. According to Hartman, if "Romantic poetry appears to the orthodox as misplaced religious feeling ('spilt religion'), to the Romantics themselves it redeems religion" (BF 305), and so the aggrandizement of art in the Romantic period

> is due in no small measure to the fact that poets like Wordsworth and Blake cannot give up one hope raised by the Revolution – that a terrestrial paradise is possible – yet are eventually forced to give up a second hope – that it can be attained by direct political action. The shift from faith in the reformation of man through the prior reformation of society to that in the prior reformation of man through vision and art has often been noted. The failure of the French Revolution anchors the Romantic movement or is the consolidating rather than primary cause. It closes, perhaps until the advent of Communism, the possibility that politics rather than art should be invested with a passion previously subsumed by religion. (BF 205 n.)

Of course, the aggrandizement of art only increased the burden on the individual poet. Of all the Romantics, Wordsworth probably felt the increased responsibility most acutely. Intensely conscious of "what great poetry was before him" (UnRW 13), he associated that burden with "the vocation and survival of imaginative power" (FR 184). It is the poet's sense of "vocation, his struggle with it, and the authenticity of that struggle" (xxiii) that Hartman studies in *Wordsworth's Poetry*. Questions concerning both his future as poet and that of poetry itself burned in Wordsworth's soul. Sharing the Romantic understanding that "the burden of the mystery was to be borne by the individual directly" (BF 136), Wordsworth came to believe (there *was* something of what Keats called the "egotistical sublime" about him) that he "alone stood between us and the death of nature to imagination. His subtlest feelings had a larger destiny. He was at a turning point in history which would see either a real marriage of the mind of man with nature or their apocalyptic severance" (WP xiv).

Hartman continues and extends Wordsworth's efforts through studies of the artistic struggle with vocation. In critics and poets alike, he traces a continuing concern with the fate (and even the very possibility) of poetry in the modern world. These historical considerations represent a perpetuation of and elaboration on the concerns we have been noting in post-Enlightenment thought and not an objective, disinterested, dispassionate account. Hartman, in other words, shares the worries of Romantic poets like Wordsworth, Blake, and Keats, and he feels the increase they have added to the burden of knowledge and response. Like those poets, but at a point in history all the more demanding, in part *because* of their contributions, Hartman feels "on the spot": "the *burden* of knowledge ... must be carried by someone." The question he poses most insistently is: "Is it too late, or can our age, like every previous one, protect the concept of art?" (FR 107).

The threats to art are now numerous, complex, and serious, and they certainly include, according to Hartman, those Wordsworth attacked, notably his age's degrading thirst after "outrageous stimulation," aroused by forces political and cultural. In our own time, factors such as the lust for intimacy, "the drive for meaning," and "the dream of communication" conspire to render the survival of art, let alone its continued effectiveness, problematical. The imagination and freedom of response are at stake, Hartman points out.

But no matter what the age, in Wordsworth's as well as our own, art has at best "a precarious status," for it exists alongside opposed and strong forces "in a world of *praxis*, a world where hasty ends and proleptic words prevail" (FR 246). For Hartman, whose ideas parallel (and no doubt have been influenced by) Malraux's, the significance of art is inseparable from its *difference*. "Art is not reality," Hartman agrees with Malraux; "the relation of the one to the other is essentially liminal; between art and its translation into immediate relevance a threshold intervenes which cannot be crossed without destroying art's very place in society" (FR 109).

What that place is, lies at the center of Hartman's work. Sometimes interpreted as an apolitical "aesthetic criticism," Hartman's thinking centers on art as "radical critique," reinterpreting, as we saw earlier, "aesthetic as a critique."[4] What he means by this is the development of

> interpretive powers that bring us closer to all types of experience, not in their immediacy but in their mediatedness. Every work of art, from this point of view, is a criticism of life in terms of a criticism of mediations: of conventions, schematisms, institutions, of art itself, and the way we think or talk about it. (UnRW 191)

Whereas "action ideologizes interpretation and keeps moving relentlessly toward an all-consuming point which is the new regime, the new order," the aesthetic, which involves an alliance between art and philosophy, is "always characterized ... by a structure of postponement; the doubting or delaying of closure, the insistence on remainders or of a return of the past, and – more problematically – on a concept of elation that embraces both the reality of history and freedom of mind" (UnRW 186).[5]

Art takes, in fact, an *active* role in opposing "politicization or the slavery of an exclusively practical thinking" (UnRW 186). Like Malraux, Hartman regards "art and the heritage of Western culture as very special weapons in an era of ideological warfare" (M viii). For novelist and critic alike, "art alone stands beyond victory and defeat, preserving to human consciousness whatever is swept aside by the sharp decisions of the immediate historical present" (M 61–2). Art becomes, then, crucial to humankind's preservation in the face of forces menacing the very idea of *man*: Hartman writes in a study of the "ground" he shares with Camus, published in *Beyond Formalism*, that from Malraux "we learn that ... all defense is related to man's artistic nature" (86). In Malraux's words, which Hartman cites at least twice, the idea of man itself "is more dependent on the evidence of the artist than on the evidence of history" (M 71; see also EP 50). Such remarks, Hartman knows, smack of the ahistorical and apolitical, though Malraux's dedication to art, he argues (with how much self-defensiveness?), "is, in reality, a very special kind of politics called forth by the failure of humanistic philosophies to produce effective men of action" (M 90). In any case, such a position as Malraux and Hartman embrace by no means obviates action. "There must be action," Hartman writes, but, like Benjamin, he recognizes that "the field of action, for the writer at least, includes the past: its relation to the crisis at hand." And the past "remains a dialectical field of forces and cannot be foreclosed by the pseudoappropriations of totalitarian propaganda. 'Only the historian,'" Hartman quotes Benjamin as saying, "'will have the gift of fanning the spark of hope in the past who is firmly convinced that *even the dead* will not be safe from the enemy if he wins'" (CW 75). "The dead" thus impose an awful responsibility upon us.

Given the foregoing, it is not surprising that (the Hebraic and Romantic) Hartman agrees with Malraux (and Joyce) that art's modern, no different from its ancient, function, "is reticence, cunning, resistance – against whatever is perceived as fate," notably including "propaganda or propagandistic versions of history" (EP 213). He finds in art several types of resistance: to "readerly appropriation" (EP 198); to ideologies and the "synchronic pressure of abstract knowledge" (FR 102, 104); to the meanings *it* provokes (CW 269); to our "lust for knowing or merging" (FR 102); to intimacy (BF 54). In its capacity of resistance, art invigorates without consoling, unsettling and perplexing rather than comforting (BF 263). Art maintains, in fact, Hartman argues, an "impregnable reserve in the midst of explanatory assaults," a reserve that stems from "the very openness of symbols to several, even opposed, kinds of meaning" and that should be understood, *pace* deconstruction, as "a reservoir of resonances rather than a mystifying void" (FR 105). That reserve and the resistance it makes possible account for art's *radical* political significance even as it actively resists specific political appropriation. So committed is Hartman to art's political potential that he calls revolutionaries "the unacknowledged poets of the world – but more naïve than the poets, more trusting in the effectiveness of a unique or single imposition" (CW 108). Art's political power, according to Hartman, derives from its opposition to that drive toward "a unique or single imposition": art "refuses to let us fall into one circumference" (BF 67); it is, in other words, "that which cannot be *gleichgeschaltet* or *aufgehoben*

– which cannot have only one dimension" (EP 215). As a result, Hartman claims, "*language* rather than politics is fate; politics is part of a counterfeit Great Tradition that arrogates to itself the impositional strength of performative language" (CW 108). Hartman's hermeneutic reflections will not satisfy those intent on immediate political action, but then his own thoughtfulness represents a powerful critique of and alternative to such "one-dimensional" efforts, an alternative that is not at all, I would insist, quietistic.

Art's broader social function, as Hartman presents it, is also tied to its capacity of resistance, specifically the way it postpones sense, point, or closure. Indeed, art not only keeps space open, despite efforts (both deliberate and inadvertent) at closure, but it also *creates* space – and with it, freedom. Rejecting what Hartman calls "a fog of intimacy hiding ... genuine difference," art makes "room for the other and even the divine" (BF 67). In an extended and important discussion entitled "The Voice of the Shuttle: Language from the Point of View of Literature," reprinted in *Beyond Formalism*, Hartman elaborates on art's capacity to "make room." Here he argues that "it makes room in meaning itself," rather than adds itself "to the world of meanings" (352). Describing art as "a vital hermeneutics," Hartman also claims that "it limits the sacred or makes room for life in life" (351). What he means by this is the following: human life, he writes, "like a poetical figure,"

> is an indeterminate middle between overspecified poles always threatening to collapse it. The poles may be birth and death, father and mother, mother and wife, love and judgment, heaven and earth, first things and last things. Art narrates that middle region and charts it like a purgatory, for only if it exists can life exist; only if the imagination presses against the poles are error and life and illusion – all those things which Shelley called "generous superstitions" – possible. The excluded middle is a tragedy also for the imagination. (BF 348)

Exploring that "middle region," which is life itself in all its muddle, art, even though demanding, "allows a response as free, imaginative, and self-tasking as its own must have been" (CW 62). So *generous* is art, in fact, that in Hartman's words, directed against E. D. Hirsch's straightened insistence on objective and Norman Holland's on subjective interpretation, it grants the understanding freedom "to produce its own form of meaningfulness" (CW 269). As it does so, Hartman writes, "art finds what can be ranged *against* assertion without being *for* weakness – that is, without allowing the vertigo of indecisiveness or nonidentity to foster by reaction even more dangerous – psychotic or Cold War – assertions" (EP 99). Though art exacts severe demands, therefore, it permits, makes room for, free (and imaginative) response – and this effect too bears radical political import. Imperiled in our world, as in Wordsworth's, the imaginative response that art both represents and demands not only keeps us functioning, but it also allows (prompts?) us to grow in humanheartedness. Art is that generous and capacious opportunity by means of which "we join our lives to a larger life that is neither alien nor mystical... but a portion of our own recovered history" (EP 177).

As important and essential as art is, it still needs defending, precisely because of its difference from the world of *praxis*. Hartman's most effective defense of art occurs, I think, in "Toward Literary History," the last chapter in *Beyond Formalism*, which extends the reflections we have been considering and offers some intriguing additional perspectives. Focusing on literary history, always his forte, Hartman confronts the then-prevailing positivistic conception of such history, which offered, in the words of Wellek and Warren, "'either social histories, or histories of thought as illustrated in literature, or impressions and judgments on specific works arranged in more or less chronological order'" (quoted 256). We are all "disenchanted," Hartman writes, "with these picaresque adventures in pseudo-causality which go under the name of literary history, those handbooks with footnotes which claim to sing of the whole but load every rift with glue" (356). What he proposes instead is essentially what he undertook six years earlier in *Wordsworth's Poetry*: "a history from the point of view of the poets – from within their consciousness of the historical vocation of art" (356). Only that, he declares, is fully responsible to the demands of art. It is, in fact, essential "for the sake of literature – it is our historical duty because *it alone* can provide today a sorely needed defense of art" (357, italics added).

If literary history is to provide that needed defense of art, Hartman maintains, it will have to confront questions of both form and the artist's historical vocation. Form thus emerges as of crucial importance, as it has, of course, throughout this most historical of Hartman's books ("There are many ways to transcend formalism," we recall, "but the worst is not to study forms" [BF 56]). In "Toward Literary History," Hartman claims that we have, in recent years, accepted an expanded notion of form, so that it can no longer, as in Pound, Eliot, and Yeats, be "narrowly linked to the concerns of a priestly culture or its mid-cult imitations" (359). In fact, Hartman hopes to persuade us that "an important new theory of form is gradually emerging" (359). He briefly takes up, and evaluates, the contributions to such a theory of Marxist criticism, Frye's notion of archetypes, and new versions of what he (I think misleadingly) calls structuralism, including the work of Lévi-Strauss as well as that of I. A. Richards and certain Anglo-American colleagues. Still missing, Hartman argues, is "a theory linking the form of the medium to the form of the artist's historical consciousness" (366).

By no means an easy task, this. The reasons are several, and many of them derive from our historical situation. Even if critics now accept an expanded notion of form, artists themselves nowadays find forms to be "conservative despite themselves," always serving to "reconcile or integrate." What appeals to them is iconoclasm:

> To create a truly iconoclastic art, a structure-breaking art; to change the function of form from reconciliation and conservation to rebellion, and so to participate in the enormity of present experience – this is the one Promethean aim still fiery enough to inspire. (367)

As Hartman quietly demonstrates, artists' concern with form is linked, inseparably, to their sense of vocation and so their relation to tradition and "prior greatness." As he puts it, "no great writer is without an identity crisis," involving "the vocational crisis that occurs in the poet as poet, in his literary self-consciousness" (367). As he develops his point, we are likely to sense, I think, autobiographical touches, reflecting Hartman's own struggle with the artistic vocation.

> A great artist has the ambition to seize (and hand on) the flame of inspiration, to identify the genius of art with his own genius or that of a particular age (genius loci). But this exacerbates the crisis of self-consciousness: of emergence and of commitment to being manifestly what one is. In the modern era with its problem of "legitimacy," the artist is especially aware of the need for self-justification. The basic problem, however, is as old as history: how is spiritual authority to be transmitted if not through an elite of persons or communities? There seems to be no recorded greatness without the driving force of an idea of election, or the search for evidences of election. (367–8)

How to reconcile such ideas, and recognitions, concerning election and "an elite of persons or communities" with an essentially democratic nature? Ambitious and forced to wrestle with the greatness that ambition at once resents, fears, and needs, the artist is, Hartman goes on, "like Hamlet" in having always to

> find his own way to "appear": he has no ritual to guide him. The presumption of his act, the daring of his art, is all. The conventions at his disposal do not lessen the agony of self-election: if he admires the ancients, he trembles to rival them; if he does not admire, he trembles before a void he must fill. (368)

In moving toward a theory of literary vocation, Hartman is explicitly phenomenological, focusing on "consciousness studied in the effort to 'appear,'" which he carries over in his next book, *The Fate of Reading*. Here, at the end of *Beyond Formalism*, he anticipates Bloom, particularly in treating the emergence of a "psychotheology" of art in Keats's *Hyperion*. That poem shows, according to Hartman, the ephebe god on the verge of replacing the sun god (who, we might say, is troped as the *son* god). *Hyperion* traces, that is, "a birth which is a forgetting, and a dying into recollection." The antelife into which Apollo dies by a "kind of platonic anamnesis" is nothing less than *tradition* – specifically, Hartman writes, "Wordsworth, Milton, Spenser, the Bible, Plato – the *paradise of poets*" (371–2). Tradition may be defined, then, as "'sovran voices' mediated by each great poet." In Hartman's helpful terms, "The fledgling god's dying into the life of recollection is ... comparable to Adam's falling into knowledge or the ambiguous career of the soul in Wordsworth's Intimations Ode, its humanizing passage from a birth which is 'a sleep and a forgetting' to the compensating radiance of the philosophic mind" (372).

Thus we reach, through reflections on the historical vocation of art, a revitalized understanding of form, which derives precisely from the inherence of the latter in the former. That is, engaged himself in historical recovery (notably here of Milton's courtly interlude *Arcades*), Hartman shows how "the idea of form merged with that of the historical vocation of art" (381). Rather than some platonic abstraction or alien imposition, form is inseparable, and in fact derives, from the individual artist's struggle with tradition, with literary history. It is a function, we might say, of his or her wrestling with the voices of the "mighty dead." Little wonder, then, that Hartman frequently describes poetry as "the working through of voices" (e.g. UnRW 100).

In "Toward Literary History," Hartman himself works through a number of voices, including Eliot. In fact, Hartman begins the essay by acknowledging that imposing figure: "The older way of achieving a form impersonal enough to allow the new to emerge was to subordinate the individual talent to the tradition" (358). Before he is done, Hartman brings forth an alternative, one that, among other things, not only rejects such subordination but also avoids the elitism that marks Eliot's writing. That alternative involves the notion of *genius loci*, which first surfaced in *Wordsworth's Poetry* and then figured prominently in other essays on Romanticism included in *Beyond Formalism*.[6] This important concept allows Hartman to define "the artist's struggle with his vocation – with past masters and the 'pastness' of art in modern society" as "a version of a universal struggle: of genius with Genius, and of genius with the genius loci (spirit of place)" (372). Art may indeed be "the offspring of a precarious marriage between genius and genius loci" (384). Whether or not that is so, Hartman (prankishly) describes "the vocation of literature as Art seeking Pop – art seeking its father figure in folk culture." Genius, Hartman concludes, "merges confusingly with genius loci as Volksboden or autochthonous art" (377). Though Hartman manages a perspective more responsive to the "social base" of literature, one more sensitive in this respect than Eliot's, he remains committed to "a principle of authority which is purely authorial: which seems to derive from art alone, or from the author's genius rather than from the genius of his age" or from that of his or her place (357). As in Romantic thought generally, so for Hartman (but not Eliot), responsibility rests with the individual. In Hartman, that emphasis on individual responsibility coexists, however precariously, with a cultural commitment that less dialectical thinkers rarely manage. Too often the possibility of both/and becomes a simple either/or choice.

The complex responsibility that Hartman regards as resting with the individual applies as much to critic as to "primary" artist. To be sure, differences exist between the responsibilities of the critic and those of the poet, but they are more of degree than of kind. We can thus rewrite Hartman's question whether it is possible "to esteem poems that do not feel liable – responsible to the great makers gone before" (BF 272) as "Is it possible to esteem *readings* that do not feel liable – responsible to the great makers gone before?" Here there may be, for once, no choice, for according to Hartman, each interpretation of a work of art "is gained only by struggling with a *chaos of texts* that is called, euphemistically, tradition, or more neutrally, literary history" (CW 239).

At any rate, the resonances that poetry produces (better: is) give it an irreducibly intertextual quality, and the understanding and appreciation of those resonances require the trained, knowledgeable ear of the interpreter. The crucial thing for Hartman, of course, is "the literary consciousness itself": that is, "the consciousness a poet [or critic, I add] has of his vocation," and by that, Hartman makes clear, he means "not the programmatic statements only, in letters and manifestoes, but principally the opus operatum, the poem [or critical essay] as recapitulating a vision of literary destiny or constitutive of it" (FR 280). Literary history, in other words, is not *outside* the text, somehow its background, but rather *within* the text, constituting its meaning and available to the interpreter whose ability to bring from the text such meaning depends on his or her immersion in literary history. Thus it is that Hartman describes "English, when it gets beyond spelling and grammar, [as] not a technique but a cultural acquisition of great complexity: a literature as well as a basic literacy" (CW 290).

The burden on the individual talent, critical as well as poetic, is more complex still. Consider again Hartman's reflections on Keats and the poetical vocation. With reference to *The Fall of Hyperion*, Hartman exclaims: "What a soul-making, to have to sustain symbols which should have sustained him! ... Poetry here is not a mediation supporting the poet. The opposite seems to be the case, for poetry now stands in dire need of Keats" (FR 67). Elaborating on "the burden of authorship" felt by Keats, Hartman says that "he is not relieved but shamed by the knowledge that the gods are born once more of him, that great poetry must survive, if at all, in a cockney's breast. His is the Way. He also, occasionally," Hartman adds, "seeks the Way Out" (FR 68–9). The survival of art does not, of course, depend, *pace* Wilde, so directly on the critic, whose position remains, even if problematically, secondary ("even the best essays," Hartman admits, "are secondary products, stimulated by the literature on which they comment" [FR 303]). Nevertheless, critics too bear responsibility for sustaining the great works and so for keeping the tradition alive. Too often, though, we seek the Way Out, accepting a purely subordinate position (such as Eliot insisted on), repressing our artistic impulses, adopting "an objective or institutionalized state of independence in exchange for a subjective state always on the point of vacillation or revolt" (CW 218), and in fact evading entailed responsibilities to "the great makers gone before."

As always, reading is the issue, and reading is "not a neutral technique"; rather, "it is shaped by the classics it in turn supports" (FR 304). As a result of the chiastic and symbiotic relation – another two-way street – between reading and the text read, the great work is preserved. "As the quantity of writing increases," Hartman writes, "the quality of reading should also increase to present the great or exceptional work as something still possible, not only as something confined to a past era and breaking out of that into present consciousness" (CW 165). "Through the work of reading," then, as the Rabbis knew of the sacred text, "the work of art never comes to rest" (CW 186). Necessary to art as art is (differently) to interpretation, the work of reading occupies a place of no mean importance in the history of art: "His words, the critic's words, should enter the world of art even as the arts and institutions he comments on have entered his. As the work of art is an event in the history of interpretation, so the work of interpretation should be an event in the history of art" (CW 215).

The necessity for "intertextual leaping" resulting from the poem's implication in "an intertextual corpus which the skilled interpreter supplies" does not absolve the reader of a responsibility to the text scrupulous and exact (UnRW 213). Hartman's position will not satisfy the literal-minded or finicky, for in his view the interpretive situation can be neither schematized nor made absolutely clear-cut: as noted earlier, Hartman believes that "no one can remove the reader's responsibility entirely: in this, to each his own conscience" (UnRW 141). The interpretive situation partakes, in fact, of the "hermeneutic perplexity" that Hartman not only finds unavoidable but embraces. In "The Work of Reading," in *Criticism in the Wilderness*, he puts it this way: "In the matter of art we cannot draw up a Guide for the Perplexed."

> We can only urge that readers, inspired by hermeneutic traditions, take back some of their authority and become both creative and thoughtful, as in days of old. It is true, of course, that today they are less *liable* for their mistakes, and that being creative is for many a defense for whatever they do. The rabbinical or patristic exegete was creative within a scrupulosity as exacting as any invented by extreme apostles of the Catholic or Puritan conscience; he pretended not to violate the letter of Scripture or else he took pleasure in the strict counterpoint

of letter and spirit, of apparent meaning and recreative commentary. The puritanism (small *p*) of so much critical writing of today, its modest but unconvincing subservience to art, comes from the realization that now it is we who put the restraint on ourselves; it is from the individual critic that the check on subjective or wild interpretation must come. (161)

Coleridge, whom Hartman quotes, provides a gloss on this last point. "As it must not, so genius cannot be lawless, for it is even this that constitutes its genius – the power of acting creatively under laws of its own origination" (quoted 269). Hartman is never more Romantic (and different from Eliot) than in making clear the demands on the individual. That the responsibility for "checking" purely subjective and willful interpretations rests, not with the policing power of "order" or tradition, but with the individual critic only adds to the burden.

With such freedom comes, not just responsibility, but also the potential for abuse. There is, in addition, the fact that the chiastic and symbiotic relationship of text and reader that Hartman advocates is precarious and unstable. As such, it cannot insure or preserve order; instead, it is radically unsettling. All of these factors worry those opponents of "creative criticism" who claim (falsely) that pride of place has shifted to the interpreter. Hartman is well aware of the problem, including the potential threat to tradition that accompanies the freedom he prizes. He acknowledges it most poignantly in discussing Benjamin and the relation between the Jewish ideas of *haggada* and *hallaka*. "One of the saddest sentences Benjamin wrote," he begins,

> concerns Kafka in relation to Jewish tradition: "He sacrificed truth for the sake of clinging to its transmissibility, its haggadic element." The distinction being made relies on the difference in talmudic writings between *haggada* (story, troping, free elaboration) and *hallaka* (law, the truth of the letter, the unmodifiable character of ritual). Truth and tradition ("transmissibility") are now in opposition. We are reminded not only of Bloom's analysis of this bind in the relation of later to earlier poet but of all contemporary criticism that presents itself as commentary on a received text yet cannot be called submissive to it. "Kafka's writings," Benjamin continues, "are by their nature parables. They do not lie modestly at the feet of the doctrine, as the haggada lies at the feet of the hallaka. Though

apparently reduced to submission, they unexpectedly raise a mighty paw against it." (CW 80)

Do these words not describe precisely the relation of the individual talent, critical or poetic, to tradition? At once responsible *to* that tradition and in some degree responsible *for* its survival, the individual may, nevertheless, raise "eine gewichtige Pranke" against it. This is indeed unsettling, though any alternative I can imagine would seem far worse. Would not, in any case, any occurring trespass or profanation ultimately be incorporated in a then-modified and expanded tradition – as prophesied in Kafka's parable of the leopards whose violation of ceremony eventually becomes part of the ceremony? Tradition subsists precisely through its incorporation and revision by the individual talent.

The responsibility involved Hartman nicely illustrates with another Jewish tale, this one from the end of his recent essay "Religious Literacy." After writing that the test of any commentary is whether it makes the text brooded upon "memorable or forgettable," Hartman cites "a drash by the Baal Shem Tov, which is exemplary for its own text-dependence. He is thinking about," writes Hartman, "the relation of tradition to the individual talent." And that he represents as follows: "In the Amidah prayer, he suggests, 'our God' indicates a personal search, 'God of our Fathers,' the tradition; and if, after having said 'God of Abraham,' we repeat 'God of Isaac,' 'God of Jacob,' this shows that Isaac and Jacob did not rely on what was transmitted but themselves went in search of the divine."[7]

6

Estranging the familiar: Hartman and the essay, or the cat Geoffrey at pranks

Is it at least *possible* for the essay to muster enough vigor to institute a renewal of ideas ... while remaining essayistic, distinct from a scientific philosophy's striving for absolute truths...? The central question, thus, is criticism, the essay, as work of art, as art genre.
Criticism in the Wilderness

We can't go back to Pater or Ruskin, or the best Hazlitt and Coleridge; the amount of positive historical knowledge we are expected to carry along is too great. But they gave the essay a dignity which it need not lose in its more specialized and burdened form.
The Fate of Reading

When Christopher Smart writes in *Jubilate Agno*, "For I pray the Lord Jesus to translate my MAGNIFICAT into verse and represent it," the pun (magnifi-cat) alluding to the "magnification" of the cat Jeoffrey and of the animal kingdom generally, corroborates what Freud says about wit both submitting to and escaping the censor. To compare a hymn (the Magnificat) associated with the Virgin Mary to the gambols of Jeoffrey is blasphemous – except that the pun remains unexplicit and the poet, in any case, "gives the glory" to God by asking Christ to make his verses acceptable. Yet the anxiety, I believe, or the pressure resulting in this kind of wit, goes deeper. It is not one outrageously smart comparison which is at stake, but the legitimacy of artistic representation as a whole. The magnifi-cat theme expresses, in its marvelous mixture of humility and daring, the artist's sense that he is disturbing the "holy Sabbath" of creation by his recreation; that he is trespassing on sacred

property or stealing an image of it or even exalting himself as a maker – in short, that he is magnifying mankind instead of "giving the glory" to God. Smart therefore atones the exposed, self-conscious self by "at-one-ing" it with the animal creation it has exploited. And, in return, he asks that his verse-representation be "represented" before God by a mediator who enters the first line of his poem as "Lord, and Lamb."
The Fate of Reading

"Eine gewichtige Pranke" ... In Kafka that paw-prank is often a startling – frightening and comic at the same time – resurrection of a casual metaphor or figure. Something apparently without guile rises up to impede the "progress" of the story and becomes a life-and-death matter.
Criticism in the Wilderness

Although frequently represented as promoting the obliteration of all distinctions between "primary" texts and those "secondary" ones we label criticism, Geoffrey Hartman insists that he continues "to believe in the separation of genres, as in the distinctness of the sexes." Accordingly, he expresses unhappiness with "certain, let us call them unisex, experiments in critical writing – which weaken the task of interpretation by spicing it up with parafictional devices." Almost in the same breath, Hartman adds, however, no doubt unsettling traditionalists buoyed by the preceding remarks, that "worthwhile critical writing carries with it the power to change not simply our opinion about art but also our very idea of art in relation to other activities; including criticism" (CW 216). Characteristically, then, even as he promotes "creative criticism," Hartman adopts a far-from-simple stance. As we have seen, for him the relation of literature and criticism can be figured, in Wordsworthian terms, as one of "mutual domination" and "interchangeable supremacy." Since criticism is, in fact, "not extraliterary, not outside of literature or art looking in [but] ... a defining and influential part of its subject, a genre with some constant and some changing features" (CW 257), the relation can no longer be understood as parasitic but instead as symbiotic.

With Hartman, emphasis shifts to the critic, to the nature of his or her response, and so to the question of style.[1] Hartman understands literature, or what we have traditionally called literature, as the representation of extra-ordinary events, the great poem in turn as an extra-ordinary language-event; therefore, "the spectacle of the polite critic dealing with an extravagant literature, trying so hard to come to terms with it in his own tempered language, verges on the ludicrous" (CW 155). In *The Fate of Reading*, Hartman animadverts against the practice and assumptions of so much critical commentary (he rarely stings, but when he does so it is generally, as here, in discussing "plainstyle" critics). In imitation of Dante (or is it Byron?), he presents "a vision of judgment," realized as he dreams of "a mob eddying about and shouting confusedly" outside the "pearly gates," a group forming, in fact, "a limbo of their own, a new circle neither in heaven nor hell, the Circle of Interpreters." Poetic and creative, Hartman's account stands in rich counterpoint to his subject. Regarding the "methodically humble" interpreter, Hartman goes on to write:

> He subdues himself to commentary on work or writer, is effusive about the *integrity of the text*, and feels exalted by exhibiting art's controlled, fully organized energy of imagination. What passion yet what objectivity! What range yet what unity! What consistency of theme and style! His essays, called articles, merchandized in the depressed market place of academic periodicals, conform strictly to the cool element of scholarly prose. They are sober, literate, literal, pointed. Leave behind all fantasy, you who read these pages.

Somewhat less pointedly himself, now considering (however ironically) the situation from the perspective he has reviled, and reining in his own "flights of fancy," Hartman acknowledges that the critic is "writing, after all, criticism not fiction." Therefore,

> he will not violate the work of art by imposing on it his own, subjective flights of fancy, however intriguing these may be. He has put off personality except for the precise amount it needs to animate his prose. Who can fault him? Is anyone against objectivity, integrity, and the scrupulous distinction of functions? (9)

Who, indeed? But other questions assert themselves about cool, controlled, and accommodated (rather than "answerable") criticism, notably including those Hartman raises in the title chapter of *The Fate of Reading*. His dialectical way of proceeding is once again on display.

> ... is criticism a yea yea, nay nay affair, best conducted in as dry a prose as possible? This admirable ideal has its shortcomings. It establishes too often a schizoid rather than useful distance between art and criticism. Under the pressure of such an ideal

writers divide into a class of artists and a class of adjudicators, each with its own prerogatives. Surely a bureaucratic or managerial, rather than a human and persuasive solution. Why shouldn't the critic be "divers et ondoyant," in the essay form at least? ... In any case, to prescribe the separateness of literary and literary-critical genres, and put down all mixed criticism as bad art, does not resolve the contradiction faced by those who want criticism to be a rigorous testing of interpretive hypotheses or clarifying of the author's intention. How will they reconcile the notion of essay – tentative, continuously self-reflective, structured, yet informal – with the rigor that evaluative or historical criticism should ideally bring to its subject? (268–9)

The issue is "creative criticism" or, as Hartman puts it, "what to make of the 'brilliance' of this phenomenon, which liberates the critical activity from its positive or reviewing function, from its subordination to the thing commented on" (CW 191). The question goes back through, among others, (and surprisingly) H. L. Mencken, who rails against the critic as pedagogue, (at least implicitly) to Pope and Dryden and even Plato; of course, Oscar Wilde represents the *locus classicus* of the argument for "the critic as artist." His considerable irony notwithstanding, Wilde's position is much less delicate and balanced than Hartman's, regarding "the work of art simply as a starting point for a new creation," one that "need not necessarily bear any obvious resemblance to the thing it criticizes."[2] The "fusion of creation with criticism" in "the new philosophic criticism" (CW 190) represents, Hartman argues, "neither an inflation of criticism at the expense of creative writing nor a promiscuous intermingling of both" (CW 202). It does, however, in the various ways it embraces mixture and impurity, avoid the reductiveness – or totality – of both "unisex" experiments and the objectivity of so much recent criticism. It also entails "a creative testing of *limits*: the limits of what Hegel called 'absolute knowledge' and Dewey the 'quest for certainty.'" That there is, rather than "absolute knowledge," a "textual infinite, an interminable web of texts and interpretations" puts *all* lines, *all* boundaries, in question, not just text and commentary or literature and philosophy but also inside and outside and even, as Hartman notes, nation and nation (CW 211). Derrida's *Glas* Hartman adduces as exemplary in showing how

> the line of exegesis will therefore tend to be as precariously extensible as the line of the text. The subject matter of exegesis

> is, in fact, this "line." Yet criticism as commentary *de linea* always crosses the line and changes to one *trans lineam*. The commentator's discourse, that is, cannot be neatly or methodically separated from that of the author: the relation is contaminating and chiastic; source text and secondary text, though separable, enter into a mutually supportive, mutually dominating relation. (CW 206)

As a result, Hartman suggests, criticism may be or become "that literature of imaginative reason" that Matthew Arnold sought. Whether or not that occurs, Hartman maintains, with due caution,

> it is not impossible that a future generation will consider some critical and scholarly essays written from Arnold's time on as interesting as the poetry and fiction of the period. It is not impossible that the creative spirit may be showing itself in such books as Hegel's *Lectures on Aesthetics*, Ruskin's *Queen of the Air*, Pater's *Renaissance*, Erich Auerbach's *Mimesis*, or certain essays of Barfield, Lukács, Benjamin, and Derrida [might one add Hartman to that list?]. Moreover, though criticism is not fiction but rather a genre in its own right, it is not impossible that, today, this genre may be changing its form and occupying more intellectual and creative space. (CW 256–7)

The form that criticism has traditionally taken is the essay, and near the heart of this matter of "creative criticism" lies the question of the critical essay, "as work of art, as art genre" (CW 203). Not exactly a new issue, but an exciting one, it emerges in the context of the current resurgence of interest in the essay generally, on the part of readers and writers alike. I have discussed "the return of/to the essay" elsewhere,[3] and so will not repeat that argument here. Instead, I will try to define Hartman's position on the essay, a bit later attending to his practice of the form.

In form, tone, and style, the essay differs significantly from the article, although we often use the terms interchangeably. Despite its protean nature – Edward Hoagland describes it as "a greased pig," Joseph Epstein as "a pair of baggy pants into which nearly anyone and anything can fit," and Elizabeth Hardwick as a "slithery form, wearisomely vague and as chancy as trying to catch a fish in the open hand" – the essay possesses certain distinctive, perhaps defining features.[4] Hartman himself describes the essay – we heard above – as "tentative, continuously self-reflective, structured, yet informal." It is also, and perhaps above all, anti-systematic, dramatizing the mind's journeys, its saunterings and maunderings, among books, ideas, and emotions, much as one savors a good book or fine wine. In keeping with the occasional status that partly accounts for that anti-systematic nature, the essay foregrounds the writer and his or her personality. Here is Edward Hoagland, one of the best contemporary essayists, on the essay's dependence on personality and with it the quality of the voice we hear speaking. Essays, he writes,

> hang somewhere on a line between two sturdy poles: this is what I think, and this is what I am. Autobiographies which aren't novels are generally extended essays, indeed. A personal essay is like the human voice talking, its order the mind's natural flow, instead of a systematized outline of ideas. Though more wayward or informal than an article or treatise, somewhere it contains a point which is its real center, even if the point couldn't be uttered in fewer words than the essayist has used. Essays don't usually boil down to a summary, as articles do, and the style of the writer has a "nap" to it, a combination of personality and originality and energetic loose ends that stand up like the nap on a piece of wool and can't be brushed flat.[5]

Echoing William H. Gass's similar point that the essay "interests itself in the narration of ideas – in their *unfolding*," Phillip Lopate has written – all of this recalls Hartman – that in this "baggy" form "the track of a person's thoughts struggling to achieve some understanding of a problem *is* the plot, is the adventure."[6] Here we would do well to remember not only Hartman's confession that *Criticism in the Wilderness* "is a book of experiences rather than a systematic defense of literary studies" (1) but also Paul H. Fry's succinct and apt description of Hartman's work: "The roundabout course of his allusiveness represents the course of interpretive discovery. His criticism is the most *realistic* record we have of what literate reading is like."[7] Hartman as *essayist*, then.

It is not so much that Hartman seems to have a special affinity for the essay form as that his thinking is of the kind characteristic of the essay. In this regard, beyond the previous points, consider W. Wolfgang Holdheim's recent claim that "the essay is the hermeneutic genre *par excellence*."[8] The claim may derive from Georg Lukács. For Lukács, maintains Holdheim, "the essay is grounded in *Leben*, in existence," it possesses a "genuinely intellectual character," and it reflects the "nondogmatic nature (questions, not answers) of that cognitive interest." The essay is, moreover, Holdheim continues, processual, enacting "a to-and-fro movement between subject and object," a movement that "presents itself, among other things, as a dialectic between developing idea and elucidated occasion."[9] In fact, Holdheim writes, the essay "demonstrates the act of knowing *in flagrante* – cognition as 'getting to know.' . . . [S]uch knowledge reflects our universal condition as finite beings that live in time, that endure only in and through change."[10] Obviously, Holdheim's points, many of them, find echoes in Hartman, whose account, for example, of his "personal and macaronic procedure" (5) in *Criticism in the Wilderness* (a "shuttling," he says) parallels that "to-and-fro" movement Holdheim describes. Such parallels between Hartman and Holdheim are not surprising, given their common grounding in hermeneutics.[11]

Although some have attempted to define the nature of the speaking voice or authorial personality necessary for or indicative of an effective essay, Joseph Epstein for one arguing that an affirmativeness or "love of life . . . is one of the qualities that all the great essayists hold in common,"[12] such narrowing – reductiveness, really – seems doomed to fail, as well as to violate the broad and open, if not dialectical, spirit of the essay. Nevertheless, I believe that a certain feminine quality does inhere in the essay. Gass maintains that the writer of essays is always initially "in a feminine mood . . ., receptive to and fertilized by texts, hungry to quote, eager to reproduce."[13] I am not so sure about all of *that*; I find more to the point Gass's distinction between the essayistic spirit and "the strenuous disciplines which define the search for truth."[14] The pointed, determined, unequivocal – in short, the masculinist – quest for certainty, unrelenting and fierce, is alien to what the essay is all about. It may be, as Gass suggests, that the essay is not for one who seeks mastery but for one who is an amateur (i.e., a lover). In any case, the tenderness that I have remarked in Hartman's writing is, I am suggesting, characteristic of the essay. In *Saving the Text*, for example, by the time we reach the section of "Words and Wounds" entitled "Soft Names," we appreciate the importance of the "affectionate sort of theorizing" (155) Hartman discusses, praises, and practices. His celebration of "the soft namings of a maternal voice" (144) reverberates upon the ear, allowing us to glimpse certain distinctions between his own speculative and open efforts, which embrace the "task of equivocation" (60), and the determined search for unequivocal truth, delivered in "the definite article," that constitutes philosophy and its relentless, masculine quest of the *savoir absolu*. As an essayist, Hartman is tender, this heart-man.

She does not refer to the essay specifically, or to its crucial difference from the (masculine) article, prized by the academic profession, but Jane Tompkins has made the point most effectively. Although the wish had been repressed by professional conventions, which would not have you "talk about your private life in the course of doing your professional work," what Tompkins now confesses to wanting to write "would always take off from personal experience, would always be in some way a chronicle of my hours and days, would speak in a voice which can talk about everything, would reach out to a reader like me and touch me where I want to be touched."[15] In other words, Tompkins adds, she wants "to speak in what Ursula Le Guin called the mother tongue. Whereas 'the dialect of the father tongue,'" she quotes Le Guin as saying, "'is the language of thought that seeks objectivity,'" the mother tongue, "'spoken or written expects an answer.'" It is, in short, "'conversation'" that is sought, perhaps in Hartman's analogous terms, response or an "answerable style." In any case, "'The mother tongue is language not as mere communication, but as relation, relationship.'"[16]

At the heart of the matter is what is happening to the essay. The situation facing the essayist today differs radically from that in the nineteenth century, arguably the heyday of essayistic art, and so the way they wrote, however appealing and deserving of praise, cannot be ours. Nor can that "teatotalling" style that developed among English critics in the period roughly from 1920 to 1950, when "an order of discourse strove hard to remain a discourse of order": "The English classical writer, even when the stakes were high, wished to please rather than teach, and to remind rather than instruct. This critical tradition, keeping its distance from sacred but also from learned commentary," writes Hartman, "sought to purify the reader's taste and the national language, and so addressed itself to peers or friends – in short, to a class of equally cultured people": the result was a "friendship style" that in its "dream of communication" privileged conversation ("T and T" 32, 33). The problem is, now, that those who

> uphold the art of criticism as conversation too often stifle intellectual exchange. The conversational decorum has become a defensive mystique for which "dialectic" and even "dialogue" (in Plato's or Gadamer's or Bakhtin's strong sense) are threatening words.... It is time to try something else. ("T and T" 38)

In Hartman's words,

> we can't go back to Pater or Ruskin, or the best Hazlitt and Coleridge; the amount of positive historical knowledge we are expected to carry along is too great. But they gave the essay a dignity which it need not lose in its more specialized and burdened form. (FR 290)

What, then, does or would the more modern, burdened and specialized yet dignified, essay look like? To repeat: "what to make of the 'brilliance' of this phenomenon, which liberates the critical activity from its positive or reviewing function, from its subordination to the thing commented on?"

In confronting these questions, central to Hartman's work, we can hardly do better than to begin with his most sustained reflection on the critical essay; that occurs in "Literary Commentary as Literature," reprinted in *Criticism in the Wilderness*. As he acknowledges there, the assertion, if not the demonstration, of the critical essay's artfulness and significance derives from Lukács's "On the Nature and Form of the Essay," written as a letter to his friend Leo Popper in 1910. Hartman devotes several pages of his own essay to consideration of his predecessor's work, to which he is "drawn strongly" (195).

He elaborates and extends Lukács's arguments, working through them towards his own interpretation of commentary's role and status. I think the strength of Lukács's attraction stems not just from Hartman's shared sense of the critic's responsibilities but also from certain important qualities they have in common. What Hartman says of Lukács might be said of himself as well: he is "as plastic as Kant or Schiller in his elaboration of distinctions, each of which is given its dignity. He is never trapped by categories" (195).

At bottom, Lukács "does not accept subordination as a defining characteristic of the essay. For him the great essayists . . . use events or books merely as occasions to express their own 'criticism of life'" (191), a position that Hartman echoes when he writes that "in criticism, we deal not with language as such, nor with the philosophy of language, but with how books or habits of reading *penetrate* our lives" (202–3). The question that Hartman then raises is that that evidently prompted Lukács's reflections: linking the essay with "negative knowledge," Hartman wonders, with Lukács, whether the essay, specifically the critical essay, has a form of its own, a shape or perspective that removes it from the domain of positive knowledge (*Wissenschaft*) to give it a place beside art, yet without confusing the boundaries of scholarship and art? Is it at least *possible* for the essay to muster enough vigor to institute a renewal of ideas ("die Kraft zu einem begrifflichen Neuordnen des Lebens") while remaining essayistic, distinct from a scientific philosophy's striving for absolute truths (the "eisig-endgültige Vollkommenheit der Philosophie")? The central question, thus, is criticism, the essay, as work of art, as art genre. "Also: die Kritik, der Essay – oder nenne es vorläufig was Du willst – als Kunstwerk, als Kunstgattung." (191)

In attempting to locate and define what distinguishes the essay "with the rigour of a law, from all other art forms" – a daunting task, all the more so because of the essay's protean nature – Lukács argues that "the critic is one who glimpses destiny in forms: whose most profound experience is the soul-content which forms indirectly and unconsciously conceal within themselves."[17] (This is not so unlike Hartman's linking of form and history in "Toward Literary History," which I discussed earlier.) Form "*is* reality" for critics, Lukács argues, "the voice with which they address their questions to life." Accordingly, Lukács maintains, the critic is "always speaking about the ultimate problems of life, but in a tone which implies that he is only discussing pictures and books, only the inessential and pretty ornaments of real life – and even then not their innermost substance but only their beautiful and useless surface."[18] Fundamental to what the essay connotes and means, to what it is, is *irony*. And whether or not the essay somehow offers a privileged access to truth, towards which it is always striving, it functions as a mode of *negative* knowledge. Rehearsing these points, Hartman notes the essay's relation to dialectic, a point he takes from Walter Pater, who, he believes, influenced Lukács. However that may be, Pater distinguished the treatise (not unlike what we call the article) as the instrument of dogmatic philosophy, from the essay or dialogue, as the instrument of dialectic, maintaining that the latter "'does in truth little more than clear the ground, or the atmosphere, or the mental tablet.'" Hartman quotes, with evident approval, Pater's embrace of "'this tentative character of dialectic, of question and answer as the method of discovery, of teaching and learning ... the position, in a word, of the philosophic *essayist*'" (193). This emphasis upon the philosophic, in Pater, Lukács, and Hartman, as well as in Theodor Adorno and Max

Bense, marks an important distinction from the tradition of the personal of familiar essay,[19] though much of what is offered concerning the critical essay applies to all forms of the genre.

Although the necessity remains, in a critical essay, one would think, to review, represent, or at least begin with a text or a theme, Lukács argues that the critic is guided by a transcendent *idea*. Denoting what is so important to Hartman, which I have called "tradition" or "literary history," Lukács claims that poetry, for instance, "is older and greater – a larger, more important thing – than all the works of poetry"; the critic, he believes, "has been sent into the world" to announce this *idea*: "to bring to light this *a priori* primacy over great and small, to proclaim it, to judge every phenomenon by the scale of values glimpsed and grasped through this recognition." Yet the critical essayist exists as only a herald, perhaps "the pure type of the precursor" of "the one who is always about to arrive, the one who is never quite there," i.e., "the great value-definer of aesthetics." The critic functions, in other words, as "a John the Baptist who goes out to preach in the wilderness about another who is still to come, whose shoelace he is not worthy to untie." For now, Lukács continues, "The essay can calmly and proudly set its fragmentariness against the petty completeness of scientific exactitude or impressionistic freshness; but its purest fulfillment, its most vigorous accomplishment becomes powerless once the great aesthetic comes."[20] Criticism in the wilderness, therefore – and so Hartman's book engages not just Matthew Arnold but also Georg Lukács in more "intertextual leaping."

Lukács offers a crucial distinction between the tragic sense and the essayistic, each with its own particular interpretation of *end*. Perhaps calling to mind that "gewichtige Pranke," which Hartman traces in Benjamin and Kafka, that rises up, seemingly out of nowhere, to impede progress, doom intention and unsettle us, Lukács writes:

> a tragic life is crowned only by its end, only the end gives meaning, sense and form to the whole, and it is precisely the end which is always arbitrary and ironic here [i.e., in the essay]....
> A question is thrown up and extended so far in depth that it becomes the question of all questions, but after that everything remains open; something comes from outside – from a reality which has no connection with the question nor with that which, as the possibility of an answer, brings forth a new question to meet it – and interrupts everything. This interruption is not an end, because it does not come from within, and yet it is the most

profound ending because a conclusion from within would have been impossible.[21]

An excellent description of the essay, of whatever kind, Lukács's account here recalls the world-shattering, even kerygmatic, power of the Hebraic *logos*, which "disconfirms" such structure as characterizes the cybernetic mythic world, allowing for the possibility of the new to break in, a point that Adorno too insists on in his counterstatement to Lukács.[22]

Of all the points Lukács makes about the essay, probably none is more important than that that concerns its *desire*, which follows from its threshold nature, its marginal status. As Hartman explains, Lukács, "more explicitly than Pater, attributes the essay form to both irony and desire (*Sehnsucht*), to a double, complementary or contrary, infinitizing. The essay lives off a desire that has an in-itself, that is more than something merely waiting to be completed, and removed, by absolute knowledge." In fact, writes Hartman, when we finish reading Lukács, "we have the uncanny impression that his exemplum has enacted the entire problem" (195) (might the same be said of Hartman's essay?). Hartman's conclusion on this point follows, and it is important:

> This "real" letter to a friend, Leo Popper, dated formally, "Florence, October 1910," is much more than the letter-preface to a book of essays, more than an essay even: it is an "intellectual poem," as A. W. Schlegel called Hemsterhuis' essays. It delimits its own position in the life of the intellect but meanwhile incorporates so much living thought that its narrower function of *Gericht* expands into the form of *Gedicht*. (195–6)

I will continue to draw from "Literary Commentary as Literature," for Hartman's immediately following remarks elaborate on this important notion of "intellectual poem" and of the desire that marks it; in so doing, they help us understand the relation to the essay tradition of Hartman's own desire.

> If the essay is indeed an intellectual poem, it is unflattering to observe that very few such poems exist in the sphere of literary or cultural criticism. The uneasy coexistence, in essays, of their referential function as commentary with their ambition to *be* literature and not only be about it makes for a medley of insight and idiosyncratic self-assertion. There is a charm, of course, to many nineteenth-century essays, which preserves them from

> this fate. Arnold or Pater on Wordsworth can be read as interesting prose, sustained by valid if occasionally dated remarks. We are not threatened, not imposed on, by the force of their observation, or not any longer. Pater and Arnold are now part of the heaven of English literature, like Wordsworth himself. The ideal proposed by Lukács is, however, a harder one, and as unlikely of realization as a poem that must carry along, and not shirk, a strong weight of ratiocination or of opinion with the force of fact. (196)

By "intellectual poem," then, Hartman means much more than artful prose or charm applied to intellectual questions. Whatever he means, it involves "insight and idiosyncratic self-assertion" and also severity; it is, in short, serious stuff.

> How scarce this commodity is, this essay which is an intellectual poem, can be gauged by a guess that, with the early exception of Friedrich Schlegel, only Valéry habitually attained it: one thinks of his masterful construction of the figure of Leonardo da Vinci or of "Poetry and Abstract Thought," both of which, it happens, raise the issue of the relation between artistic and scientific thinking. One might add such essays as Ortega's "In Search of Goethe from Within." Certain of Freud's or Heidegger's essays are also constructions of this kind, severe intellectual poems. (196)

Hartman does not have in mind at all, then, literary charm or grace of expression, nor the accessibility or forged links with the reader characteristic of the personal or familiar essay: "Tea and totality don't mix" ("T and T" 39). The essay as "intellectual poem" is demanding and philosophical, marked by its desire to be read for what it is, rather than simply for what it is about. It is severe – and defamiliarizing. Derrida is important here because, as Hartman puts it, "he exposes the privilege accorded to voice in the form of the conversational style as it aspired to Pater's 'inward' dialogue"; indeed, his deconstruction aims at "the dream of communication which that style, as the proprium of all styles, underwrites" ("T and T" 40). The issue may be that of communicating "in colloquial form the theory or methodology developed" ("T and T" 39).

Hartman advances a notion bound to recall his description of his own "personal and macaronic" procedure in *Criticism in the Wilderness* ("I allow a formal idea within critical theory to elicit the analysis of a poem and vice-versa...."[5]):

Yet neither Valéry nor Ortega nor Freud nor Heidegger engages very often in the close reading of literature or the close viewing of art. Their notion of detail, when it comes to art, is less exigent, and their exposition less grainy than ours. The critical essay today, to qualify as such, must contain some close-ups: it tends to proceed, in fact, by shifts of perspective (as in some kinds of sequential art or concrete poetry) that expose the non-homogeneity of the fact at hand, the arbitrariness of the knots that bind the work into a semblance of unity. The close-ups are not there merely to illustrate or reinforce a suppositious unity but to show what simplifications, or institutional processes, are necessary for achieving any kind of unitary, consensual view of the artifact. (196–7)

At bottom, "the critical essay is critical: we are allowed to survive but not to substantialize our illusions" (197). Often more demanding than poems, "the essays of the more intellectual practitioners of the art of literary or philosophical criticism ... make the text a little harder to understand and the visible a little harder to see" (197). In other words, they "estrange the familiar." They also "increase rather than lighten the burden of tradition, in an anti-evangelical and depressing manner" (197).

The essays Hartman celebrates are not only "less distinguished in their decorum," but most are also much more "exacting than the 'familiar' prose which aimed, in the previous century, to expand the family of readers. Hazlitt makes you feel equal to, or different only in degree from, a Wordsworth" (197). Thus reminding us that "familiar" is linked to the notion of "family," Hartman admits that "this democratic ethos" remains as valid as it was earlier, though complications exist that must be acknowledged, additional burdens that must be borne:

> the virulence of nationalistic and separatist movements has taught us how dangerous it is to assume intimacy or common standards. The labor involved in understanding something foreign or dissident without either colonizing it or becoming oneself a cultural transvestite meets us fully as the reality, the otherness to be faced. (197–8)

Once more, Hartman refuses to collapse distance and difference, to assume too quick intimacy with the other or the foreign; neither a colonizer nor a "cultural transvestite," he remains respectful of the complexities that persist in a world that we easily think of as smaller and smaller, on the model of the family.

Moreover, the difficult (and defamiliarizing) critics Hartman speaks of – in this connection he mentions specifically Adorno, Blackmur, and Derrida – "though not paralyzed by the heavy task of emulating pastmasters or alien traditions, ... know that culture has often progressed by contamination." According to Hartman, this "produces an anguish and a self-scrutiny leading to a vacillating or deeply equivocal recuperation of what Northrop Frye has prematurely named 'the secular scripture.' " Again using their differences to make his own position clear, Hartman points to Frye's suggestion that "art becomes secular by being recuperated." To this, Hartman responds pointedly: "Yet woe to him (I must add) by whom this recuperation comes! He may profane the tradition, just as the New Testament runs the risk of profaning the Old, by giving it a universality that at once redeems and cheapens the barbarous, that is, ethnocentric, element" (198).[23]

The critical essay Hartman proceeds to describe, not surprisingly, as both timely and untimely, reflecting a responsibility to tradition and the past and, at the same time, expressing desire:

> it stands at the very intersection of what is perceived to be a past to be carried forward, and a future that must be kept open. In Lukács's idealism, as in Frye's, the futuristic element is "desire," or whatever fuels wishing, and cannot achieve fulfillment.

That desire, where institutionalized, "produces superstition; kept free it produces a frivolous or disinterested irony" (199). Desire is critical, then, linked to the critical spirit – and perhaps "sacred discontent." Reflecting even more deeply on the irony and desire inherent in the essay, Hartman goes beyond and, indeed, counter to Lukács:

> It is mere common sense, then, to put the critical essay on the side of irony, but this may turn out to be more defensive than correct. What lies beyond wish fulfillment or the pleasure principle is not irony but something daemonic to which Freud ventured to give the name of reality-mastery. Lukács's career as a critic veers dialectically, and perhaps daemonically, toward a reality-mastery in which desire, wish fulfillment, and formal irony play only a subordinate role. The process of incorporating what continues to violate one's identity – I mean on the level of cultural conflict or exchange – may lie beyond the range of

values associated with such words as *pleasure, taste, civility, irony, accommodation*. This beyond may also become the domain of the literary essay, the more urgent and severe its aim. (199)

Although, as we noted, Hartman believes that "the English tradition in criticism is sublimated chatter," he insists that criticism "has an unacknowledged penchant for reversal in it," and that penchant, he adds, continuing the reflections just quoted, is "near-daemonic." In turn, *that* quality "brings it close to the primacy of art" (199). Well aware of the much-bruited claim that "'the corruption of the poet is the generation of the critic,'" Hartman acknowledges that the penchant for reversal in the essay "can be dismissed as the sin of envy: as a drive for primacy like Satan's or Iago's." Yet it is hard to disagree with Lukács:

> there *is* something ironic about the critic's subordination of himself to the work reviewed. At best he keeps testing that work, that apparent greatness, and by force of doubt or enthusiasm puts it more patently before us. He plays the role now of accuser and now of God. A judicious rather than judicial criticism will, needless to say, not try for a single verdict: like Dr. Johnson's, it will expose virtues and weaknesses, strong points and failings together. But it can also frighten us by opening a breach – or the possibility of transvaluation – in almost every received value. (199–200)

For Hartman, we reduce, or ignore, at our peril "the insufferable coexistence, even crossover, of holiness and profaneness in art." Let us hear him out on this matter:

> This crossover tears us apart; and we imaginatively take our revenge by tearing at it, or prudently and hygienically – by means of a *genre tranché* critical theory – denying the crossover, and separating the daemonry of art from the civility of criticism, or discursive from literary discourse, or person from persona, and so forth. Yet everyone has known the feeling that in Henry James or Sartre, let alone Borges, criticism is not independent of the fictional drive. The more insidious question is whether any critic has value who is only a critic: who does not put us in the presence of "critical fictions" or make us aware of them in the writings of others. (201)

Hartman is also a poet.

In at least three senses, I would say. First, there is the fact, not widely enough known, that Hartman has written a number of poems, which have appeared in major magazines and reviews, some of them reprinted in *Akiba's Children* (1978). In Appendix I venture some brief, preliminary remarks on a few of the poems, which treat themes and perform strategies analogous to those characteristic of the prose. If not always, at least some of the time, Hartman's critical work, which since 1964 has taken essay form, achieves the level of "intellectual poetry" as he describes that concept (such is my judgment, anyway). How it does so is, from one perspective, what I am discussing throughout this book and more particularly in the present chapter. One important reason for spending so much time on "Literary Commentary as Literature," and quoting so extensively from it is that I have wanted to suggest that, even in what might seem a straightforward exposition, Hartman engages a series of major issues in an unpointed manner exacting and demanding. I remarked in the opening chapter on the paratactic quality of Hartman's style, with "its refusal to subordinate arguments and observations in a hierarchically entailed manner." That description is Martin Jay's, discussing Theodor Adorno, whose metaphor of force-field (*Kraftfeld*) also applies to Hartman: "a relational interplay of attractions and aversions that constitute ... the dynamic, transmutational structure of a complex phenomenon."[24] No doubt in my own *prosaic* account I have *straightened out* Hartman's thinking, zealously obscuring the relational as I have sought to make clear the directional. Still, by providing so many of Hartman's own words, I hope to have suggested the difference in his work from simple linear development (*and* accommodation) as well as the implied resistance to easy appropriation. The thinking Hartman inspires entails circling about a topic, following him as he *relates* issues and returns, bee-like, always attentive to resonances, to previous points made, which are never completely forgotten, without ever coming to rest in anything like a thesis-statement (his essays thus body forth *desire*). There is precious little rest, ever, for the Wandering Jew. Hartman insures, damn him, that we stay with his words rather than jump quickly, assuming so much, to "meaning." What he writes of Walter Benjamin, therefore, applies to his own writing: whether or not the "curse" derives from "the Jewish imagination," these writers "cannot let go of any ideas," their "prose thickens involuntarily," and, as a result, their "crowded language" becomes "curiously unprogressive or exitless" (CW 64). In quoting so much from Hartman, I have at least stayed with his words, hoping to indicate, too, the reticence or "holding-back" typical of "the Jewish imagination."

Whereas the idea of the critical essay as "intellectual poem" centrally involves depth and severity of intellectual engagement, philosophical speculation, often philological rigor, and perhaps psychological risk, there is a third way in which Hartman is, if not a poet, at least a writer of considerable artistic accomplishment. I mean that his essays, whether or not they attain the level of "intellectual poetry," are, many of them, structured and "styled" in a way that can only be described, I think, as evocative and poetic. As more than one frustrated commentator has observed, you cannot pin Hartman down. On remarkably light feet for one bearing the burden of so much knowledge, he dances around issues and texts, brooding on them, to be sure, but never landing or zeroing in quite the way the author of an article would. "Words and Wounds" provides an example of the deftness I am laboring to describe – and of the exasperation it can produce (any number of other essays would also serve here). This particular essay is organized in fifteen sections, of varying length and difficulty, each prefaced by a more or less clever or witty subtitle and most of them given an apt quotation as further introduction. These sections function as virtually autonomous units – in the Romantic tradition, Hartman appreciates the historical link between the word *text* and the Romantic fragment and makes essays composed of fragments and *as* fragments.[25] As a result, the reader must often struggle to make connections, wondering how to get from question *x* to issue *y* – Hartman is not very accommodating. This particular difficulty is exacerbated by the paratactic and epigrammatic style. That is, Hartman punctuates long passages with pithy and memorable remarks (e.g., in "Words and Wounds": "Literature sweats balm, and heals the wound words help to produce" (134); "One breaks words with the other as one breaks bread" (137); "Goethe's 'tender empiricism' suggests an affectionate sort of thinking, on the unlikely pattern of a conversation, not excluding carnal conversation" (155) – other essays, often less determined, offer even better examples). If, in struggling with such an essay, we try to "apprehend the purposive principle immanent in the structure" of the text, which "determines the mutual interfunctioning of its component parts,"[26] we are likely to be frustrated. Swerves occur, and epigrammatic statements and clear assertions rise up, prankishly, it seems, to impede our progress, indeed to make it all but impossible to locate a simple purposive movement, consistent and totalizing. The reader (at least this reader) instinctively clutches at one or more of the powerful assertions, using it as fulcrum, focus, or argument – anything that might offer a secure handle. That, unfortunately, often proves to be a mistake, for typically, as he broods, Hartman allows his mind the run of an interpretation, rather than pursues an argument to a definite and pointed conclusion. The process, accordingly, is more important than any specific destination reached, epigrammatic statements and clever subtitles being embedded in the process (Derrida's succinct description of "seriality without paradigm" springs to mind here[27]), rather than transcending it to signal an exit into packaged meaning. Here, too, what Hartman points out concerning Walter Benjamin applies to himself as well. In the "Epistemo-Critical Prologue" to *The Origins of German Tragic Drama*, Benjamin formulated a notion of *"prose form* or *philosophical style"* that acknowledges the power of something resembling that "gewichtige Pranke" that disrupts the march of ideas towards a single, positive conclusion. Hartman quotes Benjamin's definition of philosophical style:

> *the art of interruption in contrast to the chain of deduction*; the tenacity of the essay in contrast to the single gesture of the fragment; the repetition of themes in contrast to shallow universalism; the fullness of concentrated positivity in contrast to the negation of polemics. (CW 281, italics added)[28]

The effect of such a style as Hartman's is unsettling. Unsettling, in fact, are several aspects of his essayistic efforts. These include the presence of radically different linguistic registers in a passage like the following from *Criticism in the Wilderness*:

> As long as we practice what Nietzsche called monumental history – and this kind of history is presupposed by most interpretive criticism – we must also examine what is involved in our intensive care and even canonization of certain writers.... The automatic valuing of such works of art over works of commentary, for instance (encouraging close reading of the former but considering it vainglorious to give such attention to the latter) betrays a subtle idolatry. It monumentalizes a dead man's relics, turns them into the icon of a power that continues to operate its reversals and obliterations... by means of the very act – criticism – being downgraded. (103)

The unsettling juxtaposition here of the medical (e.g., "intensive care"), the religious, and the conventional literary-critical slows us down, makes us "read" rather than merely consume the words. Moreover, the discussion obviously transcends the narrowly literary or critical, possessing religious implications, and the mixture of the literary and the religious, so closely intertwined here, is bound to disturb those who insist on neat separation, who think in categories. In fact, this passage, I am saying, requires the very effort it discusses, the close reading that works of art ordinarily receive but that works of commentary, Hartman laments, do not, being considered vainglorious.

Often, I have suggested, what Hartman writes about someone or something else recalls, or perhaps allegorically represents, him and his work (e.g., his description of Benjamin's prose as "curiously unprogressive" and "exitless" and his account of Lukács, "never trapped by categories" but "plastic ... in his elaboration of distinctions, each of which is given its dignity"). And not infrequently, Hartman's remarks on matters critical carry broad implications. Consider, for example, the essay "Literature High and Low: The Case of the Mystery," included in *The Fate of Reading*, which unsettles the line we rather glibly draw between detective fiction and the classics of our culture. Hartman does this without any suggestion that the work of Raymond Chandler or Ross Macdonald deserves a place alongside Wordsworth or Proust. By "intertextual leaping" he brings his learning and interpretive skills to bear on detective fiction, which he illuminates in juxtaposition with *Oedipus Rex*, the novels of Robbe-Grillet, films like *Blow-Up* and *Last Year at Marienbad*, and (of course) the poems of Wordsworth. Focusing on scenes of pathos, or suffering, Hartman reveals surprising similarities without minimizing differences or blurring questions of literary worth. Concerned once more with the tyranny of the eye, he emphasizes crime fiction's trust, probably excessive, in reason, and in particular its "passion," probably obsessive, for "ocular proof." Brooding on these issues produces such *aperçus* as the following:

> our eyes ache to read more, to see more, to know that the one just man (the detective) will succeed – yet when all is finished, nothing is rereadable. Instead of a Jamesian reticence that, at least, chastens the detective urge – our urge to know or penetrate intimately another person's world – the crime novel incites it artificially by a continuous, self-cancelling series of overstatements, drawing us into one false hypothesis or flashy scene after another. (218)

What *is* the subject here? The detective urge or the human? With even greater force, Hartman renders up some wide-ranging observations that stem from and transcend the specific matter of detective fiction, without, however, leaving that subject behind. The following passage carries implications with broad significance; it also reflects in important ways on Hartman's own work:

> Most popular mysteries are devoted to solving rather than examining a problem. Their reasonings put reason to sleep, abolish darkness by elucidation, and bury the corpse for good. Few detective novels want the reader to exert his intelligence fully, to find gaps in the plot or the reasoning, to worry about the moral question of fixing the blame. They are exorcisms, stories with happy endings that could be classified with comedy because they settle the unsettling. (212)

Precisely. Detective fiction thus parallels conventional criticism in strategy and desire, though Hartman does not say so directly. Yet on point after point in the passage above, detective fiction appears as the virtual opposite of Hartman's own hermeneutic labor, which seeks not to "settle the unsettling" but rather to unsettle the settling, to estrange the familiar, including, of course, mysteries.

A certain *dramatic* quality inheres, I am suggesting, in Hartman's criticism, contributing to its evocative and artistic effects. Not unlike the way, in his terms, Lukács's account of the essay enacts the problem it discusses, Hartman's essays frequently dramatize their argument. Often this dramatization, or enactment, involves a demonstration of the interimplication and mutual involvement of apparently simple oppositions. "Words and Wounds," for example, *shows* the inseparability of maternal and paternal, curse and blessing, philosophy and literature, tenderness and assertion, and other supposedly clear differences. In this essay, complications appear in small ways as well as in larger thematic terms. For example, approaching a close, Hartman writes, "Having come this far I feel that everything remains to be explained" (151). Explanation is, the reader is well aware, at issue, connoting a (masculine or paternal) belief in clear and hard truth, which Hartman's reflections suggest is problematical at best; actually, in the face of rife equivocation, explanation appears to be, literally speaking, impossible. A few pages later, Hartman declares, *explaining* – and so contradicting – himself, "I have wished to describe rather than explain" (154). Explanation cannot, then, be easily forgone, and in fact on the very next page Hartman digs an even deeper hole for himself, saying, "Let me explain" (155). What this little drama thus enacts is either a contradiction or the equivocation that Hartman argues to be unavoidable.

Various essays in *Criticism in the Wilderness* engage in similar dramatizations. When, for example, in "Understanding Criticism," after using "Leda and the Swan" as "a fable for the hermeneutic situation" (35), Hartman asserts that criticism, "a newer kind of hermeneutics, 'affirms' the power of negative thinking" (31), he indicates in one breath *both* the inseparability of affirmation and negative thinking *and* the necessity of such "hermeneutic perplexity" and "hesitation" as prevents conversion "into a positivistic and dogmatic statement" (32). The resulting criticism perplexes, and unsettles, our comfortable notions concerning the relation of commentary and art as well as the supposed ease with which we routinely think we "consume" the former.

One final example of the dramatic or performative nature of Hartman's criticism, this one larger in scope and epitomizing, I think, the way that his writing foregrounds questions of style. Few of Hartman's essays are more stylistically (and structurally) interesting, or have less conventional and more poetic form, with some special claim, perhaps, to the status of "intellectual poem," than "The Interpreter: A Self-Analysis," the introductory chapter in *The Fate of Reading*. Like "Words and Wounds," this essay consists of a number of subsections, often with playful subtitles. It "crosses over," feeling from the beginning like a "primary" text. The essay, in fact, enacts, performs its argument, which is that "interpretation is a feast, not a fast"; interpretation, that is, "imposes an obligatory excess" (18). "The Interpreter: A Self-Analysis" thus deliberately appears *excessive*: it is rich, abundant, with lots going on, not at all abstemious or restrained, but celebratory, even carnivalesque. None of the humility, objectivity, and "cool" of usual scholarly prose, which Hartman discusses, appears here. This may be "criticism on the wild side."[29] Hartman opens, daringly enough, even flamboyantly, with his "confession" of "a superiority complex *vis-à-vis* art" (3). He proceeds to echo Wordsworth in *The Prelude*, writing that "when I was young (real young) what came in through the senses was so profuse and arbitrary I had no need of heaven and hell. I lived instead in chaos . . ." (4). Then, echoing the stages of Wordsworth's evolving vision as that poet chronicles them in "Tintern Abbey," Hartman distinguishes his present understanding from that at the time he wrote *The Unmediated Vision*. Reasons for these clear echoes may be hard to determine, apart from Hartman's immersion in Wordsworth and perhaps a desire, certainly understandable, to link his confession with autobiography, one that emphasizes the growth of a mind, which happens to be what Hartman too is narrating. At any rate, he moves from his "confession" through a series of reflections and speculations concerning interpretation and the relation of commentary to art – these include "A Vision of Judgment," the Dantesque dream-vision I discussed earlier – and on to an ending that is more an "and-ing" – what Rosenzweig discusses, as Hartman elaborates in "On The Jewish Imagination." Appropriately, albeit ironically, this is "the Last Word," which begins, in fact, with a dramatized version of the interpretive situation: the interpreter asks of the Book, "Who's there?," and it responds like the sentinel Francisco to Bernardo in the opening lines of *Hamlet*, "Nay, answer me; stand, and unfold yourself." Hartman thus leaves us with questions and no (positive) solution at all. His point concerns the reversal that marks every interpretive event: "Things get crossed up in this jittery situation. It should be the interpreter who unfolds the text. But the book begins to question the interpreter, its *qui vive* challenges him to prove he's not a ghost. What is he then?" (19). What, indeed?

We are back, therefore, to the question with which I opened this chapter. In this severe "poem," Hartman both argues and enacts not only the interpreter's interimplication with what he or she interprets but also the (symbiotic) relationship of "mutual domination" and "interchangeable supremacy" that obtains between interpreter and interpreted text. Here the interpreter "comes out," presenting, or representing, himself, not unlike Christopher Smart in Hartman's account that I offer as an epigraph, Smart who responds to the demand placed on him by his "vocation." What *Hartman* presents, in this essay, is by no means an emphasis on the reader or interpreter at the expense of texts commented on but rather a sense of the mutual sustaining power, the play, the dialectic between reader and text. And since, therefore, the text interpreted is not an object, the interpreter's (answerable) style is not object-ive.

We are (still) not used to such critical writing, to such criticism, and, defamiliarizing, it unsettles. Hartman is quite clear on this point, writing in "Understanding Criticism":

> Criticism as a kind of hermeneutics is disconcerting; like logic, but without the latter's motive of absolute internal consistency, it reveals contradictions and equivocations, and so makes fiction interpretable by making it less readable. The fluency of the

reader is affected by a kind of stutter: the critic's response becomes deliberately hesitant. It is as if we could not tell in advance where a writer's rhetoric might undermine itself or where the reader might be trapped into perplexity. For the old hermeneutics the choice was clear. (CW 32)

That the choice is not – or at least no longer – clear is just the point, and so we have "negative hermeneutics," about which more in my last chapter. In Hartman, respectful of complexity, with the reticence characteristic of "the Jewish imagination" in his genes, the "response becomes deliberately hesitant" – therefore thoughtful, analogous to Keats's "negative capability." Moreover, it is difficult to "digest" or "assimilate" either the texts Hartman treats (in such "an engaged and personal way") or him. His prose shares in what he finds in Carlyle: "a dyspeptic quality" (CW 59), which does not sit lightly on the reader's stomach. Hartman's *indigestive criticism* represents a significant difference from, or reorientation of, both critical commentary and the essay, which the former has traditionally taken for its form. Such efforts he has been engaged in from early on in his career: in fact, in the Prefatory Note to the Harbinger Edition of *The Unmediated Vision*, he expressed the "hope that what follows is dry enough to prevent interpretation from being consolation, or merely that" [v]. Not the hope, this, of essayists working comfortably in the mainline of the personal or familiar tradition but of one who, while respectful of the dignity represented by those essays, accepts the burden of historical, philosophical, and theoretical knowledge. Engaging the tradition in a complex way, Hartman estranges the familiar.

And yet .... In so arguing, I may be, in giving Hartman so much credit, minimizing the *essay's* capaciousness. It may be that such strategies as I have attributed to Hartman are, in fact, what the essay is all about. Réda Bensmaïa has recently, and cogently, argued that the term *essai*, deriving from Montaigne, is "the polysemic word *par excellence*," and W. Wolfgang Holdheim has just as persuasively shown how even the familiar or personal essay, historically considered, reveals some surprising links with deconstruction, that most unfamiliar or defamiliarizing and apparently impersonal mode of thought.[30] In Holdheim's words, "the essay is less a genre than quite deliberately an antigenre, designed to flaunt the prescriptiveness in literary matters which had been inherited from a rationalistic rhetorical tradition."[31] What – I have been arguing – Hartman is doing sounds very much like the point the acknowledged "father" of the essay was engaged in centuries earlier. Holdheim (who has no axe to grind for deconstruction) specifically associates Montaigne with deconstructive efforts, writing, in fact, that the author of *Essais*

> was engaged in an *Abbau* of his tradition (the term has lately been translated as "deconstruction"). It is an active deconstruction in the genuine sense: a clearing away of rubbish, of reified sedimentation, so that issues may once again be laid bare in their concreteness. His radical presentation of discontinuity is very much a reaction against uncritically accepted accumulations of continuity; his insistence on the uniquely diverse and particular is directed against too exclusive a concern with universals.[32]

This echoes Pater's sense that the essay "does in truth little more than clear the ground, or the atmosphere, or the mental tablet" as well as Hartman's "negative hermeneutics": "On its older function of saving the text, of tying it once again to the life of the mind, is superimposed the new one of doubting, by a parodistic or playful movement, master theories that claim to have overcome the past, the dead, the false" (CW 239). So, once more the question of the relation of the individual talent to tradition – and the answer must echo that we heard in the previous chapter.

7

It's about time: negative hermeneutics and the fate of reading

Meaning is not an accumulation of positive charges but rather a serialized negative, the awareness of ranges of difference within what is posited.

As a guiding concept, indeterminacy does not merely *delay* the determination of meaning, that is, suspend premature judgments and allow greater thoughtfulness. The delay is not heuristic alone, a device to slow the act of reading till we appreciate ... its complexity. The delay is intrinsic: from a certain point of view, it is thoughtfulness itself, Keats's "negative capability," a labor that aims not to overcome the negative or indeterminate but to stay within it as long as is necessary.

Criticism, ... a newer kind of hermeneutics, "affirms" the power of negative thinking. How to define negative thinking, without converting it into a positivistic and dogmatic instrument, is of course very problematic. Not only a philosophy like that of Hegel, whose dialectic is a mode of negative thinking, struggles with this question: Keats's "negative capability" and Wallace Stevens's wish to ablute or withhold the name of the sun – to see it "in the difficulty of what it is to be" – are instances of a parallel concern.

Modern hermeneutics, ... which seems so highflying, is actually a negative hermeneutics. On its older function of saving the text, of tying it once again to the life of the mind, is superimposed the new one of doubting, by a parodistic or playful movement, master theories that claim to have overcome the past, the dead, the false.

.... having let the cat out of the bag...
Criticism in the Wilderness

The essay obviously holds special interest for Hartman. Part of its value and significance derives from its protean nature: not only is it "tentative, continuously self-reflective, structured yet informal" (FR 269), thus being well suited to his critical character, but it is also open, exploratory, and ironic, pretending to be only *about* art. Its avoidance, or at least wariness, of point marks its crucial difference from what Hartman prankishly calls the definite article; its nonassertiveness, reticence, and modesty, the way it tempers "positive or practical thought by a 'self-determined indetermination'" (FR 234). Following Lukács, Hartman believes that for all its slipperiness the essay thus has "a form of its own, a shape or perspective that removes it from the domain of positive knowledge (*Wissenschaft*) to give it a place beside art" (CW 191). As Walter Pater acknowledged, the essay resembles "that long dialogue with oneself, that dialectic process, which may be coextensive with life"; it produces no positive results, managing "in truth little more [than to] clear the ground, or the atmosphere, or the mental tablet" (quoted CW 193). As with deconstruction, which has similarly been described as "a clearing away of rubbish, of reified sedimentations, so that issues may once again be laid bare in their concreteness," so with the critical essay: negativity lies at the heart of its being.[1] That negativity reinforces Hartman's commitment to the form.

In fact, Hartman extends the essay's negative labor in estranging the familiar. His negative thinking, probably inseparable from his Hebraism, manifests itself in other ways as well; the idea of the negative subsumes many, if not most, of the concerns, strategies, and efforts we have been tracing in this study. Not unlike Freud, who "brings bad ... news about the psyche, and offers no cure except the very activity – analysis – which reveals this news" (EP 143), Hartman may well appear a Bad News Angel.

The news he brings is, however, no different from that that art delivers. Since, in Hartman's words, meaning "is not an accumulation of positive charges but rather a serialized negative, the awareness of ranges of difference within what is posited" (CW 186), immediacy, presence, and those other qualities we associate with positive being are illusory. Art, genuine art, unsettles us, and because it offers little consolation, it may well leave us, as Keats's Grecian Urn does, with "a heart high-sorrowful and cloy'd,/ A burning forehead, and a parching tongue." Art can, in any case, only *represent*: the medium never dissolves so that we come face to face with "the thing itself." Art is, then, a form of negativity that knows its nature – and so teaches those with ears to hear a painful lesson. Literature "is part of this Negative Way" on which "our illusions lead cunningly into reality" (BF x), and according to Hartman, "a genuinely poetic text makes the negative ('freedom,' 'random and mortal action') emerge from the very positivity, the impositional power of language" (CW 109); every poem becomes, in this view, "an act of ... negative creation" (BF 289). In literature, Hartman writes, "the natural positivity of the mind is engaged only to be chastened, as the literary work, whether richly obscure or puzzlingly simple (a sonnet by Mallarmé or a Wordsworth lyric), teases the reader out of thought" (BF ix).

Yet fiction is, paradoxically, "inherently affirmative" (BF 74), and its affirmative nature accounts for much of its importance. It may also make criticism necessary: so strong is the pull of the positive and affirmative that art, as resistant as it is to various appropriations, stands in need of criticism if it is to succeed in its negative labor. This point Hartman makes clear in the course of reflecting on the meaning of space in Virginia Woolf's novels, in which he discerns a powerful dialectic of affirmation and "the negative moment":

> Considered as notes toward a supreme fiction, the novels of Virginia Woolf say "It must be affirmative." They suppose a mind with an immense, even unlimited, power to see or build continuities. It is almost as if the special attribute of the unconscious, that it does not know the negative, belonged also to mind in its freest state. The artist is either not conscious of the negative (i.e., his unconscious speaks through him), or fiction is generically the embodiment of the negative – and whatever dialectic characterizes mind – in purely affirmative terms. The reader, of course, may reconstitute the negative; this task is one of the principal aims of interpretation. (BF 81)

This last statement is unusual for Hartman in its directness: reconstitution of the negative, releasing it from the bonds of the positive and affirmative, is, Hartman asserts, "one of the principal aims of interpretation." In "Virginia's Web," Hartman *demonstrates* how criticism assists art in performing "the labor of the negative," this by showing "the precarious and interpolative character of Virginia Woolf's continuities" (81). Another name for that effort, of course, is deconstruction.

As important as criticism is (to art), its effects may seem minimal. For what we gain, even from the most informed and rigorous reading, is little that is positive: what we gain, in fact, Hartman writes, is only "the undoing of a previous understanding" (CW 271). In other words, "nothing new is gained, except an indeterminacy as to the locus of meaning, or a sense of the text itself as the place of revelation, a clearing (*Lichtung*) from which language, or Being itself, speaks" (UnRW 200). That may be quite enough. It is, after all, argues Hartman, "the *commentary process* that matters": "the taking away," as well as the modification and elaboration, "of previous meanings" (CW 270).

A principal aim of interpretation being the reconstitution of the negative, Hartman proposes in *Beyond Formalism* that we imitate "a more adventurous hermeneutical tradition" than seemed generally available, at least in England and America, even if that meant "deepening, provisionally, the difference between criticism and interpretation" (125). And indeed in "Adam on the Grass with Balsamum," from which I have just quoted, Hartman performs that imitation, offering an interpretation rich, speculative, and daring, in the mode of midrash. In *The Fate of Reading*, five years later, Hartman appears to increase the difference between criticism and interpretation, and so to *perform* the work of the negative, in arguing that "we must set interpretation *against* hermeneutics": the latter, he points out, has traditionally sought direct and unmediated contact with a "great Original," expecting "to reconstruct, or get back to, an origin in the form of sacred text, archetypal unity or authentic story" (16); abused in our quest of presence and consolation, interpretation theory easily becomes a means "to limit a disturbance of the peace provoked in language by the great or difficult work of thought" (UnRW 198). In light of these problems, Hartman returns, in *Criticism in the Wilderness*, to the term he had questioned ten years earlier; by 1980, of course, *criticism* was no longer identified with and limited to exegesis (in *Beyond Formalism*, we recall, Hartman mocked exegesis as "our Whore of Babylon, sitting robed in Academic black on the great dragon of Criticism and dispensing a repetitive and soporific balm from her pedantic cup" [56]). Hartman now depicts criticism as "a newer kind of hermeneutics," one that "'affirms' the power of negative thinking," itself difficult to define "without converting it into a positivistic and dogmatic instrument" (31–2; Hartman avoids that pitfall by forgoing the temptation to define and instead juxtaposing brief comments on the Frankfurt School, as well as Hegel, with such (positive) "belief" or "provisional assent" as characterizes "the Anglo-American tradition" [31–2n.]). This "newer kind of hermeneutics," different from the older, affirmative versions perhaps still bearing vestiges of belief in a sacred text, is "disconcerting": it reveals "contradictions and equivocations" where we hoped for simple and direct truth, and it makes "fiction interpretable by making it less readable. The fluency of the reader is affected by a kind of stutter": rather than assured and unequivocal, "the critic's response becomes deliberately hesitant" (32). Think here of Gadamer, and Hartman's position emerges sharply. Acknowledging, even honoring, perplexity, modern hermeneutics is nothing less than a "negative hermeneutics," which "doubts, by a parodistic or playful movement, master theories that claim to have overcome the past, the dead, the false" (239).

Obviously sceptical, "negative hermeneutics" is by no means nihilistic. On the contrary, it is both liberating and conserving, forward-looking in its iconoclasm yet maintaining a connection with "its older function." This newer hermeneutics may be described as "creative criticism," for, in Hartman's words, it "liberates the critical activity from its positive or reviewing function, from its subordination to the thing commented on.... The new philosophic criticism" – another of its names – "has a scope that, though not autotelic, seems to stand in a complex and even crossover relation to both art and philosophy" (CW 191). Negative hermeneutics, which reflects a suspensiveness or hesitancy akin to thoughtfulness itself, appears as conservative in part because, as Hartman indicates, it refuses to be beguiled by "master theories" that would allow us to bury the dead once and for all, to forget the past, or to assume that we can be done with the false. Negative hermeneutics doubts all final solutions, perhaps even any *solution* at all. It is conservative, too, because it keeps a poem *in mind*, rather than resolving it into "available meanings." "This suspensive discourse" Hartman equates with criticism and says that it "can be distinguished from the propaedeutics of scholarly interpretation as well as from the positivity of applied teacherly interpretation" (CW 274). Keeping a text in mind, preserving and saving it, allows it to stand "'in the difficulty of what it is to be'" (quoted CW 32); rather than spiritualize it by converting its differences into meanings, it respects the text's materiality. Deconstruction illustrates this particular "labor of the negative," saving the text through its repeated demonstration that "there is no transparence of the thing to thought. The meaning cannot displace the medium. A text, precisely when authentic, will not," as Hartman puts it, "do away with itself: we never reach the luminous limit where words disappear into their objects like shadows at noon" (EP 194).

The idea of the negative represents, even in this sophisticated and sceptical age, a new orientation, particularly in England and America. The forces of modernity have combined to exacerbate "the mind's natural positivity," and so we are little inclined to honor "negative thinking": *that* smacks of the merely abstract, impractical, unreal – it seems mainly indulgent in its hesitancy and refusal to come down unequivocally on one side rather than another. Rather than work, it is often considered a plaything of the idle disaffected, for today, as Hartman puts it, "thinking is considered work only when 'productive' of some positive, tangible good" (CW 166). What "character," after all, he asks, ironically, "does one show by 'resting,' by entering the castle or garden of poetic indolence?" (UnRW 147). The question Moneta puts to the poet in Keats's *The Fall of Hyperion* Hartman thus asks of the negative thinker: "What benefit canst thou do, or all thy tribe,/ To the great world? Thou art a dreaming thing,/ A fever of thyself...." But negative thinking may do good precisely through its negativity. Being distant and distancing, alienated and alienating, it may prove "productive," almost in spite of itself.

Certainly the negative has much work to do, especially in view of our persistent and easy belief that "a direct contact with life – with things themselves – is always available" (BF 62). Paul de Man figures this as the lust for "the fresh air of referential meaning," which would, we suppose, free us from the closet of introspection and the "prison-house of language." We fear being "abstracted from realities," which is the obverse of our craving for contact.[2]

Our (still-dominant) way of reading reveals the problem. In *Easy Pieces*, Hartman addresses it in the course of discussing deconstruction and the so-called Yale School. As I have argued, his analysis echoes that offered thirty years earlier in *The Unmediated Vision*, thus supporting his claim that, in their desire "to see *through* literary form to the way language or symbolic process makes or breaks meaning" and so "to create a more dialectical and open view of how literature worked," the "Yale critics" were practicing deconstruction long before Derrida arrived with a name for that anti-New Critical effort (190). Regarding our "philosophy of reading," Hartman writes, confronting our separation of art and philosophy, *dichten* and *denken*, "literature" and commentary:

> By dichotomizing art and abstract thought we have developed a method of reading too exclusively phenomenalist in character. To read was to realize: to stress the imagistic or presentational power in words, to put creative language totally on the side of embodiment and vividness. Even if it was understood that some sort of abstract or generalizing effect inhered in figures of speech, the assumption that linked quality of life to qualitative language also favored interpreting that quality as sensuous and organic. (196)

As in *The Unmediated Vision*, Hartman opposes any incarnationist or imagistic poetics, including that of New Criticism, with its promise of presence and immediacy, and looks instead towards an "insistently linguistic rather than iconic" (197) – an aniconic – approach to verbal thinking. Hartman's Hebraism emerges clearly as he joins with Derrida in promoting "the link between word and concept rather than between word and image" (196). "Of the House of Galilee" himself (STT 19), Derrida, as Hartman says, "criticizes as 'logocentric' those who claim to think in words while thinking of words as images – as verbal icons that reflect, however faintly, the Johannine logos or incarnate Word" (196). For Derrida, as for Hartman, to read or write is not to "enhance a faded image or direct referent, and so attach an abstraction (the conceptual word) to its worldly source. Such grounding is just as reductive as the opposite move, the *relève* of scientific thought." Hartman agrees with Derrida, then, in emphasizing "the incurably conceptual force of verbal thinking, and ... identify[ing] that, even in literature, as a force rather than a failing" (197). Having brought together art and abstract thinking, the verbal and the conceptual, Hartman ends "Wild, Fierce Yale" by pointing to the inherence of the latter in the former (and so again of the negative in the affirmative); he insists, in fact, on

> the unreadability of major texts, or a residual and powerful abstractness disclosed in works that have resisted reading time after time, and so produced a more than provisional conflict of interpretations. The classic work of art becomes a classic, i.e. secular, by sustaining itself within and against readerly interpretation. As Wallace Stevens declared in "Notes toward a Supreme Fiction": *It must be abstract*. (198)

Now we understand all the better Hartman's high regard for Paul de Man, whose "reflective and intensely critical" work is rigorously abstract and fundamentally negative. "It does not," Hartman writes, "respond counterassertively to pressures from without, and is not afraid to amount to very little that is positive (or positivistic)" (FR 309). In *Blindness and Insight*, moreover, even though de Man "was without a religious bone in his body," ("BI" 29),[3] Hartman finds "a religious sense of the vanity of human understanding [combined] with a philosophical irony that insists on understanding as the only good" (FR 309).

Ironically enough, in view of the recent disclosures concerning de Man's early anti-Semitism, that "sense of the vanity of human understanding" links him (and deconstruction) not to nihilism but to the Hebraism fundamental to Hartman's thinking. In the relation to the Bible of such negative thinking as characterizes deconstruction we may glimpse more of the positive (though not positivistic) value that lies in the negative. Negative thinking may be, in fact, "good news for modern man" even if of "a somewhat unlikely kind."[4] That at least is the claim of Herbert N. Schneidau in *Sacred Discontent: The Bible and Western Tradition*. As Schneidau demonstrates, the "origin" of negative thinking lies not in Hegel or the Romantics, who, Hegel insisted, had "disclosed an abyss of negative thinking" (CW 151), but in the ancient Hebrews, whom Schneidau depicts as "demythologizers," engaged in a continuous effort to resist the lure held out by their neighbors of a "cosmic continuum" offering comfort and consolation. Before the Hebrews, as Schneidau argues, "the normal mode of knowledge was familiarization;" in the mythological world, knowledge was "immediate, empathetic, proprioceptive, an analogue of familial intimacy." With the prophets, a new and very different way of knowing is born: they know the truth "because Yahweh's message reveals their fellow men in a new light of defamiliarization: a harsh glare in which the prophets, themselves separated from the communal life and the illusions of purpose it cherishes, see men as if they were ants, swarming and scurrying."[5] Defamiliarization results in alienation, and that ensuing sense of alienation, as manifested in the Bible's "unceasing critique of itself," may well constitute that text's major contribution to culture. At any rate, according to Schneidau,

> For this critique a certain cost must be paid: we habitually call this cost "objectivity," but its original name was alienation. This critique was not couched in objective theoretical terms, a mode of discourse unknown to the Hebrews, nor was it arrived at by dispassionate analysis or ratiocination. Rather, it evolved

> from deliberately chosen and painfully intense experience of alienation: as the prophet's sense of Yahweh weighs him down, he sees man as dust, man's strivings as futility, and he feels chosen, set apart, estranged.... He judges his society only by losing his sense of brotherhood with it. He feels isolated.... The prophets look at their culture and see a myth...: they can no longer believe in it, for it is a living lie.[6]

For the Hebrews, their alienation, estrangement, and endless self-criticism – what Schneidau calls "sacred discontent" – is the price paid for understanding. A positive good thus emerges, however, from this Negative Way – but only by means of it.

Revealed, or at least implied, in the negative thinking that Schneidau traces in the Bible are both a process and a "mind-set" or inclination of the heart: the Negative Way, that is, denotes at once a journey or path along which one travels, perhaps to some enlightenment (recall here Odysseus's "journey to understanding" and Siddhartha's, for example), and an outlook or approach to things (for example, "sacred discontent"). Hartman's studies of the Romantics precisely focus on these two different interpretations of the Negative Way;[7] the sense of journey he follows in Wordsworth, that of attitude or perspective in Keats. These reflections on the negative constitute an abiding and deep engagement with large questions of "ordinary" human existence. They also point up a major reason for Hartman's admiration of deconstructive thinking.

So important is the negative to Wordsworth's spiritual struggles and development that Hartman entitles a major section of his 1964 book "The Via Naturaliter Negativa." There he approaches the heart of Wordsworth's poetic labor: Wordsworth thought, writes Hartman, that

> nature itself led him beyond nature; and, since this movement of transcendence, related to what mystics have called the negative way, is inherent in life and achieved without violent or ascetic discipline, one can think of it as the progress of a soul which is *naturaliter negativa*. (33)

What Hartman reveals in Wordsworth's intense and long struggle, particularly as "recollected" in *The Prelude* is, as we observed earlier, the dialectic of nature and imagination, each with its own special and powerful claims. As long as he remains faithful to nature, respecting its guidance, which, toward the end of making his soul more than "a mere pensioner/ Of natural forms" (VI. 937 f), leads him along a *via negativa*, he thinks he cannot lose his way. But the path turns out to be circuitous and mazy and involves false starts, numerous trials, and wrong turns; thus the end, which seemed assured, proves problematical. Wordsworth has to wrestle with the oscillating and demanding forces engaged in the dialectic: when nature or external stimulus is too strong, the poet grows silent; when, on the other hand, imagination takes charge, "an independence from sense-experience" (43) threatens an apocalyptic separation from nature that spells sterility and despair. It takes Wordsworth many years "to realize that nature's 'end' is to lead to something 'without end,' to teach [him] to transcend nature" (44). This Negative Way is a gradual rather than abrupt or violent one, culminating on Mount Snowdon in what amounts to "a divine mockery of the concept of the Single Way" (47). As he composes *The Prelude* in 1804, years after the experience represented, in a style that Hartman calls negative (it is quiet, unpointed, unremarkable, in some ways anticipating "minimalist" art, though his poems "are not yet abstract like that art: they surround familiar thoughts and happenings with an imaginative aura" [EP 179]), Wordsworth finally grasps the identity of his guide along the *via negativa*: "now he sees," Hartman writes, "that it was imagination moving him by means of nature, just as Beatrice guided Dante by means of Virgil. It is not" – and this is a crucial point – "nature as such but nature indistinguishably blended with imagination that compels the poet along his Negative Way" (48). To be sure, the end represents progress, a marked increase in understanding linked to the undoing of previous ones, but Wordsworth achieves no "absolute knowledge" such as Hegel anticipated from the grand march of dialectic; instead, there is the modest but important recognition of "a dizzy openness of relation between the human mind and nature ... to-and-fros ('traffickings') between inner and outer, literal and figurative, or present and past" (66).

When Hartman writes that the narrative weight of *The Prelude* rests on the "difficult process whereby the soul, having overcome itself through nature, must now overcome nature through nature" (WP 221), he identifies the process necessary for "transcendence" that Schneidau also describes. In our freedom, the latter maintains, we secularized (and alienated) moderns, in whom "latent Yahwism" continues to operate, may become aware of our self-deceptions, and "by pressing our self-awareness to its extreme ... become alienated from ourselves." Such "decentering," along with consciousness of "the fictionality of things," is, argues Schneidau, "the precondition of insight."[8] It involves the difficult and negative process of going through: there is no easy path to "transcendence"; the burden of the *via naturaliter negativa* is that the way out is the way in and through. Echoing the Hebraic understanding as Schneidau presents it, Hartman writes: "the self must subvert and be subverted; ... its 'alienation' is the spiritual dynamics which bring us to a higher level of awareness" (FR 300). For Hartman too, there is no escaping the call to dwell patiently "in the space of alienation" (BF 107): "the quest for a true self must go through self-estrangement" (BF 105).

Repeatedly, and in various contexts, Hartman makes the key point: any possible "solutions" result from and emerge only by way of the "problems"; they rise up, often surprisingly, sometimes prankishly, from within the difficulties experienced, rather than drop down from outside. There is no beltway that allows us to bypass those damnable "traffickings." Thus Hartman doubts that the mind "can get beyond formalism without going through the study of forms" (BF 42). Writing about a central concern in Romanticism, he similarly notes those poets' attempts "to draw the antidote to self-consciousness from consciousness itself"; in this regard, Hartman quotes Kleist: "'Paradise is locked ... yet to return to the state of innocence we must eat once more of the tree of knowledge'" (BF 300). In other words, to quote Hegel as Hartman does, "'the hand that inflicts the wound is also the hand that heals it'" (BF 301 and CW 44). Yet another way of making the point is to say that "the consolation must come from the same source as the grief" (WP 302). What Hartman thus teaches, revolves around the negative idea of "an initiation into the divine light via a divine darkness" (BF 136). To invoke the Derridean term that Hartman uses in discussing *Glas*, the Immaculate Conception, and the Crucifixion, there is apparently "a dissemination through which 'spirit' must pass before it can rise or rise again" (STT 78).

In Keats, an aspect of negativity surfaces that suggests the obverse of the transcendence finally achieved by Wordsworth via the Negative Way. I refer to the notion of "negative capability," which Keats more or less "tosses off" in the course of a letter to his brothers in December 1817: "at once it struck me," he writes,

> what quality went to form a Man of Achievement especially in Literature & which Shakespeare possessed so enormously – I mean *Negative Capability*, that is when man is capable of being in uncertainties, Mysteries, doubts, without any irritable reaching after fact & reason – Coleridge, for instance, would let go by a

fine isolated verisimilitude caught from the Penetralium of mystery, from being incapable of remaining content with half knowledge. This pursued through Volumes would perhaps take us no further than this, that with a great poet the sense of Beauty overcomes every other consolation, or rather obliterates all consideration.[9]

What Keats means by this famous phrase may be likened to love that waits faithfully (I think of Garcia Marquez's *Love in the Time of Cholera*), enduring perhaps long separation and lacking complete assurance of "success" yet persevering in hope and anticipation, for the return of its "object." What Keats evidently means also looks forward to the idea of indeterminacy central to deconstruction and rightly emphasized by Hartman. The latter explains indeterminacy, in fact, via reference to "negative capability":

> As a guiding concept, indeterminacy does not merely *delay* the determination of meaning, that is, suspend premature judgments and allow greater thoughtfulness. The delay is not heuristic alone, a device to slow the act of reading till we appreciate (I could think here of Stanley Fish) its complexity. The delay is intrinsic: from a certain point of view, it is thoughtfulness itself, Keats's "negative capability," a labor that aims not to overcome the negative or indeterminate but to stay within it as long as is necessary. (CW 269–70)

Since to stay within the negative for an indeterminate period, as when awaiting the hoped-for but by-no-means-assured return of a long-absent loved one, takes great strength and courage, as well as faith, we should perhaps define this capability, in the context of reading, as "hermeneutic heroism." This Hartman does in *The Fate of Reading*, by way of reference to Hegel. The latter reveals, he writes, "how dependent we moderns are on reflective forms that have replaced the sublimer forces of religious self-consciousness. Hegel makes us face the omnipresence of consciousness and so, in one sense, increases our burden – but it is no longer the 'burden of mystery.'" Hegel does not ask us, Hartman adds, "to shoulder a set of absurdities called history which is mystifyingly explained by another set called religion, but the power of thought in all its modes: from the simple break with sensuous immediacy to the abstractions of science." Hartman then quotes from the Preface to *Phenomenology of Mind* the following passage on "hermeneutic heroism," which he defines as the capacity of the mind "to stay with negative data, with forms so abstract or contrary that no one could plead, 'Verweile doch, du bist so schön'":

> The spirit gains its true identity only by discovering itself in dismemberment. Its power does not come from taking a positive stance that averts its face from everything negative – as when we say of something, this is nonsense, or wrong, and then, finished with it, turn to another matter. The spirit is power only by looking the negative in the face and abiding with it. This abiding (*Verweilen*) is the magic charm (*Zauberkraft*) which converts the negative into Being. (118)

"To Autumn" offers a concrete illustration of the negative power Hegel talks about. Hartman calls it "the most negative capable of all of Keats's great poems" (FR 133). Though his commentary focuses on the poem *qua* poem, it may – to invoke Lukács's point regarding the essay – contain some irony, perhaps even be allegorical; the essay, we recall, is for Lukács inherently ironical, the irony consisting

> in the critic always speaking about the ultimate problems of life, but in a tone which implies that he is only discussing pictures and books, only the inessential and pretty ornaments of real life – and even then not their innermost substance but only their beautiful and useless surface.[10]

At any rate, Hartman's account of "To Autumn," echoing some key Derridean notions, strikes chords resonant with other, different, and broader contexts: "Even [the] so-called death-stanza," he writes, referring to the third and last,

> expresses no rush toward death, no clasping of darkness as a bride, or quasi-oriental ecstasy. Its word-consciousness, its mind's weather – all remains Hesperian. As its verses move toward an image of southerly flight (the poem's nearest analogue to transcendence), patterns emerge that delay the poet's "transport to summer." Perception dwells on the border and refuses to overdefine.... The proportion of northern words increases perceptibly as if to pull the poem back from its southerly orientation. There is hardly a romance language phrase.... "To Autumn" remains a poem "in the northwind sung." Its progress is merely that of repetitions "in a finer tone," of "widening speculation," of "treble soft surmise." Yet in its Hesperian reach it does not give up but joins a south to itself. (FR 133–4)

The capability that "To Autumn" embodies doesn't come easily or naturally. It takes *work* – the work of cultivating before we reach the harvesting that poem celebrates – for it is difficult to give up our "irritable reaching after fact and reason." Patience is called for, not only to remain in the Negative Way despite the strongest contrary pressures but also to keep from converting the negative into "a positivistic and dogmatic instrument" (CW 32). *That* is a powerful temptation, all the more so because we make such conversions unawares, believing ourselves faithful to the negative even as we slide towards the comfort and security of hope realized (if only in our dreams). Required, then, is not only patience but also a tolerance of ambiguity and indeterminacy, an ability to accept a state of being perpetually unsettled, a willingness *not to know*. Not only must we work to overcome "a nervous jumping to conclusions," but we must also strive to forgo "a vampiristic assumption of intimacy with the thoughts and feelings of others" (EP 182). Such achievements define "negative capability."

Through a series of related essays reprinted in *Beyond Formalism*, Hartman elaborates on the qualities that constitute negative thinking as well as its necessity. Essentially, these essays – "The Heroics of Realism," "Virginia's Web," "Camus and Malraux: The Common Ground," and "Maurice Blanchot: Philosopher-Novelist" – confront what Hartman elsewhere describes as perhaps *the* problem with modernity. Contrary to what we non-deconstructionists ordinarily suppose, Hartman argues, the problem is not an absence of meaning, for "meaning is everywhere"; it is, therefore, "that of fullness rather than emptiness, of redundancy and insignificant signification" (BF 353). "The Heroics of Realism" addresses this situation by focusing, even more sharply than the other essays mentioned, on that easy belief I noted earlier: the logocentric, phonocentric assumption that "a direct contact with life – with things themselves is always available" (BF 62). Against that "dogmatic factor in realism" (BF 62), Hartman ranges the defamiliarizing efforts of Woolf, Camus, Malraux, Blanchot, James, and Jane Austen. In such writers, argues Hartman, "art retains its power of making room for the strange, the different, and even the divine. It is the familiar world that must now be saved – from familiarity" (BF 75). Literature has several means of achieving this (negative) effect, one of them being impersonal narration. Hartman's further reflections carry him from such specific formal and technical concerns to large questions of human relations. At the heart of the problem of realism, he argues, lies our "rage for intimacy," which subsumes so many of our efforts. "The author," he writes, "staying within realism,"

> must keep from too easy an intimacy with creation. The body of the world, the body of other persons, is a strange fact; their thoughts are a mystery; every relation includes shock and unveilings. The impersonal mode is clearly an effort at distance, one of many. It is an effort to hold back – by placing true imaginative obstacles before – the leveling and inquisitive mind. James obstacles himself; he refuses simply to know. Every mind tends to be viewed through another, and the desire to know positively (and can even the artist escape it?) is always presented as a vampirish act. A great novel does not breed familiarity; a bad novel is simply one that betrays the mystery, rapes the past, and lets us possess too quickly another person or mind. (BF 70)

In Austen's novels, Hartman finds a "proper" realism, which honors restraint and manifests respect for the thoughts, feelings, and person of the other. He centers his commentary on the late novel *Persuasion*, in which, as he says, "two estranged lovers meet accidentally after many years, and we never doubt that their reconciliation will occur, any more than that Odysseus will return home" (63–4). The drama lies in the negotiation of respect, which inevitably involves time and the (difficult) ability to abide it. The lovers, in Austen's novel, are for some time kept apart "in tense separation and have to navigate social barriers and serious obstacles of self-esteem before they reach a new mutual accord. To collapse the space of separation too soon," observes Hartman, "would be to collapse the novel, to sin at once against art, society, and some deeper sense of the necessity of a slow redemption, of having to buy back what is estranged or wasted." Hartman applauds Austen's "honesty": "So deeply does she make us perceive the gulf that might have been between the lovers; so careful is she to respect a reality of time which love might not have overcome" (64).

Especially today, Hartman believes, "when sympathies are socialized and spread so wide as to become abstract," and the human "is often a fog of intimacy hiding the generous difference" (67), we need Austen's kind of restraint, her "negative capability," which reflects a human-heartedness generous in its respect for solitude and distance: to respect the solitude in man, writes Hartman, "is to create the very space of communion" (87). The latter, in other words, doesn't come quick or easy, no matter the vanity of human wishes; communion emerges only via the (negative) path of initial separation, distance, and respect of otherness. Instead, therefore, of indulging, and fueling, "the rage for intimacy" and its confrere, the quest of quick and easy communion, the writer today – the critical essayist as well as novelist – "must somehow manage to go from intimacy ... to that natural estrangement which is Jane Austen's donnée" (64). I adduce now Hartman's further "critique of communion" offered in "Camus and Malraux: The Common Ground," which, typically, shuttles between a specific "technical" consideration and large theoretical and human questions:

> To gain the world truly, one must first learn the measure of one's distance from it; and the dehumanization of art, noticed by Ortega y Gasset, is a general symptom of this necessary recreation of distance. Ortega's highest praise was to say, as of Proust, that he invented a new discrepancy between reality and ourselves. Dehumanization, however, is the wrong word. In the abeyance of self-justifying conventions, which limit the contact of persons and encourage a language intrinsically veiled, the artist makes room in the "all too human" for a necessary angel (sometimes, a necessary devil):
>
>> I am the necessary angel of earth
>> Since, in my sight, you see the earth again,
>> Cleared of its stiff and stubborn, man-locked set.
>> *Wallace Stevens*
>
> This humanistic attack on the anthropomorphic ("man-locked") intelligence fosters techniques of perception which are dissociative rather than associative in nature. They do not make the strange familiar but estrange the familiar. One such technique (there are a great many) is Faulkner's and Robbe-Grillet's use of the "estranged consciousness." Even where it depicts an abnormal state of mind it does so by projecting reality as irreducibly, troublingly, *other*. Consciousness, for these writers, is little more than a rape, a wrong or premature intimacy. It is a moral labor to reach the innocence of things or realize their independence *vis-à-vis* ourselves. Our narcissism is endless and essential, and only by various methods of dissociation that disrupt ordinary perception can we get beyond the self to a sense of the other. (66)

A close relative of "the rage for intimacy," stemming no doubt from an indulged narcissism, is haste that cannot abide such restraint as Austen adumbrates. As Hartman shows, particularly in a series of essays this time reprinted in *The Fate of Reading*, haste figures in all our activities – and certainly infects hope: whether political or spiritual, claims Hartman elsewhere, hope "contains haste, in the form of a deep hate of medial time" (BF 159). This point he makes repeatedly, as a matter of fact, drawing out important implications (as we saw earlier, Hartman joins Benjamin in placing "hope in the past"). In an essay on Valéry's "Fable of the Bee," having claimed that "in poetry the point remains virtual and generates the poem itself as a 'prolonged hesitation' between sound and sense, or formal and referential values," Hartman proceeds to argue that the poetics of "L'Abeille" "is directed not against imaginative desire but against something far more haste-ridden and literal – which, in fact, was threatening to annul that desire. The sting in real life," he prankishly adds, intertextually linking Valéry to Wordsworth, who similarly animadverted against *his* age's degrading thirst after "outrageous stimulation," "is a massive need for intoxicants, raising perpetually the threshold of stimulation, and so shortening, and perhaps injuring, the very *durée* of thought." Hartman then quotes from Valéry's too-little-known "Le Bilan de l'Intelligence" this powerful indictment of the modern sin against time and distance:

> As for the most central of our senses, our inner sense of the interval between desire and possession, which is no other than the sense of duration, that feeling of time which was formerly satisfied by the speed of horses, now finds that the fastest trains are too slow, and we fret with impatience between telegrams. We crave events like food that can never be highly seasoned enough. If every morning there is no great disaster in the world we feel a certain emptiness: "There is nothing in the papers today," we say. We are caught red-handed. We are poisoned. So I have grounds for saying that there is such a thing as our being intoxicated by energy, just as we are intoxicated by haste, or by size.... We are losing that essential peace in the depths of our being, that priceless absence in which the most delicate elements of life are refreshed and comfortable, while the inner creature is in some way cleansed of past and future, of present awareness, of obligations pending and expectation lying in wait.[11] (246–7)

For Hartman, whose reflections on time are equally rich, even if they occur – ironically – as interpretations of texts from Marvell to Malraux and from Wordsworth to Heidegger, the humanities offer us moderns the best chance of recouping those losses incurred by speed and haste. Especially in *Criticism in the Wilderness* and *Easy Pieces*, Hartman not only bears witness to the power of the humanities, but he also openly addresses their irreducible function in a world dreaming of communication, craving intimacy, and lusting for meaning. For Hartman, like Valéry as well as Wordsworth and also Benjamin, the issue is about time: as he insists in *Beyond Formalism*, the mind must be "given enough natural time in which to reflect" (293); it cannot "know or resolve itself except by a temporal run" (20). This idea of a "temporal run" is an analogue of, or maybe just another name for, the *via negativa*: there is simply a "*durée* of thought," perhaps a natural process that cannot be foreshortened or avoided except at our peril; it has to be *gone through*. This Valéry calls "the sense of duration," that "interval between desire and possession." Hartman calls it "due process" and rests his defense of the humanities on the way they encourage us to take our time. A split thus develops between the humanities and "the world in which speed is encouraged" (EP 175). Though they lack *positive* force in that world, the humanities are what keep us functioning. They are, Hartman writes, "always in 'slow motion' compared to the sciences or to the immediate demands of the practical world" (EP 176). Their calendar, "like the religious calendar, though not confined to fixed dates, allows the store of experience to come before us once again, as we incline – fast and forgetful – into the future. Here and there contact is made between these calendars or wheels moving at different speeds; and the meshing that occurs," Hartman adds, "which can be very powerful indeed, not only at the point of contact but as it provides a design for mutual and coordinated work, is what we call experience." The humanities are, then, "the slowly moving wheel that allows us to connect with past traditions at different points in our precipitous careers." They also "sustain the contemplative life in us" (EP 177). They are what Walter Benjamin treats and dramatizes in such essays as "The Storyteller," "On Some Motifs in Baudelaire," and "The Work of Art in the Age of Mechanical Reproduction."

Responding directly to the question what the humanities can offer a society "in which 'communication' is the operative ideal," Hartman focuses on the "delay time" they encourage; they provide, he writes, "mainly doubt and delay, but a methodical doubt (like that of Descartes) and a testing kind of delay." Elaborating, he links "delay time" to "negative capability" as well as to an understanding of how words operate (i.e., *against* "the dream of communication"), present in his own work as early as *The Unmediated Vision*: Keats, he begins,

> coined the term "negative capability," meaning by it the opposite of a nervous jumping to conclusions or a vampiristic assumption of intimacy with the thoughts and feelings of others. The study of literature is a help in avoiding such abuses because words, as the most intimate and ready means of communication we have, are most likely to be abused by impatience and vampirism. When we realize that words are never simply promissory notes, that they are never straightforwardly referential, that they are mediating rather than immediate and therefore cannot be evaluated without a constant awareness of their verbal and situational contexts, then we marvel that they signify at all and that the "delay time" required for their proper understanding does not extend into infinity. (EP 182–3)

Hartman ends *Criticism in the Wilderness* with a description of humanistic work that brings together many of the strands we have been following. Though I have referred to it before, I will quote it here. Humanists, he writes, "bring their own set of qualities to every task."

> They will not easily sacrifice anything to anything else: they take their time, and ponder – often elaborately – whether a new step does not entail an exclusion rather than an advantageous change or transformation. So the inspiring teacher in the humanities will always be pointing to something neglected by the dominant point of view, or something blunted by familiarity, or despised by fashion and social pressure. He is incurably a redeemer – not in the highflying sense but in the spirit-embedding sense. His active life is spent in uncovering and preserving traces of the contemplative life – those symbols and inscriptions – buried in layers of change. Like Wordsworth's poet, the humanist recalls forgotten voices, arguments, artifacts, "things silently gone out of mind and things violently destroyed." He *reinscribes* us, to use a current expression; and the expression is good, because life in culture is a palimpsest that can only be deciphered by a species of "thick description." It is a mistake to think of the humanist as spiritualizing anything: on the contrary, he materializes us, he makes us aware of the

material culture (including texts) in which everyone has always lived. Only the passage of time spiritualizes, that is, volatilizes and deracinates; we are in transition; our life remains a feast of mortuary riddles and jokes that must be answered. In the shape of that answer everyone participates who takes time to think about time. (300–1)

To an extent, of course, Hartman is describing himself here: he too is engaged in redemptive work, preserving, calling voices out of silence, textualizing and materializing us, responding to "a feast of mortuary riddles and jokes," wandering in the wilderness, in no apparent hurry to reach a definite point, conscious of time and respectful of it. Engaged in negative thinking, he refuses to travel one-way streets. He writes essays rather than articles. Like Heidegger, he "does not worry about 'correct' readings," for he understands that "the only error (since the condition of language at present is itself error) consists in closing the circle of understanding prematurely – foreclosing it – and so evading the intimate otherness of a text linked to the intimate otherness of Being itself" (CW 168).

"What to do with *time*" remains the issue (CW 165). In "The Work of Reading," Hartman reflects on the relation of reading to time, of reading with watching, as he laments its current situation. Rather like writing, which, he says, "has become in most Western countries a mixture of entertainment, confession, symbolic protest, and the endless retailing of accumulated knowledge," thus lacking the necessary "critical and dangerous factors," reading now seems "arbitrary, opinionated, and spotty, rather than interpretive and authenticating" (165). For an alternative, Hartman returns to Plato, who is at once essayistic and negative, knowing what to do with time. The goal is a "maieutic rather than evangelical and news-oriented understanding of reading," and the Socratic dialogues, writes Hartman,

cannot be reduced to a pedagogically accommodated instruction or to a remystifying of knowledge directed against the Sophists' claim that knowledge is merely know-how and should be marketed as a commodity. The dramatic and ironic quality of the Socratic dialogues, removed from the pressure of the great tragedies and their driving stichomythia, conveys a peculiarly satisfying sense of our relation to time. Socrates needs time to "deliver" the truth. So do we; his rhythm is our rhythm. It is this matter of the relation of thought to time and language – and of the relation of time and language to each other – that also preoccupies Heidegger, Wittgenstein, and Derrida. (166)

And Hartman, I would add. His essays, like the Socratic dialogues, exploratory, exposing wrong turns and quack responses, thus engaged in a clearing of the ground, and therefore negative, are also like Wordsworth's poems, unpointed, perhaps plotless, even – in a sense – unremarkable: they do not sting. As such, they too convey "a peculiarly satisfying sense of our relation to time."

Like Emerson, the "giant" (essayist), whom, he insists, we must think through, allowing him "to invade our prose" (CW 19), Hartman knows that "the moral difficulty" we all face, not merely in our reading, lies "in being patient (on ice) while waiting for the promised end" (CW 185). Waiting, and the watching that should accompany it, are negative work, and Hartman, the Wandering Jew, regards them as "a religious duty as well as a symptom of alienated labor" (CW 130).

The cat being out of the bag, what more needs to be said?

Appendix I

Though small, the body of poetry Hartman has produced is hardly negligible. In addition to individual poems in various periodicals, he has published *Akiba's Children* (the reference is to Rabbi Akiba, who lived between 50 and 135 and greatly influenced, if he did not determine, the future of rabbinical interpretation).[1]

It should come as no surprise that Hartman's poetry is highly intertextual, intense, brooding, allusive, and Hebraic in subject matter and perspective, notably including a deep suspicion of visual images and the tyranny of the eye that stems at least from the time of *The Unmediated Vision*. "The Silence," for example, marks "a hell of helplessness before the image," though hope returns, albeit problematically, in questions that can still be asked.[2] The poem raises the possibility that hope for survival resides in the revival of the word, which allows us not so much to see as to think, question, and write. So wary is Hartman of the visual image that he works towards its subversion. Such an effort characterizes "Aubade," appropriately enough the opening poem in *Akiba's Children* and one in which the intellectual and the playful, the intertextual and even the prankish, coexist. Indeterminacy clothes the figure of the cock, itself rich in tradition, of course, literary and otherwise, and the reader must bear the various conventions in mind. But it is impossible to say exactly what the cock represents here. It is obviously many things, some religious, some bawdy, but it is not an image. Perhaps it is best thought of as a process reflecting the multivalence of both language and experience.

> The cock wakes the dawn
> Scarlet as the coxcomb on its head:
> But I wake the voice of the cock
> In the barn of the dead.

> Swiftly the rooster congregations
> Laud with great gorge the soul's repair
> Pecking at seeds of prayer
> Like small ships pitching at anchor.
>
> The whole sky crows with satisfaction,
> Its nether-wing uncovers Abraham,
> That early riser, with two cocks:
> The kindled ears of man.[3]

The first stanza here perhaps inevitably suggests the relation of commentator to poet: if the latter responds to nature's call, the former awakens later that responsive voice otherwise silent "in the barn of the dead."

The last poem in the collection, "In Honor of the Master of the Good Name," collects many of the themes treated in other poems, including writing, interpretation, and aspects of the Jewish imagination, and richly elaborates on them. It does so in a way that is at once intellectual (and scholarly) and playful. The "Master of the Good Name," Israel ben Eliezer, or Bal Shem Tov, ignited the movement known as Hasidism, a kind of mysticism that, at least according to Martin Buber, founds redemption in the "here and now."[4] (Might that be a parallel to Wordsworth?) In this poem, the "speaking voice" begins with what has already begun, that interminable web of language and texts that we can only enter. The issue, we might say, is, as always, the word, pregnant with possibility, which we strive to hear and understand through the rich text(ile) it weaves. I quote the last two verse paragraphs:

> But as Beginning capsized into End
> A voice in the navel-dark an alphabet
> Lit, a beam of day more trenchant than
> Sinai's gimlet hole; my lips threaded light,
> Hemmed hope, stuttered and stitched until
> Errands of space appeared, looser darks
> Moving to the memory of dawn:
> Then in one crowing the master womb
> Ousted the contour of a master cry
> Voided the great blackness a breath-breadth

Voiced it as vowels a wind, and I heard:
OUT OF MY FULNESS have I flung your name.
Take that mercy-space, O fighter of God
Made of your name: I have leeched myself smaller
Exiled my strength for your name's sake,
Hastened the beginning, goaded the day of the world.
Sound the abyss, make visible the void
Leaping toward me, the mark spirits breathe,
Ayin or Aleph bellow it upwards.
Behold the BESHT: his strength is in the word
Between the word, and he eats his tongue like grass.

What lies "in the word/ Between the word," as between reading and writing perhaps, provides sustenance and gives strength. It is not a positive or absolute knowledge, there being only "a textual infinite, an interminable web of texts or interpretations." Note, by the way, that in the first verse paragraph I quoted, the first letter of the lines literally spells out the name Bal Shem Tov, the "Master of the Good Name," whereas the last verse paragraph repeats that procedure in reverse order, adding a significant extra line at the end (or is it the beginning?). The cat at pranks.

Appendix II

Anyone knowledgeable of Hartman who reads Martin Jay's impressive monograph introducing the work of Theodor Adorno must be struck by the analogues among Adorno's writing, that of Hartman, deconstruction, and Judaism. As to the last, although Adorno was only half-Jewish by birth, after Auschwitz especially he "came to acknowledge the true ramifications of his Jewish heritage" ("To write poetry after Auschwitz is barbaric," he insisted). According to Jay, "the major lesson Adorno drew from the Holocaust was ... the link between anti-Semitism and totalistic thinking. The Jew, he now came to understand, was the most stubborn repository of that otherness, difference and non-identity which twentieth-century totalitarianism had sought to liquidate." Moreover, like his collaborator in the Frankfurt School, Max Horkheimer, Adorno "justified his refusal to spell out the utopian alternative to present-day society by reference to the Jewish prohibition on picturing God or paradise."[1]

For such reasons, Jay finds that Judaism constitutes one of the stars in the "constellation" of ideas characterizing Adorno's thought, another of which is deconstruction. Indeed, Terry Eagleton has remarked,

> The parallels between deconstruction and Adorno are particularly striking. Long before the current fashion, Adorno was insisting on the power of those heterogeneous fragments that slip through the conceptual net, rejecting all philosophy of identity, refusing class consciousness as objectionably "positive," and denying the intentionability of signification. Indeed, there is hardly a theme in contemporary deconstruction that is not richly elaborated in his work.[2]

Adorno's fundamental emphasis on non-identity and difference, no doubt affected by if not actually deriving from his Jewish heritage, solidifies the link with deconstruction, and I shall return to it directly. For now I restrict myself to a parallel that at once recalls Derrida's basic point, which I cited above, and Hartman's analogue to it. In *Negative Dialectics*, Adorno asserts that "it is not the purpose of critical thought to place the object on the orphaned royal throne once occupied by the subject. On that throne the object would be nothing but an idol. The purpose of critical thought is to abolish the hierarchy."[3] Crucial points, these, and they are now frequently termed Derridean.

As with Hartman, "it is impossible to understand Adorno's ideas," claims Gillian Rose, in a book on Adorno entitled *The Melancholy Science*, without understanding the ways in which he presents them, that is, his style, and without understanding the reasons for his preoccupation with style."[4] Even though Adorno's writing is notoriously difficult, his work was, as Jay has written, "essentially essayistic in spirit," its form open and experimental, reflecting the anti-system that, in his own terms, constituted his program.[5] Adorno wrote on the essay in "The Essay as Form," not available in English until 1984; it is a major reflection, rivaling Lukács's "On the Nature and Form of the Essay," to which it acts as a counterstatement.[6] Whether or not his various kinds of writing – on politics, music, literature, linguistic questions – can justly be called anti-texts, they tend to be fragmentary in nature, and they are written, as Rose notes, in a variety of styles. In general, however, Adorno's style, almost always demanding, is "paratactic, anti-systematic, non-cumulative," untotalizing and apparently – but only apparently – shapeless.[7] Parataxis is, in fact, crucial to Adorno's project, his *Aesthetic Theory* being written "concentrically, in equally weighted, paratactic parts which are ordered around a middle point which is expressed by the constellation of the parts." As to why he wrote in this manner, Adorno once explained that

> from my theorem that there are no philosophical first principles, it follows that one cannot construct a continuous argument with the usual stages, but one must assemble the whole from a series of partial complexes ... whose constellation not [logical] sequence produces the idea.[8]

If this stylistic feature suggests an analogy with Hartman, Adorno's preference for chiasmus makes that similarity seem all the greater. Indeed, as Gillian Rose has remarked, in place of the norms of usual philosophical argumentation Adorno substitutes the figure of chiasmus, which functions in his work as somewhere between trope and argument. This interest in style, if not the particular features of his own writing, suggests that for Adorno, as for Hartman, "much of his critical writing aspired to the level of art." Like Hartman, too, whether thinking of his own work or that of others, Adorno "called into question the very boundary between criticism and creation, without, however, ever effacing it entirely."[9]

Again like Hartman, Adorno was simply haunted by questions of style. In Rose's words, Adorno

> discussed his method and style in everything he wrote, often at the expense of discussing the ostensible subject of the piece.... His articles on literature are largely concerned with language and style.... Every initial essay on another's work emphasizes the relation between thought and its presentation.... Almost every page of these works includes a self-conscious reference to method and style.[10]

Consider, moreover, "The Essay as Form." Adorno agrees with Lukács that the essay is a "modest" form, the form, in fact, "best suited to a philosophy which has renounced the philosophical system." Opposing Descartes's rules in *Discourse on Method*, Adorno considers the essays of Lukács, Benjamin, and others, intent on "prescribing how the essay should be constructed and how it should function." As Rose finely observes, "Adorno starts from the assumption of a split and antagonistic reality which cannot be adequately represented by any system which makes its goals unity and simplicity or clarity." In the face of such a system comes the essay, which "thinks in breaks because reality is brittle and finds its unity through the breaks, not by smoothing them over." Leading towards a philosophy of culture, the essay is, for Adorno, the "critical form *par excellence*."[11]

For reasons already apparent, especially in his foregoing comments on style, Adorno asserted that "the whole is the false." Opposed to any totalizing, stylistic, cultural, or political, an opposition no doubt stemming at least in part from his Jewish heritage, Adorno insisted on *critical* reflection, believing that "open thinking points beyond itself" rather than comes to rest in any system or blindly commits itself to any single course of action. Indeed, fearing "premature unification," as Martin Jay puts it, "Adorno insisted on the ideological dangers of overcoming in thought what was still split in reality."[12] Adorno felt, in fact, what can only be described as "the tyranny of identity," which in the "administered" world of bourgeois life, threatens the collapse of all difference and the effacement of otherness, precisely the impetus behind the Holocaust, of course. Recalling Hartman's insistence, borrowed from Wordsworth, on "mutual domination" and "interchangeable supremacy," Adorno, in Jay's words, worked towards "a dialectic of mutually supportive non-identity."[13] Instead, then, of "the recovery of a perfect wholeness or original plentitude," Adorno, proto-deconstructively, sought "the restoration of difference and non-identity to their proper place in the non-hierarchical constellation of subjective and objective forces he called peace." Again recalling Hartman's Wordsworthian understanding, "rather than giving priority to one or the other, a negative dialectics played off nature against history or society and vice versa chiasmically."[14]

Among the many reasons Adorno set such a high store by art is, not just its insights concerning the plight of the modern subject, but also its inherently critical power, as well as the fact that "in art, unlike more theoretical activities, conceptual domination of the natural world was checked by sensuous receptivity."[15] By no means conceived of as a simple mirroring, art figured for Adorno as "the most likely repository of negation in the administered world," possessing, indeed, a "genuinely emancipatory potential."[16] Entailing theoretical reflection, aesthetic experience could release such potential, Adorno came to believe, more powerfully than politics. In place of "that domination of nature so basic to the dialectic of enlightenment" might be "an essentially aesthetic relationship between man and the natural world," a conclusion shared by Malraux as Hartman describes it in his 1960 monograph.[17]

Because of such a position, and because his real interests lay in culture, society, and the human psyche, Adorno has not infrequently been labeled an "apolitical aesthete," not unlike Hartman, a charge that the former roundly rejected just as the latter would. Still, Adorno clearly chose aesthetics over politics, defending "only those modernisms that withdrew from direct political or social commitment." But though many have spotted a "political deficit" in his theory, it must be granted that even Adorno's choice of aesthetics was deeply political, for he held that "genuine art contained a utopian moment that pointed to a future political and social transformation."[18] According to Adorno, in the essay "Lyric Poetry and Society," sounding a theme prominent in Hartman as well and in fact anticipating the latter's close to *Criticism in the Wilderness*:

APPENDIX II

> We must be especially wary of the present, insufferable tendency to drag out at every slightest opportunity the concept of ideology. For ideology is untruth – false consciousness, a lie. It manifests itself in the failure of art works, in their own intrinsic falsehood, and can be uncovered by criticism.... The greatness of works of art lies solely in their power to let those things be heard which ideology conceals.[19]

This wariness and restlessly critical spirit, whether or not partly attributable to Adorno's Jewish heritage, bears, like his highly charged sense of art's cultural and social mission, significant analogy to the work of Hartman. I think Adorno could endorse Hartman's critical position that "the one-dimensional progressive claims of conqueror or would-be conqueror are disabled by hermeneutic reflection."

Notes

1 READING HARDMAN

1 Daniel T. O'Hara, *The Romance of Interpretation: Visionary Criticism from Pater to de Man* (New York: Columbia University Press, 1985), p. 114.
2 The Hartmanian mode of criticism differs from a plainstyle, relatively unphilosophical and often uncompromisingly social criticism – the American way of Edmund Wilson, Alfred Kazin, and Irving Howe, for example, and the British way inaugurated by Matthew Arnold. Hartman has thus been roundly criticized by those who find in such features of his work as I have described in this chapter a confusion of creative and critical writing, a pretentious style, over-abstractness or over-intellectualized instead of humanistic concerns, and so on. Among the complaints, see Eugene Goodheart, *The Skeptic Disposition in Contemporary Criticism* (Princeton: Princeton University Press, 1984). See also Christopher Norris, *Deconstruction: Theory and Practice* (London: Methuen, 1982).
3 Martin Jay, *Adorno* (Cambridge, Mass.: Harvard University Press, 1984), p. 15.
4 Hartman gives Anatole France's definition of the critic in *Criticism in the Wilderness*, p. 11. On the inseparability of reading and thinking in Hartman, see Donald G. Marshall's Foreword ("Wordsworth and Post-Enlightenment Culture") to *The Unremarkable Wordsworth*, pp. vii–xxiii.
5 Virginia Woolf, *A Room of One's Own* (New York: Harcourt, Brace, 1929), p. 84.
6 Georg Lukács, *Soul and Form*, trans. Anna Bostock (Cambridge, Mass.: MIT Press, 1974), p. 9.
7 Helen Vendler, "Critical Models," *New Yorker*, 58 (3 May 1982), 158.
8 Vendler, p. 161.
9 Vendler, p. 158.
10 Vendler, p. 158.
11 Vendler, p. 158.
12 George Steiner, "The Archives of Eden."
13 Deconstructing without a license, Cynthia Ozick reads Steiner's either/or as a both/and, suggesting his "hope for having it both ways": "to have an 'authentic culture' with a 'fabric of high literacy' not only flourishing in a context of morality, responsibility, and answerability, but actually

determining and stimulating these" (*Metaphor and Memory* [New York: Knopf, 1989], p. 75).
14 Vendler, p. 161.

2 A MATTER OF RELATION: A QUESTION OF PLACE

1 Jonathan Swift, *The Battle of the Books*, in *Gulliver's Travels and Other Writings*, ed. Louis A. Landa (Boston: Houghton Mifflin, 1960), pp. 366–7.
2 See *Reading Deconstruction/Deconstructive Reading* (Lexington: University Press of Kentucky, 1983), esp. pp. 49–57. This paragraph, in fact, repeats, with some significant modification, points made there.
3 See Sarah Lawall, *Critics of Consciousness: The Existential Structures of Literature* (Cambridge, Mass.: Harvard University Press, 1968).
4 For de Man's "Semiology and Rhetoric," see *Allegories of Reading: Figural Language in Rousseau, Nietzsche, Rilke, and Proust* (New Haven: Yale University Press, 1979), pp. 3–19.
5 Hartman quotes here Barbara Herrnstein Smith, *Poetic Closure: A Study of How Poems End* (Chicago: University of Chicago Press, 1968), p. 250.
6 *Deconstruction and Criticism*, by Bloom *et al.* (New York: Continuum–Seabury Press, 1979), p. ix.
7 *Deconstruction and Criticism*, p. vii.
8 *Deconstruction and Criticism*, p. viii.
9 At one point in *Criticism in the Wilderness*, Hartman notes "the direction in which I would have to revise my discussion of 'Pure Representation' in *The Unmediated Vision*" (p. 112n.).
10 Paul H. Fry, *The Reach of Criticism: Method and Perception in Literary Theory* (New Haven: Yale University Press, 1983), p. 200.
11 Hartman enigmatically dedicates *Saving the Text* to "the Subject."
12 *Deconstruction and Criticism*, p. 195.
13 de Man, Foreword, *The Dissimulating Harmony: The Image of Interpretation in Nietzsche, Rilke, Artaud, and Benjamin*, by Carol Jacobs (Baltimore: Johns Hopkins University Press, 1978), pp. ix–x. Of course, in 1954, Hartman regards the poem's "betrayal" as indicative of Wordsworth's *poetic* failure rather than an inevitable consequence of the power of language and texts to wreak havoc with intention, no matter how accomplished the writer.
14 Derrida, *Of Grammatology*, trans. Gayatri Chakravorty Spivak (Baltimore: Johns Hopkins University Press, 1976), p. 62.
15 "Words, Wish, Worth: Wordsworth," in *Deconstruction and Criticism*, p. 209. See also pp. 210, 211.
16 Cynthia Ozick, *Metaphor and Memory* (New York: Knopf, 1989), pp. 276, 277.
17 However unconsciously and presciently deconstructive in attitude, aim, and strategy, Hartman appears to remain, at least through 1975, caught in the web of logocentrism that Derrida everywhere confronts and challenges. In the important title chapter of *The Fate of Reading*, which I shall return to in a later chapter, Hartman displays "the standard logocentric 'symptoms'... hierarchical thinking, nostalgia, and an insistence on original authority" (Brigitte Sandquist, in an unpublished paper, "Geoffrey Hartman and Logos-(epi)-centrism," p. 2; I am much indebted to

this fine analysis). In fact, privileged hierarchies appear throughout "The Fate of Reading," most strikingly perhaps in the assumptions shared with Milton that books are infused with the "life-blood of a master-spirit" (247). Hierarchization grounds, as a matter of fact, the sexism that permeates the essay: consider the unchecked use of the third-person masculine pronoun, the unfortunate claim that reading is "like girl-watching, a simple expense of spirit," and the comparison of the critic to a cricket; only *male* crickets, of course, produce the at-once charming and damnable chirping characteristic of crickets: Hartman's audience, thus, "must be master-cricket-critics, not mistress/would-be critics" (Sandquist 4). Hartman's (logocentric) nostalgia for an earlier, greater past is hardly less pervasive; it appears in his elevation of reading "old-style" and his call for a "re-nascence of wonder," this latter menaced by modern critics who have converted expression into "generative codes needing operators rather than readers," including by deconstructionists for whom the Word, once "spermatic and vernal," becomes "the mode for an anti-renaissance, a de-nascence of wonder" (252). As to the matter of an origin-al authority, consider Hartman's claim that "though a text is discontinuously woven of many strands or codes, there is magic in the web. The sense of an informing spirit, however limited or conditioned, or outwitting those limits and conditions, is what holds us" (254).

And yet Hartman appears "aware that he holds these views in a world affected by deconstructionism. He writes self-consciously and self-critically" (Sandquist 6). It may be, as Brigitte Sandquist perceptively argues, not only that Hartman's logocentrism represents a commitment to the Logos but also that his Logos-centrism is "epi"-centric, suggesting a horizon on which issues are played out while displaying an ultimate return to the center. In Sandquist's words:

> Hartman's notion of the will and literary authority is not centered or closed. Instead, it is "epi-centered": existing on a receding horizon away from the center but constantly reflecting or referring back to an (absent) center – the Logos. Perhaps we can understand Hartman's Logos-(epi)-centrism as the position of a Romantic practicing the "minor mode of prophecy called literary criticism" and living in a post-structuralist world. He realizes that the Romantic view of the author is like the Garden of Eden ("In the beginning..."). We cannot return to the Garden, just as we cannot expect the full presence of the Logos, but we can try to recapture it and approximate it here on earth with the power of words as logos. "He mourns a fading gift, but he mourns it on a golden footstool made of its radiant words." (15)

The uneasy combination of deconstructive aims and strategies and stubborn logocentrism points up Hartman's unsystematic thinking, everywhere marked by just such impurity.

3 THE WANDERING JEW

1 See, for example, Edmond Jabès, *The Book of Questions*, trans. Rosemarie Waldrop (Middletown, Conn.: Wesleyan University Press, 1976);

Emmanuel Levinas, *Quatres Lectures Talmudiques* (Paris: Editions de Minuit, 1968), and "To Love the Torah More than God," trans. Helen A. Stephenson and Richard I. Sugarman, *Judaism* 28 (1979): 216–23; José Faur, *Golden Doves with Silver Dots: Semiotics and Textuality in Rabbinic Interpretation* (Bloomington: Indiana University Press, 1986); Susan A. Handelman, *The Slayers of Moses: The Emergence of Rabbinic Interpretation in Modern Literary Theory* (Albany: State University of New York Press, 1982); and Herbert N. Schneidau, *Sacred Discontent: The Bible and Western Tradition* (Baton Rouge: Louisiana State University Press, 1976).

2 Hartman says his remarks "rely mainly on 'Das Neue Denken' (1925), a series of supplementary remarks" to Rosenzweig's *The Star of Redemption*, in *Kleinere Schriften* (Berlin, 1937), pp. 373–98.

3 Imre Salusinszky, *Criticism in Society: Interviews with Jacques Derrida, Northrop Frye, Harold Bloom, Geoffrey Hartman, Frank Kermode, Edward Said, Barbara Johnson, Frank Lentricchia, and J. Hillis Miller* (New York: Methuen, 1987), pp. 75–6.

4 See my "Dehellenizing Literary Criticism," reprinted in my *Reading Deconstruction/Deconstructive Reading* (Lexington: University Press of Kentucky, 1983), pp. 34–48. I quote here John Dominic Crossan, *The Dark Interval: Towards a Theology of Story* (Niles, Ill.: Argus, 1975), p. 43. See also the title essay in Cynthia Ozick, *Metaphor and Memory* (New York: Knopf, 1989), pp. 265–83.

5 See, in this regard, Hartman's contributions to *ORIM: A Jewish Journal at Yale*.

6 For an interesting, different attraction to midrash, indeed a hope for "the creation of a literature of *midrash*, or fictive commentary," see Ozick, *Metaphor and Memory*, p. 223. Her essay "Ruth," included there, is a brilliant "fictive" reading of that Hebrew figure.

7 All of this resonates with Hartman's later attempt to deal with the de Man "scandal."

8 *The Lesson of Paul de Man*, ed. Peter Brooks, Shoshana Felman, and J. Hillis Miller, *Yale French Studies*, no. 69 (1985), p. 7.

9 *The Lesson of Paul de Man*, p. 7.

10 Preface, *Deconstruction and Criticism*, by Harold Bloom *et al.* (New York: Seabury Press, 1979), p. ix.

11 After I finished writing the foregoing analysis of "Blindness and Insight," Hartman published a longer essay entitled "Looking Back on Paul de Man" (in *Reading de Man Reading*, ed. Lindsay Waters and Wlad Godzich. Theory and History of Literature 59 [Minneapolis: University of Minnesota Press, 1989]). This essay brings together, in revised form, "Blindness and Insight" and a piece that originally appeared in the *London Review of Books*, 15 March–4 April 1984. "Looking Back on Paul de Man" presents the current controversy in the large context of de Man's work generally. Interestingly, its two sections are entitled "Radical Patience" and "Radical Impatience"; as I discuss elsewhere in this book, the idea of patience, "negative capability," or the ability to abide time lies at the very heart of Hartman's work, paralleling, in fact, Wordsworth's turn from forms of *apocalyptic* thinking. In Hartman's words, in the recent essay, "I was impressed by de Man's radical patience; now the early articles show that

he passed through a phase of radical impatience" (22). Though a new thematic emphasis emerges in the revised essay (that of patience), that revision does not, I feel, essentially alter the basic analysis I have offered. It is true, however, that Hartman now appears defensive, somewhat anxious about his own commentary on his friend (e.g., "this is said not to extenuate de Man..." (23)), and apparently concerned to put some distance between himself and de Man (e.g., he declares that he describes "rather than endorse[s]" de Man's analysis, "self-serving or not," of the linguistic nature of selfhood (21)). In the same vein, perhaps, appears Hartman's conclusion, which I quote in its entirety, for it represents an elaboration on many of the points I have discussed and an indication of the tone characteristic of this revised essay:

> That de Man concealed his past casts a shadow on our analysis of his mature criticism. To fall, however, into a pattern of either/or, of denunciation or defense, is a trap that shows the poverty of our speech when it comes to moral statement. The integrity of the later work has been questioned: it is necessary to read it again, testingly; only then can its value be clarified. The debate could be fruitful, if it leads to more than an exchange of hostilities. It does not seem excessive to ask that people at least read the essays in question rather than accepting hearsay distortions about deconstruction. It also seems appropriate to have those who were close to the Yale critic tell us what they know of his character.
>
> Some mystery will remain: the same that always dogs us when we try to join the literary work and the life. My own attempt in that direction must remain speculative. It sees in de Man's essays not an elaborate, evasive masking of a discredited point of view but rather a severe, generalized reflection on rhetoric, spurred by the experience of totalitarianism. I do not know why de Man did not say as much directly; despite his own attitude on "excuses" such forthrightness might have been more effective, as well as morally clear. But his turn from the politics of culture to the language of art was not, I think, an escape into but an escape from aestheticism: a disenchantment with that final aestheticizing of politics (blatant in many of his own early pieces) that gave fascism its false brilliance. De Man's critique of every tendency to totalize literature or language, to see unity where there is no unity, could be a belated, but still powerful, act of conscience. (23)

Hartman later made a third (and he told me final) attempt to deal with the de Man matter. Entitled "History and Judgment: The Case of Paul de Man," this appeared in *History and Memory*, edited at Tel Aviv University. What is new here – this is not a rehashing of the previous articles – includes an analysis of the reaction to de Man in the context of a thoughtful discussion of judgment. Hartman now appears less defensive, able to reflect critically on his own earlier treatment of the "case," still critical of deconstruction's failure to make clear enough its "situatedness," and quite clear as to his own assessment of de Man. Balanced, sensitive, and also confident, that includes the following judgment:

NOTES

> Some public acknowledgment was necessary, whatever the causes behind his silence. For de Man to disclose his past would have been morally correct and clarifying. At issue is not just the silence about his past, but – as in Heidegger – about an ideology implicated in genocide. It is not disavowal alone we look for, but an open reflection on the error (whether personal, collective or both) that led into an enormous human and moral catastrophe. (77)

Here too I will quote Hartman's last few sentences, which address finely the involved issue of judging:

> My conclusion is not that we suspend judgmental or moral reflection, but that we think more about the aims of this kind of discourse. The aim of judgment in historical or literary-critical discourse – a forensic rather than judicial sort of inquiry – is not that of determining guilt or innocence. It is to change history into memory: to make a case for what should be remembered, and how it should be remembered. This responsibility converts every judgment into a judgment on the person who makes it. (80)

12 Preface, *Deconstruction and Criticism*, p. ix.
13 Of course, Henry James describes the critic as a knight "who has knelt through his long vigil and who has the piety of his office" (*The Art of Criticism*, ed. William Veeder and Susan M. Griffin [Chicago: University of Chicago Press, 1986], p. 235).
14 Donald G. Marshall, Foreword ("Wordsworth and Post-Enlightenment Culture"), *The Unremarkable Wordsworth*, p. xvii.
15 Marshall, Foreword, p. xxii.
16 Salusinszky, p. 75.
17 "Religious Literacy," *Conservative Judaism*, 40 (1988), 30.

4 CALLING VOICES OUT OF SILENCE

1 The idea of communion resonates with Hartman's description, in *Criticism in the Wilderness*, of "hermeneutics as our daily bread" (245). These metaphors resonate, in turn, with Hartman's contention that interpretation "is a feast, not a fast" (FR 18). Nevertheless, Hartman grants that critical reading produces indigestion: the interpreter "evokes the writers of the past in such an engaged and personal way that it is *more* difficult for us to 'digest' or 'assimilate' them." Another aspect of these metaphors emerges when Hartman claims that books are "a feeding source" (CW 220). He is concerned, in other words, with "body images" and the role of "lower forms of need or desire," from which the "polite critic" seeks to free himself, believing that he "stands outside the 'corpus' of literature" (CW 216, 217). His point may be clearest in the following note: "Only Emerson, perhaps, among transcendental interpreters knows that reading is based on something analogous to physical need, as in this sublime and sublimating passage, from 'Quotation and Originality' " (*Letters and Social Aims*, 1883):

> Whoever looks at the insect world, at flies, aphides, gnats, and innumerable parasites, and even at the infant mammals, must have remarked the extreme content they take in suction, which constitutes the main business of their life. If we go into a library or newsroom, we see the same function on a higher plane, performed with like ardor, with equal impatience of interruption indicating the sweetness of the act. (CW 217n.)

2 John D. Caputo, *Radical Hermeneutics: Repetition, Deconstruction, and the Hermeneutic Project* (Bloomington: Indiana University Press, 1987), p. 81.
3 Lacan, in Anthony Wilden, *The Languages of the Self: The Function of Language in Psychoanalysis* (Baltimore: Johns Hopkins Press, 1968), p. 20. Quoted in STT, p. 109.
4 Shoshana Felman, *Jacques Lacan and the Adventure of Insight: Psychoanalysis in Contemporary Culture* (Cambridge, Mass.: Harvard University Press, 1987), p. 115.
5 Felman, p. 118.
6 Jacques Lacan, *Ecrits: A Selection*, trans. Alan Sheridan (New York: Norton, 1977), pp. 86–7.
7 Felman, p. 119.

5 "DYING INTO THE LIFE OF RECOLLECTION"

1 T. S. Eliot, *The Sacred Wood* (London: Methuen, 1920), pp. 52–3, 53–4, 58.
2 Eliot, p. 49.
3 Eliot, pp. 49–50.
4 See, for example, Michael Sprinker, "Aesthetic Criticism: Geoffrey Hartman," in *The Yale Critics: Deconstruction in America*, ed. Jonathan Arac, Wlad Godzich, and Wallace Martin. Theory and History of Literature 6 (Minneapolis: University of Minnesota Press, 1983), pp. 43–65.
5 Here Hartman obviously means something different from the (conventional) meaning of aesthetics he implies in *Criticism in the Wilderness*. There, discussing Benjamin, he writes: "Aestheticism was never the answer. There must be action" (75).
6 Lest there be some misunderstanding that the notion of the *genius loci* entail some jingoistic nationalism (he distinguishes "national" from "nationalistic") Hartman adds the following elaboration:

> If art is the offspring of a precarious marriage between genius and genius loci, the place of which it is the genius is not necessarily a nation-state. Art can express a people (an emerging class or suppressed majority), a region (a Galilee whose genius becomes triumphant), or a speech-community (as large as an Empire, as small as a professional body). Hence literary study often combats the premature universalism that urges the institution of a common tongue or perfect language. (BF 384)

The position Hartman espouses here provides insight into his (increasing) efforts on behalf of Jewish studies. It may also help us appreciate his

contention that "genius, in expelling a false or discovering a true genius, discovers itself and enlarges us" (BF 378).
7 "Religious Literacy," *Conservative Judaism*, 40 (1988), 33.

6 ESTRANGING THE FAMILIAR

1 For an interesting, intelligent account of style in significant ways parallel to Hartman's, see Richard Lanham, *Literacy and the Survival of Humanism* (New Haven: Yale University Press, 1983).
2 Oscar Wilde, "The Critic as Artist," in *Literary Criticism of Oscar Wilde*, ed. Stanley Weintraub (Lincoln: University of Nebraska Press, 1968).
3 See "The Return of/to the Essay," forthcoming in the *ADE Bulletin*. See also my forthcoming essay "Critical Writing and the Burden of History."
4 Edward Hoagland, *The Tugman's Passage* (rpt. New York: Penguin, 1983), p. 25; Joseph Epstein, *Plausible Prejudices: Essays on American Writing* (New York: Norton, 1985), p. 400; Elizabeth Hardwick, ed., *The Best American Essays 1986* (New York: Ticknor and Fields, 1986), p. xv.
5 Hoagland, pp. 25–6.
6 William H. Gass, *Habitations of the Word: Essays* (New York: Simon & Schuster, 1985), p. 23; Phillip Lopate, "The Essay Lives – In Disguise," *The New York Times Book Review*, 18 November 1984, p. 47.
7 Paul H. Fry, *The Reach of Criticism: Method and Perception in Literary Theory* (New Haven: Yale University Press, 1983), p. 200.
8 W. Wolfgang Holdheim, *The Hermeneutic Mode: Essays on Time in Literature and Literary Theory* (Ithaca: Cornell University Press, 1984), p. 30.
9 Holdheim, pp. 28–9.
10 Holdheim, p. 29.
11 But, I should point out, Holdheim situates a good deal of his introductory discussion precisely counter to Hartman, the disagreement centering on purported differences as to hermeneutics and especially questions of the self and the subjective.
12 Epstein, p. 405.
13 Gass, p. 26.
14 Gass, p. 30.
15 Jane P. Tompkins, "Me and My Shadow," *New Literary History* 19 (1987), 169, 173.
16 Tompkins, pp. 173–4.
17 Georg Lukács, *Soul and Form*, trans. Anna Bostock (Cambridge, Mass.: MIT Press, 1974), p. 8.
18 Lukács, pp. 8, 9.
19 Emerson should enter here. Rather unusually for an American, he reveals at once a grounding in philosophy and an intense, bitter struggle with it. In terms of aims national and personal, as well as of style and commitment to the essay, he deserves comparison – and contrast – with Hartman.
20 Lukács, pp. 16, 17.
21 Lukács, p. 14.
22 Herbert N. Schneidau, *Sacred Discontent: The Bible and Western Tradition* (Baton Rouge: Louisiana State University Press, 1976), pp. 295–6. See Adorno's "The Essay as Form," trans. Bob Hullott-Kentor, *New German Critique*, 32 (1984), 151–71.

NOTES

23 In this regard, see Hartman's "Religious Literacy," *Conservative Judaism*, 40 (1988), 26–34.
24 Martin Jay, *Adorno* (Cambridge, Mass.: Harvard University Press, 1984), pp. 14, 15.
25 Cf. CW 212.
26 Walter A. Davis, *The Act of Interpretation: A Critique of Literary Reason* (Chicago: University of Chicago Press, 1978), p. 2.
27 Jacques Derrida, "Living On: Border Lines," in Harold Bloom *et al. Deconstruction and Criticism* (New York: Seabury Press, 1979), p. 130.
28 Hartman provides, I am tempted to say, a window onto the process of thinking so that we can watch him thinking, watch him writing, struggling with texts, ideas, and emotions, showing, in fact, how reading leads to writing, which, as he notes, is the difference that reading most often makes. But of course, as he has helped teach us, no language exists as a transparent window. Thus, as I have tried to indicate, we must *read* his words.
29 See Christopher Norris, *Deconstruction: Theory and Practice* (London: Methuen, 1983).
30 Réda Bensmaïa, *The Barthes Effect: The Essay as Reflective Text*, foreword Michèle Richman, trans. Pat Fedkiew. Theory and History of Literature 54 (Minneapolis: University of Minnesota Press, 1987), p. 96.
31 Holdheim, p. 20.
32 Holdheim, p. 21.

7 IT'S ABOUT TIME

1 W. Wolfgang Holdheim, *The Hermeneutic Mode: Essays on Time in Literature and Literary Theory* (Ithaca: Cornell University Press, 1984), p. 20.
2 Paul de Man, *Allegories of Reading: Figural Language in Rousseau, Nietzsche, Rilke, and Proust* (New Haven: Yale University Press, 1979), p. 4.
3 He was thus unlike the other "Yale critics."
4 Herbert N. Schneidau, *Sacred Discontent: The Bible and Western Tradition* (Baton Rouge: Louisiana State University Press, 1976), p. 49.
5 Schneidau, pp. 17–18.
6 Schneidau, pp. 16–17.
7 Hartman thinks the two different interpretations of the Negative Way incompatible, but the journey *through* may result in a state (by no means static) purged of wrong desires.
8 Schneidau, p. 49.
9 *Selected Poems and Letters by John Keats*, ed. Douglas Bush (Boston: Riverside–Houghton Mifflin, 1959), p. 261.
10 Georg Lukács, *Soul and Form*, trans. Anna Bostock (Cambridge, Mass.: MIT Press, 1974), p. 9.
11 Hartman quotes from that 1935 text as translated in *The Collected Works of Paul Valéry*, ed. Jackson Mathews, vol. 10, *History and Politics*, trans. Denise Folliot and Jackson Mathews (New York: Pantheon, 1962), pp. 141–2.

APPENDIX I

1 Only 350 copies were printed of *Akiba's Children*.

NOTES

2 Jill Kruger-Robbins, in an unpublished paper, "The Work of Reading: Geoffrey Hartman," p. 6. This is the only substantial discussion I know of Hartman's poetry, and I am much indebted to it.
3 Cf. the poems "Abraham" and "Tanges Tamen Aethera," the latter of which, with the almost infinite number of questions it raises, leaves the reader at best unsettled.
4 The meaning of Hasidism is a matter of considerable controversy, Gershom Scholem engaging in an often bitter controversy with Buber over traces of messianism and Gnosticism in the movement. See David Biale, *Gershom Scholem: Kabbalah and Counter-History* (Cambridge, Mass.: Harvard University Press, 1979), esp. pp. 165–70.

APPENDIX II

1 Martin Jay, *Adorno* (Cambridge, Mass.: Harvard University Press, 1984), pp. 19, 20. The quotation of Adorno is from *Prisms: Cultural Criticism and Society*, trans. Samuel and Shierry Weber (London: Neville Spearman, 1967), p. 34.
2 Terry Eagleton, *Walter Benjamin or Towards a Revolutionary Criticism* (London: Verso, 1981), p. 141. Jay quotes this passage and rightly calls attention to another analysis of the similarities betwen Adorno and deconstruction, that by Michael Ryan: *Marxism and Deconstruction: A Critical Articulation* (Baltimore: Johns Hopkins University Press, 1982), pp. 73–80.
3 Theodor Adorno, *Negative Dialectics*, trans. E. B. Ashton (New York: Herder and Herder, 1973), p. 65.
4 Gillian Rose, *The Melancholy Science: An Introduction to the Thought of Theodor W. Adorno* (New York: Columbia University Press, 1978), p. 11.
5 Jay, pp. 12, 53, 57.
6 Adorno, "The Essay as Form," trans. Bob Hullott-Kentor, *New German Critique* 32 (1984): 151–71.
7 Rose, pp. 12, 58, 155.
8 See Rose, p. 13.
9 Rose, pp. 13, 111–12.
10 Rose, p. 12.
11 Rose, pp. 14, 15.
12 Jay, p. 87.
13 Jay, p. 80.
14 Jay, pp. 68, 69.
15 Jay, p. 76.
16 Jay, pp. 125, 154.
17 Jay, p. 100.
18 Jay, pp. 130, 155.
19 Adorno, "Lyric Poetry and Society," *Telos* 20 (1974), 57–8; quoted in Jay, p. 155.

Index

accommodation 51–2, 104, 118
Adorno, Theodor 3, 15, 111, 113, 116, 118; and deconstruction 151–2, 154; on the essay 152–3; his Jewishness 151, 153, 155; and politics 154–5; his preoccupation with style 152–3; prizes art 154–5; questions boundary between criticism and creation 153; and totalitarianism 151, 153; his work as essayist 152
aesthetic, the 60, 91
akedah 55, 60
Akiba, Rabbi 37, 148
Ancients-Moderns 14
answerable style 2, 30, 69, 77, 104, 109, 124
apocalyptic 9, 11, 45, 55–7, 60, 136; defined 59
Aristotle 28 (quoted)
Arnold, Matthew 9, 62, 80 (quoted), 106, 112, 114
art 36, 80, 83, 96, 116, 133; Adorno on 154–5; its difference 91, 94; makes room 93–4, 140, 142; minimalist 136; and the negative 128–9; and politics 91–4; as radical critique 91; and religion 89; as resistance 92–3, 129; its significance 91–2, 94; *see also* Hartman
Auerbach, Erich 106
Austen, Jane 140, 142; her negative capability 141; *Persuasion* 141
authority 23, 95, 97

Bachelard, Gaston 16 (quoted)
Bakhtin, Mikhail 15, 109
Barfield, Owen 106
Bate, Walter Jackson 87–8
Benjamin, Walter 9, 15, 44, 92 (quoted), 100 (quoted), 106, 112, 143–4, 153; on philosophical style 120; the quality of his prose 118, 121; sees hope in the past 92, 143
Bense, Max 111
Bensmaïa, Réda 125 (quoted)
Blackmur, R. P. 116
Blake, William 2, 47, 50 (quoted), 56 (quoted), 59, 86 (quoted), 90
Blanchot, Maurice 6, 140
Bleich, David 15
Bloom, Harold 15, 47, 80, 86–8, 96, 100; Hartman distinguishes from other Yale critics 20, 43; Hartman's critique of 83–4
both/and 14, 20, 33, 35–6, 40, 97
Buber, Martin 15, 37, 65, 149
Budick, Sanford 37
Bultmann, Rudolf 15
burden 48, 51, 60, 62, 68, 71, 80, 137–8; of artistic vocation 84, 88–90, 94–8, 124; of knowledge 88, 90, 119; of the past 88; of tradition 68, 87, 100, 115
Burke, Kenneth 15, 18, 44, 71–2 (quoted), 85

Camus, Albert 91, 140, 142
Caputo, John D. 65–6 (quoted)
Carlyle, Thomas 125; *Sartor Resartus* 10

INDEX

Chandler, Raymond 121
chiasmus 18, 29, 59, 75, 153
Claudel, Paul 25 (quoted)
Coleridge, Samuel Taylor 100 (quoted), 109; *The Ancient Mariner* 53–4, 71
coming out 2, 6, 37, 96, 124
commentary: impossibility of separating from literature 75, 78–9; relation to literature 29, 97–100, 103, 123–4, 132–3, 153; symbiotic nature of relation to literature 25, 33, 79, 99–100, 103, 124; *see also* criticism
criticism: changing its form 106; as creative 68, 99-100, 103, 105–6, 131, 153; and the essay 105–6, 109–17, 125; and fiction 104, 106, 117; irresponsibility in 12; as literature 6, 103, 105–6; and midrash 38; plainstyle 2–3, 104, 156 n. 2; as sublimated chatter 10, 117; as suspensive 131; as symbiotic 79, 99–100, 103, 124; *see also* commentary; style
criticism of consciousness 16, 24
Crossan, John Dominic 37 (quoted)
culture: as cultivation 55

Davis, Walter A. 119 (quoted)
deconstruction 26–8, 30, 35, 41–2, 125–6, 128–9, 131–2, 134–5; Hartman's relation to 18–29, 42, 92, 135; and indeterminacy 138; and the negative 129; and New Criticism 21, 23–4, 74, 132; and totalitarianism 42, 44–5; *see also* de Man; Derrida; Hartman
defamiliarizing 114–15, 122–4, 140; and alienation 134–5
delay time 6, 60–1, 145
Deleuze, Gilles 65
de Man, Paul 26, 39–45 (quoted 42–3), 132–4 (quoted 132); Hartman's differences from 18–20, 84; Hartman's response to his collaborationist writings 37, 41–5, 159–61 n. 11; *see also* deconstruction
demand/response 80

Derrida, Jacques 18–23, 35, 37, 66, 84, 116, 120 (quoted), 146, 152; Hartman's counterstatement to 73, 77, 79; Hartman's reading of 73–7; his Hebraism 133; and intellectual poetry 106, 114; *Of Grammatology* 28 (quoted); *Glas* 19, 22, 73–8, 105, 137; *see also* deconstruction
detective fiction 121–2
Dilthey, Wilhelm 15
dissemination 74

Eagleton, Terry 151 (quoted)
ear 71, 74; versus the eye and its tyranny 68, 75, 121, 148
Ebeling, Gerhard 15
echo 64, 73, 75, 77–9
echoing response 69–70, 78, 84
echo-structure 7, 71, 76
Eliot, T. S. 9–10, 47, 94, 97–8, 100; Hartman's differences from 85–8, 97; "Tradition and the Individual Talent" 85 (quoted); *The Waste Land* 86
Emerson, Ralph Waldo 147
Empson, William 18, 73
Enlightenment 52, 62, 154; and fiction 49; and poetry 48–9, 89; and religion 55–6; *see also* Romanticism
Epstein, Joseph 106 (quoted), 108 (quoted)
equivocation, task of 74, 108
error 32, 34, 40, 42–3, 74, 146
essay, the 32, 120, 122; as antigenre 125, as art 106, 110–11, 117; and the burden of knowledge 109–10; and creative criticism 105–6, 113; and deconstruction 125–6; described 106–17; and desire 113, 116, 118; and the feminine 108; as intellectual poem 113–15, 119; and irony 111–12, 116–17, 128, 139; and negative knowledge 110–11, 126, 128; the personal form of 107, 111, 114–15, 125; reversal in 116–17; as unpointed 128; versus the article 5, 108–9, 111, 128; *see also* Adorno; Hartman; Lukács

167

INDEX

essayistic, the 108, 112
estranging 51, 115, 122, 125, 128, 135, 142
exegesis 2, 105–6, 130

Faur, José 33
Felman, Shoshana 66–7 (quoted)
Fish, Stanley 15, 138
France, Anatole 5 (quoted), 65 (quoted)
Frankfurt School 9, 130, 151; *see also* Adorno
Freud, Sigmund 23, 115, 116, 128
Fry, Paul H. 22 (quoted), 107 (quoted)
Frye, Northrop 9, 18, 84, 95; Hartman's differences from 50–2, 116
Fuchs, Ernst 15

Gadamer, Hans-Georg 15, 17, 109, 131
Garcia Marquez, Gabriel 138
Gass, William H. 107–8 (quoted)
genius loci 49, 95, 162–3 n. 6; and artist's struggle with vocation 97
Gombrich, Ernst 15

Handelman, Susan A. 33
Hardwick, Elizabeth 106 (quoted)
Hartman, Geoffrey: abides time 6, 62, 159 n. 11; accused of obliterating distinctions 103; and the aesthetic 60, 91–3, 162 n. 5; and American taste and educational practice 9, 11–12; and Ancients-Moderns 14; animadverts against practical criticism 2–3, 104–5; and the apocalyptic 11, 45, 55, 59–60, 159 n. 11; his appeal as critical reader 64; and aura 51; as Bad News Angel 8, 128; believes in separation of genres 103; and Bloom 83–4, 88; his complicating, double, or balanced perspective 6, 16–21, 32, 38–41, 43, 51, 103–4, 115, 122, 125; on concluding 6; as conservative 8, 30; his counterstatement to Derrida 73, 77, 79; his critical character 128; his criticism not easy to distinguish from text commented on 14; and criticism of consciousness 8; his dehellenizing efforts 37; and de Man 18–19, 26, 40–5, 133–4, 159–61 n. 11; his difference 2, 6; the difficulty of reading him 5–6, 11, 75–7, 107–8, 119–20, 128, 146–7; and the difficulty of transcending forms 16, 137; the dramatic, performative quality of 122–4, 130; drawn to Wordsworth 32, 47–8, 59; his ear for sounds 8, 38, 64, 68, 71–5; his efforts on behalf of Judaism 37; and Eliot 85–8, 97; as essayist 5–6, 107–8, 128, 146–7; his essays as intellectual poetry 118–19, 124; on the fate of poetry 90; flees Germany 36; and forms 16–17, 95–7; and the fragment 119; and Frye 50–2, 116; has no method 2, 24, 64–5; and Hebraism 5, 10–11, 29–30, 32–46, 92, 133–4, 137; his hermeneutic reflection 8, 14, 19, 30, 60, 71, 93, 155; and a history of forms 94; and the humanities 6, 59–60, 144–6; the impure nature of his work 3, 14, 16, 158 n. 17; his indigestive criticism 125, 161–2 n. 1; his intertextual leaping 64, 71–2, 99, 112, 121; and Lacan 66; and the literature of imaginative reason 62; as Logos-epi-centric 157–8 n. 17; and Lukács 8, 110–13, 116, 128; on the lust for intimacy 90, 92, 115, 140–5; on method 64–5; his mixed style 3, 120–1; and the necessity of distance 140–3, and New Criticism 15, 21, 23–4, 27, 30, 132–3; as not merely a critic 8; opposes totalitarian thinking 18, 35–6, 45; other voices in 15; his paratactic style 3, 34, 118–19; and pathos 20, 43, 121; his personal, intuitive way of reading

INDEX

61, 64–5; his place 15, 29–30, 32; and the place of art 18, 91–4; his poetry discussed 148–50; and political responsibility 39; and the profession 1–2, 8; and purity 36; and reader-response 15; relation of early and later work in 21–30, 37–8, 125, 132, 145, 148; relation of thinking and writing in 32, 64; relation to deconstruction 18–29, 42, 92, 135; relation to hermeneutics 17; relation to New Criticism 15, 21, 23–4, 30, 133; relation to phenomenology 16–17, 65; relation to psychoanalysis 18; relation to rhetorical studies 18–19; reorients commentary 125; reorients the essay 125; and Romanticism 5, 30, 32, 47, 58, 92; as a Romantic 27, 50, 58, 90, 97, 100, 119; and Steiner 11; his style studied 119–21; his theory of form 94–8; his theory of literary vocation 96, 98; his theory of reading 72–3, 76–7; and tyranny of the eye 68, 121, 148; his unpointed style 4–5, 118, 147; unsettles 5, 11, 30, 75, 100, 103, 120, 122–4; and voice 25–6, 37, 52, 96–7; and Wilde 98, 105; as the Wandering Jew 8, 29, 32, 46, 118, 147; wants expanded role for criticism 10; "of" Wordsworth 79; and the Yale School 20–1, 23, 43, 132

Works (treated in some detail): "Adam on the Grass with Balsamum" (BF) 37–8; "Aubade" (*Akiba's Children*) 148–9; "Blindness and Insight" 41–5, 159–61 n. 11; "The Heroics of Realism" (BF) 140–2; "In Honor of the Master of the Good Name" (*Akiba's Children*) 149–50; "The Interpreter: A Self-Analysis" (FR) 3, 104–5, 123–4; "On the Jewish Imagination" 32–6; "Literature High and Low: The Case of the Mystery Story" (FR) 121–2; "Literary Commentary as Literature" (CW) 110–18; "Memory, Error, Text" 39–41, 43; "The Sacred Jungle 1: Carlyle, Eliot, Bloom" (CW) 86–7; *Saving the Text* 73–7; "'Timely Utterance' Once More" (UnRW) 71–2; "Toward Literary History" (BF) 94–8; "Understanding Criticism" (CW) 67–8, 123; *The Unmediated Vision* 21, 24–9; "The Use and Abuse of Structural Analysis" (UnRW) 60–2, 72; "Words, Wish, Worth: Wordsworth" (UnRW) 22–3; "Words and Wounds" (STT) 119, 122–3

Hasidism 149
haste 9, 55, 59–60, 143–4
Hazlitt, William 109, 115
Hebraism 5, 29–30, 68, 86–7; and *akedah* 55; as anti-apocalyptic 34; its associative, paratactic style 34; and deconstruction 40, 45–6, 134; and the mythic 113, 134; and the negative 37, 128, 134–5; pseudoepigraphic impulse in 34; remembrance in 37; its reticence 34–5, 45, 118, 125; and Romanticism 46; and time 34–5; versus Christianity 33–4, 40; and voice 37; and writing 33–5; *see also* Hartman; the Jewish imagination
Hegel, Georg Wilhelm Friedrich 9, 35, 39, 105–6, 130, 131 (quoted) 136, 137–9 (quoted)
Heidegger, Martin 15, 65, 79–80, 84, 115, 144, 146
hermeneutics 9, 17, 30, 32, 65, 99, 108, 123–5, 130–1; *see also* negative hermeneutics
Hirsch, E. D. 7, 93
Hoagland, Edward 106–7 (quoted)
Holdheim, W. Wolfgang 107–8 (quoted), 125–6 (quoted)
Holland, Norman 15, 93
hope 9, 34, 44, 59–60, 76, 89, 92, 138, 140, 143, 148
Hopkins, Gerard Manley 24

INDEX

Horkheimer, Max 151
human-heartedness 8, 48, 57–8, 62, 94, 141
imagination defined 53; *see also* mind (or imagination) and nature
immanentism 24–5, 37
indeterminacy 19, 130, 138, 140
interpretation: as anaclitic 80; as reconstitution of the negative 129–30; versus hermeneutics 130
Iser, Wolfgang 15

Jabès, Edmond 33
James, Henry 140-1
Jauss, Hans-Robert 15, 140
Jay, Martin 3–4 (quoted), 118, 151-4 (quoted)
Jewish imagination, the 11, 29, 32–6, 118, 125, 149; *see also* Hebraism
Joyce, James 73, 92; *Finnegans Wake* 77

kabbalah 86
Kafka, Franz 76, 86, 100–1, 112
Keats, John 5 (quoted), 54, 57, 62, 90 (quoted), 128 (quoted), 135, 137–8 (quoted); "To Autumn" 139 (quoted), 140; *Fall of Hyperion* 98, 132 (quoted); *Hyperion* 96; *see also* negative capability
Kierkegaard, Søren 83
Klein, Melanie 66
Kleist, Heinrich von 137 (quoted)

Lacan, Jacques 15, 18, 65–8 (quoted 66–7), 71
Lamb, Charles 53 (quoted)
language: its evocative nature 66–7
Le Guin, Ursula 109
Lentricchia, Frank 21
Levinas, Emmanuel 33
Lévi-Strauss, Claude 95
literary history: as defense of art 94; and form 95; as within the text 98
Lopate, Phillip 107 (quoted)
Lukács, Georg 8 (quoted), 106–7, 111–12 (quoted), 114, 121–2, 139 (quoted), 152–3; on desire 113, 116; on the essay 107, 110–11; on form 111; Hartman on 8, 110–13, 116, 128; on irony 111, 116–17, 139

Macdonald, Ross 66, 121
Malraux, André 91–2, 140, 142, 144, 154
Marshall, Donald G. 56–7 (quoted), 64 (quoted)
Marvell, Andrew 9, 144
Marxist criticism 95
Mencken, H. L. 10, 105
merging of creation and response 75, 77–8, 80, 105
midrash 37–8, 61, 71, 130
Miller, J. Hillis 16, 20, 25
Milton, John 10, 65 (quoted), 88, 96; and romance 49–50; *Paradise Lost* 37, 50 (quoted), 72
mind (or imagination) and nature 22–3, 28, 61–2, 69, 72, 78, 83, 135–6
Montaigne 5, 125–6
mutual domination/interchangeable supremacy 7, 23, 29, 78–9, 103, 106, 124, 154

negative, the 6–7, 30, 40, 51, 56, 110–11, 123, 125, 128–40, 144, 146–7; and deconstruction 129; and defamiliarization 134–5; and the Hebrews 37, 128, 134–5; literature and 129, 140; reconstitution of as aim of interpretation 129–30; its relation to affirmation 129, 132–4, 137
negative capability 30, 125, 137–8, 140–1, 145, 159 n. 11
negative hermeneutics 17, 30, 125–6; defined 131
New Critical 10, 24, 74, 132
New Criticism 21, 23–4, 27, 30, 133; and deconstruction 21, 23–4, 74, 132
New Critics 15, 23, 27
Nietzsche, Friedrich 20 (quoted), 39, 120

INDEX

Norris, Christopher 21, 123 (quoted)

O'Hara, Daniel T. 1 (quoted)
Ortega y Gasset, José 115, 142
oscillation of mastery 22–3, 78; *see also* mutual domination/interchangeable supremacy

Pater, Walter 106, 109, 111 (quoted), 113–14, 126 (quoted), 128 (quoted)
patience 6–7, 60, 140, 147, 159–60 n. 11
phenomenology 16–18, 24, 65
Plato 105, 109, 146
poetical character 48
poetry, fate of 48–9, 83, 89–90
point 4–6, 30, 58, 93, 107–8, 118, 136, 143, 147
poststructuralism 28, 74
Poulet, Georges 16
prior greatness 81, 83–4, 87, 95–6
priority, question of 77, 80–1, 83–4, 88, 90, 95, 97–9
profanation: *see* trespass
purity 36–7, 41–2, 60
purity perplex 14, 37
psychoanalysis 18, 27, 30, 32, 47, 71

reader: relation of to text 7, 29, 40, 67–72, 78–80, 99, 106; repeats poet-nature relation 60–2, 68–9, 78; his or her role 15, 70–2, 78; *see also* mutual domination/interchangeable supremacy; reading
reader-response: Hartman's difference from 15, 30
reader-responsibility 15, 67, 70, 97, 99
reading: as active hearing 70–1; discloses words within words 64, 71; as error 74; Hartman's theory of 72, 76–7; and hermeneutic heroism 138; its relation to writing 68; as negative 130; the work of 7–8, 15, 80, 99, 146
Reagan, Ronald 37, 39

realism 92, 140–1
reception 7, 67–8, 77, 86
reciprocity 28–9, 69, 71, 78, 80
recognition 7, 65–8, 76–7
relation 27–8, 33, 57, 65–6, 77–8, 87, 109, 118
response 7, 39, 66–72, 77–9, 90, 94, 109; as creative 61, 78
responsibility 7, 39, 60–1, 64, 67–8, 72–3, 79, 81, 88, 90, 98–101, 116
Richards, I. A. 18, 80, 95
Ricoeur, Paul 17
Riffaterre, Michael 60
Rilke, Rainer Maria 24
romance 49–50, 52, 54–5; and Milton 49–50; *see also* Romanticism
Romanticism 5, 25, 30, 32, 36, 45–7; and the Enlightenment 48, 50; and human-heartedness 57; and imagination 53–4; and the negative 134–5; its relation to contemporary criticism 47; and religion 53–7, 89; and romance 49–50, 52; and self-consciousness 53–5, 137
Rose, Gillian 152–3 (quoted)
Rosenzweig, Franz 35, 36 (quoted), 124
Ruskin, John 106, 109

Salusinszky, Imre 36 (quoted), 59 (quoted)
Sandquist, Brigitte 157–8 n. 17 (quoted)
Saussure, Ferdinand de 15, 25, 70
Schliermacher, Friedrich 57
Schneidau, Herbert N. 33, 134–7 (quoted)
self-consciousness 52–5, 57, 137
semiotics 65
Shelley, Percy Bysshe 47
Smart, Christopher 66, 77, 89, 124
Smith, Barbara Herrnstein 19 (quoted)
Socrates 146
Socratic dialogues 147
sound reasoning 77
Starobinski, Jean 15, 70

INDEX

Steiner, George 11 (quoted); and Hartman 11
structuralism 27, 65, 74, 95
style 3–5, 68, 103–4, 123; accommodated 10; affectionate 119; friendship 109; and the negative 136; philosophical (Benjamin) 120; teatotalling 11, 109, 114
surmise 5–6
Swift, *Battle of the Books* 14 (quoted)

time: 34–5, 40, 61; and distance 143; and the durée of thought 144; the need to abide 141; and reading 146; respect for 141; *see also* delay time
timely utterance 68–9, 71–2
Tompkins, Jane 109
Tov, Bal Shem (Israel ben Eliezer) 101, 149–50
trace 28
tradition 84, 86–8, 98, 100–1, 112, 116, 125–6; its burden 87, 100, 115; defined 87, 96
trespass or profanation 86, 101

Valéry, Paul 24, 115, 143–4 (quoted)
Vendler, Helen 9–11 (quoted 9–10)
vocation 94–5, 124; burden of 15, 30, 84, 88, 90, 98; and consciousness 96, 98; and the Enlightenment 89; in France 89; and the genius loci 97; in Milton 88; as religious 89; in Wordsworth 90

voice 25, 37, 52, 70, 87, 89, 96–7, 107, 109

Warren, Robert Penn 94 (quoted)
Wellek, René 94 (quoted)
Wilde, Oscar 98, 105
Woolf, Virginia 7 (quoted), 129, 140
Wordsworth, William *passim*; and the apocalyptic 59; and the burden of vocation 90; Hartman is drawn to 32, 47–8, 59; and Hebraism 57; his human-heartedness 57–8; and the negative 135–7; as poet of the human heart 57; his return to nature 54–8; and religion 56; and the struggle of consciousness 52–5; "Boy of Winander" 7, 69–70 (quoted), 81 (quoted); *The Excursion* 26 (quoted); "Intimations Ode" 68 (quoted), 96 (quoted); "I wandered..." 67 (quoted); Preface to *Lyrical Ballads* 55 (quoted); *The Prelude* 4 (quoted), 52, 55 (quoted), 58 (quoted), 62, 77 (quoted), 123, 135–6; "Tintern Abbey" 54 (quoted); *see also* Hartman; mind (or imagination) and nature; mutual domination/interchangeable supremacy; Romanticism

Yale School 20–1, 47; differences among 20, 43; and New Critics 23–5, 132
Yeats, William Butler 19, 95